Fourth Edition

Skills for Preschool Teachers

Janice J. Beaty

Elmira College

Merrill, an imprint of
Macmillan Publishing Company
New York

Maxwell Macmillan Canada
Toronto

Maxwell Macmillan International
New York   Oxford   Singapore   Sydney

Cover Photo: © David Young-Wolff, photo edit
Editor: Linda A. Sullivan
Production Editor: Mona Bunner
Art Coordinator: Mark D. Garrett IV
Production Buyer: Pamela D. Bennett

This book was set in Souvenir Light by Clarinda and was printed and bound by R. R. Donnelley & Sons Company. The cover was printed by New England Book Components.

Macmillan Publishing Company
866 Third Avenue
New York, NY 10022

Macmillan Publishing Company is part of the
Maxwell Communication Group of Companies.

Maxwell Macmillan Canada, Inc.
1200 Eglington Avenue East, Suite 200
Don Mills, Ontario M3C 3N1

Library of Congress Cataloging-in-Publication Data
Beaty, Janice J.
    Skills for preschool teachers / by Janice J. Beaty. — 4th ed.
        p.   cm.
    Includes bibliographical references and index.
    ISBN 0-02-307680-1
    1. Education, Preschool. 2. Child development. I. Title.
LB1140.2.B413   1992
372.21—dc20   91-13735
                                                                                   CIP

Printing: 3 4 5 6 7 8 9   Year: 2 3 4 5

Photo credits: Janice Beaty, pp. 14, 24, 34, 57, 76, 80, 100, 110, 137, 154, 158, 170, 177, 186, 195, 204, 211, 222, 228, 238, 245; Macmillan Publishing, pp. 38, 50; Ben Chandler, pp. 120, 266.

In memory of a special teacher and friend

Kathryn L. Jenkins

About the Author

Janice J. Beaty, professor of Human Services at Elmira College, Elmira, New York, is director of the Human Services and Early Childhood graduate and undergraduate programs at the college. Dr. Beaty teaches courses in early childhood, children's literature, and Mark Twain studies. She is an author of children's books, teacher training textbooks, and a co-author with her husband, Dale H. Janssen, of books on Mark Twain's life, lecturing, and travels. Dr. Beaty has developed training materials and films for the Child Development Associate program, and has traveled around the country to make presentations at CDA Training Institutes and workshops. Her interest in people of other cultures has lured her to such diverse locations as the island of Guam in the western Pacific and the island of San Salvador in the Bahamas. Her present studies focus on young children's learning through self-discovery with materials in their environment.

Preface

This introductory text presents and discusses basic classroom skills for preschool teachers. It is designed for use by college students preparing to be teachers in kindergarten, prekindergarten, nursery schools, Head Start programs, and day-care centers. It is also useful for inservice teachers and assistant teachers who are updating their skills or preparing for the national Child Development Associate (CDA) credential.

The skills for working with 3- to 5-year-old children in a classroom setting are presented in 13 chapters. Each chapter is a self-contained learning module with objectives, text, learning activities, questions sheets, lists of supplementary texts, videotapes, and an evaluation sheet. Students may progress through each chapter at their own pace using the self-taught module approach; teachers can use the text for assigned readings in college courses. To gain the greatest value from this program, the student should be in a position to apply the ideas presented with young children in an early childhood classroom. Many college programs place students in a nursery school setting for several mornings a week so that they may accomplish the prescribed learning activities with young children.

College programs that use this text as a resource for a practicum or internship experience often expect students to complete 3 to 4 modules in one semester. To determine which module chapters a student should work on, some programs carry out an initial assessment of students as they work in an early childhood classroom. The instructor or trainer uses the Teacher Skills Checklist as an observation tool in an initial assessment of the students' skills. Students are also asked to complete a self-evaluation using the Teacher Skills Checklist as described in "Initial Assessment." The instructor and each student then have a conference, during which they compare Checklist results and determine on which of the 13 skill areas the student needs to concentrate, thus providing an individualized training program based on student strengths and needs.

Observation tools in the text that focus on the strengths and needs of young children include: Large Motor Checklist, Small Motor Checklist, Language

Assessment Checklist, Self-Concept Checklist, Social Skills Checklist, and Child Involvement Checklist. The physical environment and materials of the early childhood classroom are assessed with observation tools such as: Activity Area Checklist, Classroom Safety Checklist, Classroom Cleanliness Checklist, and Book Selection Checklist.

The 13 chapters of the text are arranged in the same order as the skills in the Teacher Skills Checklist and the 13 CDA Functional Areas. Each chapter provides theoretical background on the particular skill as well as ideas for practical application in working with young children and their families in an early childhood classroom.

New Features in the Fourth Edition

The Teacher Skills Checklist has been revised to include space for evidence of teacher performance of each skill and to compress the Checklist into a more convenient and usable format.

New or expanded topics include: safety, with a new Classroom Safety Checklist and expanded discussion on traffic safety, personal safety, poisonous plants, field trip safety, and weather emergencies; health, with a new Classroom Cleanliness Checklist and expanded discussion of washing, symptoms of illnesses, and ideas for involving children in healthy practices; new children's books diverse in culture and language, including African, African-American, Amish, Appalachian, Caribbean, Hispanic, Japanese, Native American, Russian, and Vietnamese; a new Social Skills Checklist; a rewritten chapter on guidance including positive prevention measures, positive reinforcement techniques, and positive intervention methods to help children control and eliminate negative actions while learning appropriate positive behavior.

A rewritten chapter on family involvement discusses the role of parent visitors and volunteers in the classroom and focuses on families in different situations, including single-parent, blended, and culturally diverse families, working parents, and families under stress. The chapter on program management offers new ideas for overcoming team management problems and includes guidelines for team dialogue. Finally, the chapter on professionalism presents new information on licensing and credentialing, and gives two alternate methods for acquiring a CDA Credential: the Professional Preparation Program and the Direct Assessment Program.

An expanded list of topical references and children's books concludes each chapter.

Use as a Companion Text

This fourth edition of *Skills for Preschool Teachers* is designed to be used as a companion volume with the author's text *Observing Development of the Young Child* (Merrill, 1990). While *Skills for Preschool Teachers* is intended as a teacher development textbook, the companion volume *Observing Development of the Young Child* is a child development book, focusing on six major areas of development: emotional, social, motor, cognitive, language, and creative.

Like this text, *Observing Development of the Young Child* is based on an observational checklist, the Child Skills Checklist, with each major area of the

Checklist represented by a chapter in the book: Self-Identity; Emotional Development; Social Play; Prosocial Behavior; Large Motor Development; Small Motor Development; Cognitive Development: Classification and Seriation; Cognitive Development: Number, Time, Space, Memory; Spoken Language; Written Language; Art Skills; and Imagination. The observational items on the checklist represent subheadings in each chapter, just as they do in this text.

Observing Development of the Young Child presents ideas and activities to promote child development in each of the child skill areas. Planning for individual children based on checklist results helps student interns as well as teachers to provide developmentally appropriate activities for their children.

Students and teachers are encouraged to obtain a copy of *Observing Development of the Young Child* to be used in conjunction with this fourth edition of *Skills for Preschool Teachers*.

Acknowledgements

Many thanks to Bonny Helm, Elmira College CDA Field Supervisor, who read the original manuscript and suggested appropriate changes and additions; to Mary Maples, Elmira College CDA Field Supervisor, who also gave valuable suggestions; and to the many students, trainers, education coordinators, college instructors, and people in the field who have used the text and offered their ideas for improvement. I also wish to thank the reviewers for their helpful comments and suggestions: Nancy Hamilton, Edison Community College—Florida; Anita McCloud, Greenville Technical College—North Carolina; Marcia Rysztak, Lansing Community College—Michigan; Patricia Shanahan, Western Kentucky University; and Kathleen Sparkes, Onondaga Community College.

Janice J. Beaty

Contents

CHECKLISTS

Introduction

THE SELF-TAUGHT MODULE APPROACH

This text introduces a unique approach to training teachers, student teachers, and teaching assistants in early childhood classroom skills: the self-taught module training program. It is based on the premise that people learn more effectively when they become deeply involved in their own instruction. The self-taught module approach allows students to: (a) help determine their own needs; (b) participate in selecting a trainer; (c) assist in setting up a training prescription; (d) work at their own pace in an early childhood setting; (e) help determine when they have accomplished their objectives and finished their training; and finally, (f) contribute to their own evaluation of skills gained from the training.

The approach is the same as for children in the preschool setting. They also strive to become independent and self-directed in their learning. Thus it is appropriate that their teachers develop classroom skills to assist them toward that end through the process of self-taught training.

The self-taught approach is also based on the premise that training in classroom skills should be individualized to be effective. This program contains 13 module chapters that can be prescribed separately, or in any combination or sequence, to meet the individual's training needs.

Each chapter in the program is self-contained and can be used independently to upgrade particular skills during in-service training. For college students in pre-service training, all of the chapters can be used when appropriate to provide them with the basic skills necessary for successful preschool teaching.

The skills derive from the original six Competency Goals developed by the Administration for Children, Youth, and Families and refined by the Council for Early Childhood Professional Recognition (1718 Connecticut Ave. N.W. #500, Washington, DC 20009). These goals represent basic competencies for persons with primary responsibility for groups of young children 3 to 5 years of age:

1. To establish and maintain a safe, healthy learning environment
2. To advance physical and intellectual competence

1

3. To support social and emotional development and provide positive guidance
4. To establish positive and productive relationships with families
5. To ensure a well-run, purposeful program responsive to participant needs
6. To maintain a commitment to professionalism

From these Competency Goals, 13 key words have been extracted to serve as the focus for teacher training. These key words, known as Functional Areas, are as follows:

1. Safe
2. Healthy
3. Learning Environment
4. Physical
5. Cognitive
6. Communication
7. Creative
8. Self
9. Social
10. Guidance
11. Families
12. Program Management
13. Professionalism

Each of these 13 Functional Areas serves as the basis for 1 of the 13 chapters in this textbook. Each of these 13 Functional Areas also appears as a heading for the items on the Teacher Skills Checklist. *Skills for Preschool Teachers* has thus integrated the CDA competencies into a college-based teacher preparation program, as well as an in-service training program for teachers and assistants already on the job.

True learning occurs when students have opportunities to make practical applications of theoretical ideas. Therefore, the classroom skills acquired through this self-taught approach should be performed in actual preschool settings. If already serving as a teacher, assistant, or volunteer in a Head Start, day care center, nursery school, parent cooperative, Montessori, kindergarten, or prekindergarten program, the student may use the children's classroom as the location for completing the prescribed module chapters. If enrolled in a college early childhood program, the student will need to volunteer at least 3 mornings a week in a nearby preschool classroom.

Students will also need a trainer to assist with their progression through the training program. The trainer will help with each student's initial assessment, review answers to question sheets, observe students in the early childhood classroom, and meet regularly with the student to provide support and assistance as the learning activities are completed.

The trainer, in other words, serves as a support and resource person who responds to the student's work and activities. The primary responsibility for progress through the self-taught module training program belongs to the student. Students will be involved in activities such as:

1. Initial assessment of student's present skills in an early childhood classroom based on observations by the trainer using the Teacher Skills Checklist
2. Self-assessment of present skills by the student, using the Teacher Skills Checklist
3. An assessment conference with the trainer to discuss and compare results of the two checklists
4. Development of a training prescription, consisting of particular module chapters based on the results of the assessment conference
5. Step-by-step, self-directed progression through each of the assigned chapters
6. Observation by the trainer in the preschool classroom as the student carries out chapter activities
7. Regular meetings with the trainer to discuss assigned chapter activities

The intent of the self-taught module training program is to assist the student in acquiring classroom skills through a wide variety of learning techniques. Viewing a Videopak, reading from the text, writing answers to questions, responding orally to a trainer's questions, performing focused observations of children, making file cards of classroom activities, creating special games and activities to meet children's needs, demonstrating evidence of competence through classroom performance— all of these learning activities are a part of each chapter. The Videopaks listed at the end of most chapters are available from McGraw Bookstore, Elmira College, Elmira, NY 14901.

This fourth edition of *Skills for Preschool Teachers* is a comprehensive multimedia program for training primary caregivers in early childhood programs. For those already employed in programs, it will help them assess their areas of need and strengthen their skills. For those preparing to work in such programs, it will help them develop entry-level skills in a classroom setting. And for everyone who qualifies, it will prepare them to be assessed for the Child Development Associate credential.

Initial Assessment

Students in the self-taught module training program begin with an initial assessment to help them determine what classroom skills they presently possess and what skills they will need to strengthen through training. The initial assessment is a threefold process involving both the student and the trainer and consists of:

1. A classroom observation of the student by the trainer, using the Teacher Skills Checklist
2. A self-evaluation by the student using the Teacher Skills Checklist
3. A conference between the student and the trainer to compare checklist results and develop a personalized training prescription

In a self-taught program, the student is always the initiator of any activity. Therefore, it is up to you, the student, to begin the process.

SELECTING THE TRAINER

First, you will need to arrange for a trainer to make the initial assessment of you in an early childhood classroom. If you are a college student, your early childhood instructor or supervising teacher may automatically become your trainer. In other instances, someone in the early childhood program where you work or volunteer may serve as the trainer.

If you are employed in an early childhood program, it is possible for a master teacher, educational coordinator, or director to be your trainer. Or your program may wish to contract for the services of an outside trainer through a local college, university, or Head Start office.

It is important that the trainer be someone you can have confidence in. The trainer you select should be someone who has had experience in an early childhood classroom, can evaluate your classroom skills objectively, and will help and support you throughout your training program.

6

TEACHER SKILLS CHECKLIST

This checklist was developed and field-tested by the author for use as an initial assessment instrument and training tool by college students as well as CDA trainees and candidates. It is based on the previously mentioned Competency Goals and Functional Areas developed by the Council for Early Childhood Professional Recognition.

Each item of the checklist stands for one Functional Area and contains three representative indicators that demonstrate competence in the particular skill area. Each chapter of the text then discusses one of these Functional Areas, with the indicators serving as specific objectives for the chapter, and as subheadings within the chapter. Thus the Teacher Skills Checklist serves not only as an initial assessment tool but also as an outline for the text. It is important for the student to refer to the particular sections of the text to clarify or interpret the various checklist items.

ASSESSMENT BY THE TRAINER

Again, it is up to you, the student, to arrange for an initial assessment by the trainer. The assessment should take place as soon as you are comfortably involved with the children and their activities. If you are a volunteer, you may want to wait for several weeks until you feel perfectly at ease in the classroom and know both the children and the program. Then you can invite the trainer to make the observation. The trainer will place a checkmark next to each item on the Teacher Skills Checklist that you are observed performing and indicate the "evidence" for each checkmark.

SELF-ASSESSMENT

Next, you should go through the same process yourself, checking off the items on the Teacher Skills Checklist that you are performing. Be honest; check only those items you have actually performed. A self-assessment is often a difficult type of evaluation. But you need to do it carefully and accurately for your training plan to be effective. If you are not sure about an item, put down a question mark instead of a checkmark. Your responses on the checklist are just as important as the trainer's in determining your training prescription. After each item, you should also write down the evidence on which you base your checkmark. For example, for the item, "Encourages children to follow common safety practices," you might briefly describe an activity you have directed, such as: "I played a stoplight game with the children in preparation for going on a field trip across the street."

ASSESSMENT CONFERENCE

When both you and the trainer have completed your Teacher Skills Checklist, arrange a meeting to discuss the results. At this time, you should review the two checklists together, discussing the items that were checked as well as those that were not checked. If one checklist has a blank for a particular item, while the other has a checkmark for the same item, this may be an area of confusion you will want to clarify. If both checklists contain a blank for the same item, this may serve as a focus for the training to come.

TRAINING PRESCRIPTION

The training itself should be designed around the strengths of the student as indicated by the checkmarks on the checklist. As you and your trainer go over the checklist together, jot down these areas of strength on the Training Prescription form. (See Training Prescription, p. 12.) Then indicate the training needs as indicated by blanks on the checklist. To determine what Learning Activities should be prescribed, you and your trainer can choose module chapters that address the particular needs indicated and follow the Learning Activities listed at the end of those chapters.

TEACHER SKILLS CHECKLIST: INITIAL ASSESSMENT

Name: _____

Observer: _____

Teacher Skills Checklist

Name _____ Observer _____

Program _____ Dates _____

Directions
Put √ for items you see the student perform regularly.
Put N for items where there is no opportunity to observe.
Leave all other items blank.

Item	Evidence	Date

1. SAFE
_____ Promotes common safety practices within each activity area.
_____ Encourages children to follow common safety practices.
_____ Stops or redirects unsafe child behavior.

2. HEALTHY
_____ Encourages children to follow common health and nutrition practices.
_____ Provides and uses materials to insure children's health and cleanliness.
_____ Recognizes unusual behavior or symptoms of children who may be ill and provides for them.

3. LEARNING ENVIRONMENT
_____ Determines what activity areas should be included in classroom on basis of program goals, space available, and number of children.
_____ Separates activity areas and places them in appropriate spaces.
_____ Arranges equipment and materials so that children can make choices easily and independently.

4. PHYSICAL
_____ Assesses physical needs of individual children and makes appropriate plans to promote their development.
_____ Provides equipment and activities to promote large and small motor skills in and out of classroom.
_____ Provides opportunities for children to move their bodies in a variety of ways.

Item	Evidence	Date

5. COGNITIVE

_____ Helps children use all of their senses to explore their world.

_____ Helps children develop such concepts as shape, color, size, classification, seriation, number.

_____ Interacts with children in ways that encourage them to think and solve problems.

6. COMMUNICATION

_____ Interacts with children in ways that encourage them to communicate their thoughts and feelings verbally.

_____ Provides materials and activities to promote language development.

_____ Uses books and stories with children to motivate listening and speaking.

7. CREATIVE

_____ Arranges a variety of art materials for children to explore on their own.

_____ Accepts children's creative products without placing a value judgment on them.

_____ Gives children the opportunity to have fun with music.

8. SELF

_____ Accepts every child as a worthy human being and lets him or her know with non-verbal cues.

_____ Helps children accept and appreciate themselves and each other.

_____ Provides many activities and opportunities for individual children to experience success.

9. SOCIAL

_____ Provides opportunities for children to work and play cooperatively.

_____ Helps, but does not pressure, the shy child to interact with others.

_____ Provides experiences that help children respect the rights and understand the feelings of others.

Item	Evidence	Date

10. GUIDANCE

_____ Uses positive prevention measures to help eliminate negative behavior in the classroom.

_____ Uses positive reinforcement techniques to help children learn appropriate behavior.

_____ Uses positive intervention methods to help children control their negative behavior.

11. FAMILIES

_____ Involves parents in participating in children's program.

_____ Recognizes and supports families of different make-ups.

_____ Supports families and children under stress.

12. PROGRAM MANAGEMENT

_____ Uses a team approach to plan a flexible classroom schedule.

_____ Uses transitions and small group activities to accomplish the goals of the program.

_____ Plans for individual needs based on child observation and interpretation.

13. PROFESSIONALISM

_____ Makes a commitment to the early childhood field.

_____ Behaves ethically toward children and their families.

_____ Takes every opportunity to improve professional growth.

TRAINING PRESCRIPTION

Student _____ Date _____

Trainer _____ Center _____

STRENGTHS

1. _____
2. _____
3. _____
4. _____
5. _____

TRAINING NEEDS

1. _____
2. _____
3. _____
4. _____
5. _____

LEARNING ACTIVITIES

1. _____
2. _____
3. _____
4. _____
5. _____

1 Maintaining a Safe Classroom

General Objective

To be able to set up and maintain a safe classroom environment, and to reduce and prevent injuries.

Specific Objectives

- ☐ Promotes common safety practices within each activity area.
- ☐ Encourages children to follow common safety practices.
- ☐ Stops or redirects unsafe child behavior.

S afety is a basic concern for all teachers of preschool children. Before we can offer developmental activities for children who come to center-based programs, we must first guarantee them a safe environment. Their parents assume this to be the case. As a child caregiver, you make the same assumption. But you have the responsibility to see that your classroom is truly safe. You must inspect each activity area in the room before the children's daily arrival and again while children are playing busily with the equipment to be sure the safety hazards sometimes found in particular areas are not present in yours.

In addition, you must check the condition of the bathroom, the exits, the stairs, and the outdoor play area daily to be sure each is clean, clear, and safe. Although a maintenance person may have the responsibility for cleaning and repairing the building and grounds, it is also up to you as the leader of a group of young children to see that the environment is truly safe.

Making your classroom safe can prevent injuries if you are aware of the potential dangers of sharp objects, hazardous materials, falling, electric shocks, burns, and poisonous materials. Children need to learn how to keep themselves safe in the classroom, on the playground, and on the streets by following the common safety practices you present to them. You need to learn how to help children remain safe even when unsafe conditions are present.

Safety Checklist

A safety checklist is one of the most effective methods for establishing and maintaining a safe environment. It will help you to set up the classroom initially with safety in mind and will assist you in checking daily on the condition of the classroom. The Classroom Safety Checklist shown in Table 1.1 serves this purpose. Consider the items under

TABLE 1.1   Classroom Safety Checklist

Art Area

_____ Scissors use supervised

_____ Water spills cleaned up

_____ Hazardous materials eliminated (sprays, solvents, glazes, permanent markers)

Block-Building Area

_____ Building space adequate

_____ Blocks free from splinters

_____ Construction height within limits

_____ Toy accessories free from sharp edges, broken parts

Book Area

_____ Floor area covered

_____ Heating vents, pipes covered

_____ Rocking chairs away from children on floor

Computer Area

_____ Electric cords, plugs out of children's reach

_____ Location away from water

_____ Children seated with computer on low table or stand

Cooking Area

_____ Cooking appliances in compliance with local safety codes

_____ Electric appliances, microwave ovens controlled by adult

_____ Sharp implement use supervised by adult

_____ Number of children in area limited

Dramatic Play Area

_____ Clothes hooks away from eye level

_____ Plastic dishes, cutlery unbroken

_____ Play jewelry, earrings, beads unbroken

_____ Dolls, toys with no small removable parts (e.g., buttons)

Large Motor Area

_____ Climbing, sliding equipment cushioned

_____ Wheeled vehicle use controlled

_____ Safety rules established and enforced by adult

Manipulative Area

_____ Tiny beads, counters eliminated

_____ Sharp or pointed objects eliminated

_____ Objects with splinters, peeling paint, broken parts discarded

Music Area

_____ Cords on record players, radios, tape recorders out of reach

_____ Equipment using small batteries eliminated

Sand/Water Area

_____ Sand or water spills cleaned up

_____ Broken, rusty, or sharp-edged toys removed

_____ Glass implements eliminated

_____ Safety goggles used at sand table

Science/Math Area

_____ Aquarium and incubator wires out of reach

_____ Houseplants nonpoisonous

Woodworking Area

_____ Adult-size tools supervised

_____ Safety goggles used

_____ Safety rules established and enforced by adult

_____ Number of children limited

General Room Conditions

_____ Floor covering smooth, unbroken, and untorn

_____ Traffic patterns between areas clear

_____ Heaters, pipes, vents covered and sectioned off

_____ Electric cords, wires, plugs out of children's reach

_____ Electric outlets covered

_____ Smoke detectors in appropriate locations

_____ Fire extinguishers accessible

_____ Peeling paint removed, refinished

_____ Broken furniture, toys removed, repaired

_____ Sharp corners of room dividers padded

_____ Emergency procedures, phone numbers, clearly posted

Bathroom

_____ Sinks, toilets child-size

_____ Stands, stools sturdy

_____ Slippery floors cleaned up

_____ Cleaning & disinfecting materials locked up

_____ First aid kit out of children's reach; accessible to adults

TABLE 1.1 (continued)

Stairs/Exits

_____ Exits clearly labeled

_____ Stair steps smooth, unbroken, of nonskid material

_____ Carpeting, mats smooth, untorn, not slippery

_____ Stair railings reachable by children

_____ Two exits in every classroom

_____ Stairs well lighted

Outdoor Playground

_____ Playground enclosed with fence

_____ Debris, broken glass removed

_____ Cushioning under climbers, slides

_____ Large equipment anchored in ground

_____ Swings of safe material (belts, tires)

_____ Young-child-size equipment used

_____ Railings around high platforms, on steps

_____ Sharp edges, missing or loose parts, splinters on equipment corrected

_____ Adequate supervision when in use

Permission is granted by the publisher to reproduce this checklist for evaluation and record keeping.

"General Room Conditions" to make sure that the physical environment is free from problems such as floor obstructions, heating and electrical dangers, sharp corners, broken furniture and toys, or peeling paint. In addition, be sure that safety implements such as smoke detectors and fire extinguishers are available, with emergency procedures clearly displayed. Then you can check on each activity area to be sure it also conforms to the safety standards you have established for your classroom.

PROMOTES COMMON SAFETY PRACTICES WITHIN EACH ACTIVITY AREA

Art Area

Sharp scissors are safer for young children to use than dull ones, which may slip and cut a child. Small sharp scissors can also help young children develop manipulative skills safely. A nearby adult should keep a watchful eye when scissors are out, however, and put them away when not in use.

Replace art materials that are hazardous with nontoxic materials. Instead of aerosol sprays of paint or lacquer, use water-based paints for spattering. To prevent children from inhaling the dust from powdered tempera paints and powdered clay, mix these in a well-ventilated area away from the children. Some glazes contain lead, and solvents such as turpentine contain toxic substances. Even rubber cement is toxic if inhaled. Instead, use water-based, nontoxic paints and glues. Rather than use instant papier-mâché materials that may contain asbestos or lead, make your own papier-mâché from newspaper and white paste (Marotz, Rush, & Cross, 1985). Because children tend to breathe faster than adults, they may inhale two to three times as much of a toxic substance per unit of body weight as an adult. Thus it is important to eliminate toxic substances from the children's art area (Noyes, 1987).

Block-Building Area

The principal safety feature of block-building areas is the height of constructions. Some teachers permit a child to build with wooden unit blocks or large hollow blocks only as high as the child's height. Others allow children to climb on chairs to build towers as high as they can reach. The danger of this practice is that the tall building may fall on another child, or the climbing child may fall and be injured. You must decide if this situation poses a particular problem with your children. If this is a safety priority with you, you will want to establish block-building rules with children at the outset.

Since preliterate children are not able to read written rules, why not make illustrated rules for them to follow? You could draw an outline of a block building next to the outline of a child to show the allowable height. Then repeat the drawing with a too-tall building and a line drawn through it to indicate "not allowed." Below each picture write a simple rule, such as "Just Right" or "Too Tall." Some children will figure out what the words say, as well as what the illustration means.

Book Area

Your library or reading corner should be a comfortable place for children to stretch out on the floor or curl up on a pillow to read. Make sure that the floor is covered with a rug to keep it warm enough in cold weather, and that the area is free from drafts. If you use pillows on the floor, make sure there are no heat vents that might be covered accidentally. If you have a rocking chair, help children learn to control it. They tend to get carried away with child-size rockers, and may tip over or rock on someone's fingers.

Computer Area

This is a new area in many preschool programs. Young children teach themselves to use these powerful interactive learning tools if teachers set up the area for their convenience and safety. Children should sit and not stand when using this valuable piece of equipment. Two children can sit in child-size chairs in front of one computer on a low table. Electric cords should be plugged into a wall outlet behind the machine and out of the children's reach. Do not use extension cords. Keep water and sticky fingers away from the keys.

Cooking Area

You will have to learn the local safety code governing hot food preparation in your community. Some schools do not allow electric appliances, microwave ovens, or blenders in the classroom. Some use only special kitchen areas for hot cooking, while food preparation without heating is carried out in the classroom. Whatever the case, an adult should always be in the area during food preparation. Young children can use knives and scrapers safely, but an adult should supervise.

Programs limited to food preparation without heat may enjoy books such as *Kids Cooking Without a Stove* (Paul, 1975) or *Cool Cooking for Kids* (McClenaham & Jaqua, 1976).

Dramatic Play Area

Toy safety is a particular concern in this area. Check dolls for small parts that a child could twist off and swallow accidentally. Remove dolls with buttons, glass eyes, and beads that are sewed or wired on. Be sure earrings are large and strings of beads unbroken. Tiny objects sometimes find their way into young children's noses or ears. Also remove toys with springs, wires, or sharp parts.

If you use plastic dishes, knives, or spoons, make sure they are not broken. Sharp knives, of course, should not be used for play.

Large Motor Area

Climbing equipment should be cushioned with pads or other materials thick enough to prevent injuries in case a child falls. Establishing safety rules for climbers at the outset is important; in addition, an adult should supervise the area when it is in use. If you have wheeled riding vehicles, establish safety rules, such as "no bumping" with illustrated traffic signs and safety games.

The teeter-totter is one of the most dangerous pieces of large motor equipment. Even on a small indoor teeter-totter, a child can be thrown off the higher end if the child at the lower end jumps off unexpectedly. The safe use of a teeter-totter is a complex concept for 3- and 4-year-olds to learn; most teachers prefer not to use them at all.

Children with physical handicaps should be involved in all of the activity areas of the classroom, including the large motor area. Find ways to give them safe access to large motor experiences. Children in wheelchairs can throw and catch large, soft, or inflated balls. True *mainstreaming* means that all children are included in classroom activities wherever possible. Use your ingenuity to accommodate everyone. For example, in a catch-and-toss game, have everyone sit in chairs just as physically handicapped children would.

Choose equipment of appropriate sizes for young children for both indoor and outdoor play. Slide steps should have a railing as well as a railed platform at the top. The "Outdoor Play Structures Buying Guide" article (Morris, 1990, p. 58) lists 23 manufacturers of outdoor play structures, and mentions such concerns as "size of bars and angles of components to avoid entrapment of a child's head or body part." Recommendations from the Consumer Product Safety Commission include a minimum 8-foot safety zone around a play unit, as well as a resilient safety surface under and around each unit. In addition, a staff member needs to supervise large motor climbing, swinging, and sliding equipment both indoors and out.

Manipulative Area

If you have 3-year-olds or younger in your program, be sure the stringing beads and counters are large. Three-year-olds often put small objects into their mouths, noses, and ears. Check games and toys for broken parts, and discard anything with splinters, wires, or peeling paint.

Music Area

Cords on record players, tape recorders, and electronic keyboards should be out of children's reach. Children should not be allowed to plug or unplug the equipment. Use battery-operated players, when possible, but avoid equipment with small mercury-type batteries that could be swallowed accidentally.

Sand/Water Area

While playing at the sand table children should wear safety goggles, to keep sand out of their eyes. Most will enjoy wearing them. Spilled water and sand are slippery and should be cleaned up. Keep a mop and broom with handles cut down to child-size in the area, so that children can help with clean-up. Not only will they take pride in themselves and their classroom by performing this adult-type task, but they will also learn safety practices useful in other settings. To prevent spills in the first place, keep water and sand at low levels in the play tables. Children can have just as much fun and learning with 2 inches of water as they do with a filled-up water table—and they will keep drier.

Be sure toys and implements for sand and water play are not broken, rusty, or sharp-edged. Instead of glass containers, such as baby food jars or glass eye droppers, use plastic cups, containers, bottles, funnels, droppers, and basters.

Science/Math Area

Small counting and sorting items, such as buttons, seeds, or beans, pose problems for the youngest children, who tend to put such things in their mouths. Certain seeds and beans may be poisonous as well. Such children's collections can be displayed under clear plastic wrap instead of being left open for handling.

Certain houseplants are highly poisonous and thus pose a serious hazard to young children, who may be tempted to eat a leaf or berry. If you have plants in your classroom, keep them out of reach. Indoor plants that are poisonous include philodendron, dieffenbachia, amaryllis, mistletoe berries, and poinsettia leaves. Outdoor poisonous plants include holly, hydrangea, azalea, rhododendron, lily-of-the-valley, bittersweet berries, rhubarb leaves, mustard, buttercup, castor bean, yew, mushroom, black locust tree, and cherry tree.

Rather than warning children against eating such leaves or berries, it is better to remove the temptation. If you stress "no eating," certain young children who had no notion of eating a plant part will try it just because you mentioned not doing it!

Woodworking Area

In woodworking, as in playing with sand, children should wear safety goggles, and most will enjoy the experience. Use adult-size hammers, saws, pliers, and screwdrivers, since most children's toy sets are not made for use with real wood and nails. Children can learn how to use tools safely if an adult such as you or a parent, or even an experienced child, demonstrates how to do so. Limiting the number of children in the area will also reduce safety hazards.

Woodworking generates much interest for both boys and girls. They should be encouraged to learn the skills of pounding and sawing, with an adult supervising. Roofing nails and ceiling tiles are easier for beginners to use successfully. To cut down on noise, put rug squares under the pounding materials.

General Room Conditions

Check the heating system in your room. Exposed pipes should not be allowed unless they are thoroughly protected with non-asbestos insulation. Radiators and space heaters should be sectioned off to prevent children's direct contact. Portable electric or kerosene heaters are usually prohibited by fire codes or insurance regulations.

Electric cords and wires should not be accessible to children. Avoid the use of extension cords whenever possible. Place aquariums, incubators, and other such items near electrical outlets that are inaccessible to little hands.

Check your walls, furniture, and cupboards for peeling paint. Children love to pick off the pieces and put them in their mouths. Be sure the surfaces are sanded down and refinished with non-lead paint. Remove broken toys and furniture and have them repaired. Don't wait until someone gets hurt. Check wooden equipment and room dividers for splintery surfaces and have them refinished if necessary. What about the corners of the room dividers? If children stumble against them, will they be hurt? You may need to tape padding onto sharp edges.

Check the physical environment of your classroom to see if you need to modify it for children with handicapping conditions. You may need shelves or water containers at special heights. What about emergency exiting? Will you need a special ramp or other device? Should special railings or handholds be attached to stairways and bathroom walls? Should one of the classroom staff assist the child with special needs in moving safely in and out of the building? It is important for the adults in the classroom to avoid overprotectiveness, so that the child with special needs can develop independence. On the other hand, a situation that involves safety precautions may require adult help.

Bathroom

Slippery floors may be the most common cause of injuries in bathrooms. Make it a practice to check bathroom floors from time to time during the day, and clean them whenever there are spills.

Always store bathroom cleaning and disinfecting materials in cabinets out of the children's reach and be sure that cabinets containing caustic or poisonous materials are locked.

If first-aid kits or materials are stored in the bathroom, keep them out-of-reach for children, but accessible to adults.

Stairs/Exits

What about stairs into or out of the building? Can children reach the railings? Are steps sturdy and unbroken? If covered with carpet, is the carpeting smooth and in good condition? As a teacher of young children, you are accountable for all aspects of their safety in the building. Others may be responsible for repairs and replacements, but it is up to you to ensure safety.

Outdoor Playground

Is the equipment on your playground in safe condition? Check to make sure there are no loose parts, sharp edges, or slivers, as well as for adequate cushioning under climbers and slides. A cushioning of sand, wood chips, bark, or pebbles is preferable to grass or blacktop.

Belt or tire swings are preferable to swings with hard seats since the latter cause many accidents. Use child-size equipment with railings and platforms on slides. Eliminate teeter-totters and merry-go-rounds from your playground. Climbing, sliding, and swinging equipment should be securely anchored in the ground with concrete. Your playground should also be sectioned off with a fence from roads, driveways, or parking lots. Check daily to make sure there are no broken bottles or other dangerous debris on the grounds.

ENCOURAGES CHILDREN TO FOLLOW COMMON SAFETY PRACTICES

Modeling Safe Behavior

You are the model of safety behavior for your children. When they see you taking precautions with saws, hammers, knives, or electrical equipment, they will imitate you. Your behavior is much more effective than your trying to tell or "teach" children the proper rules. As you practice normal adult safety behavior, you should express it

Children should practice emergency exiting so that everyone can do it without panic.

verbally to the children. "See how I cut the pumpkin? I move the knife away from me so I don't get cut. Now you try it."

You and your staff, including volunteers, should discuss safety practices in the classroom so that all of you agree on the limits you will set for children, and will thus be able to enforce the limits consistently. Young children do not necessarily understand rules by being told. Most often, they learn by doing, by being involved in the situation. For instance, you could demonstrate at the workbench how to hold the saw and make it work, or have a carpenter come in and demonstrate. Then let each child try it. When a child has learned to use the saw, let him show the next child how to use it. If one child can show another child how to perform the task, then he has really learned it himself.

Involving Children in Safety Rules

Let the children be involved in helping to decide on the safety rules for each classroom area. All of you should agree on the rules. How many children should be allowed in the woodworking area at one time? How high can a block building be built and still be safe? Should a child be allowed to stand on a chair to make the building higher than she can reach from the floor? The children need to know this. If they help make the rules, they will be more willing to follow them.

Do not overburden children with rules. Make simple ones that everyone understands and that you can easily enforce. Children should be concerned with the safety basics, such as not hurting themselves or others. We adults are sometimes overly concerned about rules and regulations. If there are too many rules, young children simply will not respond. Keep rules simple, basic, and few in number.

Teaching Car Safety Through Dramatic Play

Most states have enacted legislation governing car safety for young children. The laws state that children under 4 years of age must sit in state-approved car seats when riding in private cars. As a teacher, you can encourage children to follow this practice through classroom play activities. Bring in a car seat, and let them practice using it themselves or with dolls during dramatic play. Or fasten a seat belt to a chair, and let children pretend to be riding in a car.

Teaching Traffic Safety with Signs and Games

Children can learn about safety signs and signals on field trips. Follow-up activities in the classroom can help reinforce these learnings. Through games, songs, and stories, they can learn that red means "stop" and green means "go." Make a traffic light from a half-gallon milk carton. Cover it with dark vinyl adhesive paper and cut three holes in a vertical row through one side. Cover the holes with red, yellow, and green cellophane or tissue paper. Make three small holes on the opposite side of the box, large enough to shine a pen flashlight through. Let the children play a Red Light-Green Light game by marching around in a circle while someone shines the flashlight through the hole to signal "stop," "wait," or "go."

You can also make cardboard stop signs and other traffic signals for the children to use in block play. Follow up this activity with a visit by a police officer or school crossing guard to demonstrate street-crossing safety. Although videos on this topic are available for children, young preschoolers do not learn concepts as well from videos and films as they do from active involvement with learning. Sitting still and listening to a teacher or a video is not as effective a learning strategy as the more interactive activities mentioned.

Using Books as Follow-up Safety Reinforcers

Once a concept is clear to children, books serve as a good follow-up when they are read to individuals and small groups. Trying to teach a safety concept to a large group of children by reading a book is much less effective, because children need to be close enough to the reader to see the illustrations. They need to be able to respond individually to the teacher's questions, such as, "Can you find the traffic light in the picture? What color is it? Does it tell the driver to stop or go?"

Two excellent books for reinforcing traffic safety concepts are the classic picture book *Red Light Green Light* (McDonald, 1944) and the wordless picture book *Truck* (Crews, 1980). Let the children make up their own story as they watch Crew's 18-wheeler following traffic signs through the city and onto the highway. Be sure to have a selection of toy cars and trucks in the block area after reading these books. Watch and listen to the children's dramatic play, and you will soon learn whether the children really understand these safety concepts.

Another wordless picture book is *First Snow* (McCully, 1985), about a family of human-like mice going for an outing in the snow. Winter ice-skating and sledding safety can be featured when the children make up stories to go along with these pictures. *Not So Fast Songololo* (Daly, 1985) is a simple story about a South African boy who helps his Granny go shopping in the crowded city. In addition to the traffic lights they encounter, this book with its sensitive illustrations shows people from another culture involved in safety problems similar to those of American children.

Practicing Emergency Exiting, Fire Drills, and Weather Emergency Procedures

Certain situations demand rules and order. Emergency exiting from the building is one of those situations. Children should practice this over and over so that everyone understands how to do it without panic. Do not wait for a fire inspector to make this happen. It is your responsibility to yourself, the children, and their families to see that fire drills, emergency evacuations, and weather emergency procedures are accomplished with ease. In case of a tornado, typhoon, hurricane or earthquake, different rules are in order. Learn those rules and practice them with your children.

Preparing for Field Trips

Field trips require special regulations. Teachers need to familiarize themselves with the field trip site to prepare the children. Are there special safety hazards that need to be addressed? On a visit to a farm, how close should children get to the animals? What about riding on a tractor? On a visit to a fire station, will the children be allowed to climb into a fire truck? In addition, children may need to learn how to walk in pairs or groups, how to cross busy thoroughfares, or how to wait for the teacher before they go forward. The adults as well as the children need to understand such procedures ahead of time. If children are transported in cars, buses, or subways, they and the drivers must be aware of safe and unsafe child behavior in a vehicle.

To anticipate the safety problems inherent in any field trip, you should make a preliminary visit to the site, if possible using the same mode of transportation the children will use. Then you can make notes about safety situations to prepare the staff and the children for the trip. Talk to the people at the site as well, in case they have safety rules or advice you will need to know ahead of time. As you look at the field trip site, try to anticipate the kinds of exploring your active children will attempt to do. Would any of these things be dangerous? What about children becoming separated from the group or going off by themselves? One of your staff members could be assigned to check on these possibilities.

In addition, you may want to practice field trip behavior ahead of time with your children in the classroom. Reading a book such as *Don't Worry, I'll Find You* (Hines, 1986) to individuals or small groups helps children to understand what to do if they get separated. Have children role-play such a situation with a doll from the dramatic play area if the story appeals to them.

Preparing for Accidents

Post emergency telephone numbers for the local police, sheriff, fire department, doctor, ambulance, hospital, and poison control center near your phone. All adults in the classroom should know where to find these numbers. Also, post directions for handling emergencies there, written in two languages if your program is bilingual. A list of children's home telephone numbers and the names of others to contact when no one is home should be available near your phone as well.

A first-aid kit should be available, and at least one member, but preferably all, of the classroom staff should know how to use it. Your program should consider devoting a staff meeting once a year to emergency procedures and first aid. A simple book for a staff member to have at hand is *A Kid's Guide to First Aid* (Freeman, 1983). Real emergency situations are illustrated in pen and ink drawings on every two pages, with simple numbered directions on what to do.

Children can also prepare for first-aid situations by hearing stories about helping someone who has been injured, or by playing doctor or nurse in the dramatic play area. You could read them a story such as *Maybe a Band-Aid Will Help* (Hines, 1984) about a little girl who tries to help her "injured" doll.

Preparing Children for Personal Safety

The personal safety of the children in your care includes protecting them from harm or victimization by predatory adults. Sexual abuse of children by adults is one of the primary dangers. Although this is a very real threat to certain young children, many professionals feel that the child care community has overreacted to the threat in ways that are potentially harmful to children.

Not only have young children in centers been alerted to "stranger-danger" with films, diagrams, games, and exhortations by their teachers, but children have also been made to feel that it is their responsibility to protect themselves from such adults. We delude ourselves if we believe that 3-, 4-, and 5-year-old children can successfully ward off the advances of adults who intend to abuse them. When young children are being abused but find that they can't control the situation, guilt feelings may add to the psychological damage of the abuse. After all, since they have been taught what to do but cannot prevent the abuse, they may come to believe it is their own fault.

As a result of this kind of overreaction to the situation on our part, we find many children in child care centers who are afraid of the other adults in the building, who run from friendly college students, who will not let health professionals examine them, or who may even show fear when their parents undress them for bed or a bath.

In addition, many child care professionals themselves worry that entering the bathroom area with the children in their care or helping children clean themselves after accidents may cause children to overreact and report to their parents that they were touched. Male child-care workers are especially vulnerable to such charges, resulting in driving out of the child care profession the much-needed male role models for young children.

We need to step back and think about the effects of instilling this kind of fear in young children. Not only does fear inhibit learning, but this kind of fear makes children all the more vulnerable to victimization. We also need to realize that most child sexual abuse occurs in the home, and that 85% of such abuse is perpetrated by someone the child knows (Hull, 1986, p. 18).

What, then, should be our role in protecting the children in our charge? We should use common sense in helping children learn not to go with strangers or accept rides from people they do not know. However, scare tactics are out of place; so is the constant bombardment of children with "stranger-danger" films and lessons.

We as teachers are the ones who really need to be educated in this matter. We should look carefully at the message we want to get across to children. It should not be one of "overkill"—that there is danger in every stranger. It should not be one of "good touches" and "bad touches." How is a preschooler to distinguish between the two? With such messages, we may be producing a generation of paranoid children who will keep their distance from one another as adults. Do we want to live in a society where caring, touching, and loving are perceived as threatening acts?

Instead, what we should do is to encourage children to talk to a trusted adult when they feel uncomfortable; to go only with a trusted adult on the street or in a car; and to ask a trusted adult when they are unsure of what to do.

The child care staff and parents need to have sensitive discussions and decide how to handle this issue in the center and at home. You may want to invite psychologists or health professionals to contribute their expertise. A positive approach, in which children learn to feel good about themselves and the people around them, should be your goal for the children's personal safety.

STOPS OR REDIRECTS UNSAFE CHILD BEHAVIOR

Anticipating Unsafe Behavior

Unsafe child behavior can take many forms. It may consist of running in the classroom or halls, pushing other children, climbing too high, playing too roughly, or using materials in unsafe ways. You may be able to eliminate much unsafe behavior by anticipating it ahead of time. Arrange the physical environment so children do not have room for uncontrolled running. Have children walk with partners in the halls or on city streets. Carefully supervise potentially dangerous situations. For example, you may know that young children are more adept at blowing out of straws than sucking up through them. You might want to demonstrate this skill at the water table when suds and straws are used, and thus prevent children from sucking up and swallowing soapy water.

Children love to play with water. If they squirt it on the floor of the classroom or the bathroom, they have created a slippery condition for others. You need to stop them firmly, not harshly, and redirect them by involving them in helping you to clean it up. Make the task interesting, not a punishment.

Redirecting Unsafe Behavior

Telling a child to stop climbing so high or to stop building such a tall block building will not resolve the safety problem. Commands like these only encourage young children to climb and build higher. A sensitive teacher knows that the best way to deal with such situations often requires redirecting unwanted behavior, not by referring to it, but by calling the child's attention to something else.

Go to the child personally rather than shouting across a room. Ask the child to show you how he can climb horizontally or swing hand over hand, or to show you how a very wide building would look. Giving a child another challenge will often redirect potentially dangerous behavior into something constructive.

Demonstrating Safe Behavior

An adult must be nearby to supervise the use of hammers, saws, paring knives, and pointed scissors. Children can and should learn to handle these implements safely. If you stop their unsafe use, you should then demonstrate the proper method and let the user try again.

If all the adults in the classroom take time to demonstrate safety regulations consistently, children will not only learn to copy such behavior, but will also help you by showing others the safe way to live in their classroom.

SUMMARY

Information from this chapter should help you set up and maintain a safe classroom environment and reduce and prevent injuries. You should be able to assess the activity areas in the room for possible safety hazards such as electrical cords, exposed heating pipes or vents, slippery floor conditions, rugs that do not lie flat and could cause tripping, and rough edges and sharp corners on room dividers. You should understand how to promote safety in each area with illustrated signs, simple basic rules, and supervision where necessary. You should know how to anticipate and redirect unsafe child behavior, as well as how to use role-playing to demonstrate safe behavior.

Children can learn the safety precautions they must practice on stairs and exits, in the bathroom, on field trips, and in cars. You can hold or attend workshops or discussions about first aid, emergency situations, and children's personal safety. As a role model for safe behavior in the classroom, you will be taking the first step to assure children and their families that your program is making a serious commitment to each child's well-being.

LEARNING ACTIVITIES

1. Read Chapter 1, "Maintaining a Safe Classroom," and answer Question Sheet 1–A.
2. View Videopak H, "Outdoor Play Equipment," and answer Question Sheet 1–B.
3. Read one or more of the books or articles listed under Suggested Readings. Begin a card file with 10 file cards that describe ideas from the reading for promoting safety in your classroom. Include the reference source on the back of each card.
4. Assess the safety of your classroom using the Classroom Safety Checklist. What changes can you suggest?
5. Have one of your staff members hold a fire drill or emergency exiting drill. Observe and record what happens. Write up the results and make recommendations for improvement.
6. Help a small group of children learn a particular safety concept using ideas and techniques from this chapter. (Your trainer can visit and observe.)
7. List the contents of your classroom first-aid kit and describe a use for each item.
8. Arrange and conduct a field trip for some or all of the children, during which you make appropriate use of safety measures. Write up the results and suggestions for improvement. (Your trainer can go along.)
9. Complete the Chapter 1 Evaluation Sheet and return it to your trainer or college supervisor.

QUESTION SHEET 1–A

(Based on Chapter 1, "Maintaining a Safe Classroom")

1. Who is responsible for providing and maintaining a safe classroom environment, and what does that responsibility entail?
2. With what safety factors should classroom caregivers be concerned? How does your classroom fare?

3. What are some of the dangerous materials a classroom might contain? Does your classroom have any of these?

4. What dangers exist for young children as they enter and exit a building? How can such dangers be overcome?

5. How can you, as a teacher, model specific safety practices for your children?

6. How do children learn safety rules? Give examples.

7. What are the safety aspects of field trips with which you should be concerned?

8. How would you handle an emergency situation such as a child falling and being injured?

9. How can you help children maintain their personal safety without frightening them?

10. What unsafe child behavior might occur in your classroom, and how could you correct it?

QUESTION SHEET 1–B

(Based on Videopak H, "Outdoor Play Equipment")

1. What should be your main concerns when equipping your playground?

2. What is the most dangerous aspect of climbers? How can you minimize this danger?

3. How should you prepare playground cable spools to eliminate safety hazards?

4. How can the dangerous aspects of slides be overcome? How is this done on your playground?

5. What materials can be used for cushioning under equipment?

6. What is the most dangerous aspect of swings, and how can this danger be minimized?

7. How can you overcome the dangerous aspects of teeter-totters?

8. How should your playground equipment be located to overcome safety hazards?

9. What should you do on a daily basis to keep your playground safe?

10. How can blacktop surfaces be used with a minimum of danger?

SUGGESTED READINGS

Comer, D. E. (1987). *Developing safety skills with the young child.* Albany, NY: Delmar.

Esbensen, S. (1987). *The early childhood playground: An outdoor classroom.* Ypsilanti, MI: High/Scope Press.

Freeman, L. (1983). *A kid's guide to first aid.* Seattle, WA: Parenting Press.

Green, M. (1977). *A sigh of relief: The first-aid handbook for childhood emergencies.* New York: Bantam.

Hill, D. M. (1977). *Mud, sand, and water.* Washington, DC: National Association for the Education of Young Children.

Hull, K. (1986). *Safe passages: A guide for teaching children personal safety.* Dawn Sign Press.

Marotz, L., Rush, J., & Cross, M. (1985). *Health, safety, and nutrition for the young child.* Albany, NY: Delmar.

McClenahan, P., & Jaqua, I. (1976). *Cool cooking for kids.* Belmont, CA: Fearon Publishers.

Morris, S. (1990). Outdoor play structures buying guide. *Child Care Information Exchange, 75,* 55–58.

Noyes, D. (1987). Indoor pollutants: Environmental hazards to young children. *Young Children, 42*(6), 57–65.

Paul, A. (1975). *Kids cooking without a stove.* Garden City, NY: Doubleday.

CHILDREN'S BOOKS

Crews, D. (1980). *Truck.* New York: Greenwillow.

Daly, N. (1985). *Not so fast Songololo.* New York: Viking Penguin.

Hines, A. G. (1986). *Don't worry, I'll find you.* New York: E.P. Dutton.

Hines, A. G. (1984). *Maybe a band-aid will help.* New York: E.P. Dutton.

McCully, E. A. (1985). *First snow.* New York: Harper & Row.

McDonald, G. (1944). *Red light green light.* Garden City, NY: Doubleday.

VIDEOTAPES

Beaty, J. J. (Producer). (1979). Outdoor play equipment (Videopak H), *Skills for preschool teachers* [Videotape]. Elmira, NY: McGraw Bookstore, Elmira College.

KRMA-TV, Denver (Producer) (1980). A Good Measure of Safety (Program 5), in *Spoonful of lovin'* [videotape]. Bloomington, IN: Agency for Instructional Technology.

CHAPTER 1 EVALUATION SHEET
MAINTAINING A SAFE CLASSROOM

1. Student _____

2. Trainer _____

3. Center where training occurred _____

4. Beginning date _____ Ending date _____

5. Describe what student did to accomplish General Objective

   _____

   _____

6. Describe what student did to accomplish Specific Objectives

   Objective 1 _____

   _____

   Objective 2 _____

   _____

   Objective 3 _____

   _____

7. Evaluation of student's Learning Activities
        (Trainer Check One)   (Student Check One)

   _____ Highly superior performance   _____

   _____ Superior performance   _____

   _____ Good performance   _____

   _____ Less than adequate performance   _____

Signature of Trainer: Signature of Student:

_____   _____

Comments:

:05 —
:15 — Small Groups (Story)
:25 — Downstairs
:45 — Dismassal

2 Maintaining a Healthy Classroom

General Objective

To be able to set up and maintain a healthy classroom that promotes good child health and nutrition and is free from factors contributing to illness.

Specific Objectives

- ☐ Encourages children to follow common health and nutrition practices.
- ☐ Provides and uses materials to insure children's health and cleanliness.
- ☐ Recognizes unusual behavior or symptoms of children who may be ill, and provides for them.

H ealth practices, like those of safety, are best taught to young children through behavior modeling on the part of classroom adults, as well as through games, stories, and real experiences in which children can become involved.

Nutrition facts, for example, become meaningful for young children not by memorizing basic food groups, but through classroom experiences with real food. Children learn to wash their hands before meals not because they know it kills germs, but because they see the teacher doing it.

ENCOURAGES CHILDREN TO FOLLOW COMMON HEALTH AND NUTRITION PRACTICES

Exercising

While large motor equipment provides children the opportunity to exercise their large muscles, you should also plan a time for strenuous running and movement in a gymnasium or on an outdoor playground. If neither is available, you can take your children for a follow-the-leader run around the building instead, inside and out. For programs that do not have an indoor or outdoor space large enough for running, have children run in place to a chant. Start out slowly and increase the speed with every verse.

> Step, step, step,
> Make your feet trep, trep,
> Make your legs hep, hep,
> As you keep in step.

Trot, trot, trot,
Make your toes dot, dot,
Make your heels hot, hot,
As you trot, trot, trot.

Canter, canter, canter,
You don't have to stop to banter,
Or to listen to a ranter,
When you canter, canter, canter.

Faster, faster, faster,
Make your feet go faster, faster,
Make your legs go even faster,
And you won't have a disaster.

STOP!

Allow children who cannot run to play catch with a beanbag, or provide some other activity that encourages them to move. For example, have wheelchair-bound children touch their toes, knees, shoulders, and head to a different chant while seated. Make up your own chants with the children, and you may be surprised at the creative rhyming words they invent.

Resting

Healthy young children seem to be perpetual motion machines, never stopping to take a breath. Yet they do need to practice a balance of active and quiet activities. It is up to the classroom staff to make sure a rest time is part of the daily program.

This does not mean the teacher should make the children put their heads down on the table for 15 minutes every morning at 10 o'clock, whether they need a rest or not. Rest time should come as a natural follow-up to exertion, rather than as a formal period at a certain time of day. If there has been no strenuous activity during the morning, a group rest time is unnecessary. If you schedule one anyway, you will probably spend most of the time trying to keep the children quiet. On the other hand, when children are truly tired, they welcome a quiet period.

Children with physical handicaps may tire more quickly than others. It is up to you to recognize the situation, provide a quiet place for such children, and make sure they stop to rest when they need it.

Some programs have a quiet period just before lunch when the children put mats on the floor and pursue quiet activities by themselves. Solitary activity is a refreshing change if a child has been with a large, active group all morning.

If yours is an all-day program, you should provide a formal nap period in the afternoon. Use cots or mats wherever you have extra space. If you are using the regular classroom space, section off an area for children who no longer take afternoon naps. Dim the lights in the room, but after the nappers have fallen asleep, you can whisper to the non-sleepers that they may go to this special area and play quietly. Individual mats help make this a quiet time for non-sleepers as well.

To encourage resting, you may want to read a story at the beginning of the quiet period. *Goodnight Moon* (Brown, 1947) is a quiet story in which a little bunny is encouraged to go to sleep as the room grows progressively darker on every page. *Close Your Eyes* (Marzolla, 1978) is a warm-hearted story about a father getting his little girl ready for bed and encouraging her to use her imagination when her eyes are closed. Following a similar theme, *Flocks of Birds* (Zolotow, 1965) is about a girl who is not sleepy; her mother suggests that she imagine flocks of birds moving as she lies in bed.

Washing

Children must learn to wash their hands upon arrival, before meals, after using the bathroom, and after handling pets. Do you serve as their model? They will do it because you ask them to and because it is an interesting sort of task, but you should model the same behavior. They should see you washing your hands, too. Demonstrate with liquid soap how a person should wash the front and back of the hands, between the fingers, and under the fingernails. Then dry your hands with a paper towel, turn off faucets with paper towel, and dispose of it in the trash container. Be sure you wash your own hands upon arrival, before preparing food, before eating, after helping a child use the toilet, and after wiping a child's nose. All of the classroom staff and volunteers should do the same.

It is essential to have a sink in the classroom as well as in the bathroom. If you do not have a sink, set up a hand-washing stand with plastic basins for washing and rinsing, and set up a method for disposing of the water after every use.

You can promote the practice of cleanliness through washing in other ways. For example, have the children bathe the dolls in the dramatic play area once a week. If the classroom does not have a toy sink in the area, bring in a plastic tub. Both boys and girls can have an enjoyable time with water, as well as practicing cleanliness. Let them wash the dolls' clothes as well. This is the time to talk about cleanliness and how it keeps us healthy.

Children generally love to play with water, so approach these activities with a sense of pleasure rather than drudgery. Hand-washing may be a daily routine, but you and the children can make it fun. Read children the light-hearted story of *Harry the Dirty Dog* (Zion, 1956) about a dog who wouldn't take a bath and finally got so dirty that his family didn't recognize him. Perhaps your children would like to bathe plastic animals from the block area after this story.

Nutrition

Children learn very quickly what foods we consider important, not by what we say, but by observing the kinds of food we serve in the classroom. Do you serve cookies and milk for a snack? Do you serve cake or cupcakes for birthdays? If you want children to become acquainted with delicious fruits and interesting vegetables, plan some exciting food activities with these foods as well.

How about making "Banana Surprise" or "Frozen Fruit Slush" or "Hairy Harrys" from the book *More than Graham Crackers* (Wanamaker, 1979) for a birthday celebration? The children can have the fun of making their own party refreshments as well as eating them. "Banana Surprise" uses bananas, graham cracker crumbs, and peanut butter, and gives children practice with the small motor skills of peeling, cutting, spreading, and rolling. If you substitute raisins for the cracker crumbs, you will be making "Ants on a Log." "Frozen Fruit Slush" uses orange and lemon juice, mashed bananas, honey, and milk, and requires a refrigerator with a

Children learn very quickly what foods we consider important by observing what we serve in the classroom.

freezer and ice cube trays. You can also teach the concept of freezing with this activity. "Hairy Harrys" consist of apple slices spread with peanut butter and topped with alfalfa sprouts and raisins. The children can even make their own peanut butter.

In addition to making refreshments for parties, let the children also make their own daily snacks, such as "Stuffed Celery" from the book *Good Times with Good Foods.* Children will practice scrubbing and cutting celery, and they can make a variety of fillings—cottage cheese, cream cheese, or peanut butter. This book contains an excellent collection of nutritious recipes, each illustrated with simple, step-by-step picture directions that you can copy onto a large newsprint recipe chart for the children to follow as they prepare the food.

Once children have experiences with real foods, teachers can introduce other fun nutrition activities. Food puppets can visit the class to talk about their favorite foods. How about a "junk food puppet" who thinks everyone should eat nothing but candy bars, potato chips, and soda? How will your children respond? This may be the time for the book *Gregory, the Terrible Eater* (Sharmat, 1980), the hilarious story of a little goat who craves human food, but must learn to eat "correctly" by being served one piece of goat food at a time, for example, "spaghetti and a shoelace in tomato sauce." Can your children make up nutritious menus for their own pets? For themselves?

To grow up healthy and strong, children need to eat a balanced diet as well. Your youngsters will enjoy hearing you read *Much Bigger than Martin* (Kellogg, 1976) about a little boy who tries to make himself bigger than his older brother by stuffing himself with apples.

Besides recipes, the book *Cool Cooking for Kids* (McClenahan, 1976) has many pages of ideas for puppets and food games. One is a "Shoe-box Train," with decorated shoe boxes representing each of the four basic food groups. Children have to choose which cut-out food pictures belong in each of the train cars. You should have pictures of food from the "meat group" (including poultry, and fish), the "milk group" (including yogurt, cottage cheese, and other dairy products), the "vegetable and fruit group," and the "bread and cereal group" (including whole-grain bread, rice, and pasta). You could also ask the children to drive their train over to the dramatic play area and pick up some play fruits, vegetables, and food.

Medical Tests and Examinations

Although a classroom teacher is not usually responsible for setting up medical tests and examinations for the children, you can certainly support the health specialist who does. You and the specialist need to work together to plan and carry out classroom activities to acquaint children with these examinations to make them less threatening.

Before an eye test, let children practice holding a card over one eye and responding to an eye chart. Later they can give a similar "test" to the dolls in the dramatic play area. Before an ear test, have the health specialist demonstrate or talk to the children about what will occur. The nurse in one Head Start Program pasted together a three-dimensional model of an ear inside a shoe box. Through a hole in one end the children could shine a pen flashlight to see the inner parts of the "ear" just as the doctor would.

Be honest with children about what will happen. If their fingers will be pricked to draw blood, have a pretend demonstration with a nurse officiating. Invite a dental hygienist to demonstrate a dental checkup. Read a book to individuals or small groups. *My Dentist* (Rockwell, 1975) is a simple story about a little girl who goes to a dentist's office for a checkup, and features well-illustrated dental tools and equipment.

Take your class on a visit to a clinic. Afterwards, put out medical and dental props for children to play with in the dramatic play area. Listen to what they say to learn how much they have learned about health checkups. Read *Curious George Goes to the Hospital* (Rey, 1966) about a mischievous little monkey who has a minor operation but major fun in the children's ward of a hospital.

It is important for young children to act out their feelings about doctors and nurses, about getting shots and going to the hospital. Medical role-playing in the dramatic play area of the classroom serves a therapeutic as well as an educational role for youngsters. Some children can pretend to be doctors or nurses giving shots to other children or dolls, and others can pretend to be patients, rolling up their sleeves for a shot. This is scary business for youngsters. Working out their fears of doctors and shots in this non-threatening manner helps children to prepare for the real thing.

As a follow-up to this medical role-playing, you can read the book *No Measles, No Mumps for Me* (Showers, 1980) about a little boy who is immunized against the childhood diseases. In simple terms and illustrations, the story explains what happens inside the body when a person gets an immunization shot.

Other Health Practices

Again, you are the model for the children to follow. Be sure your own health practices are worth following. If you want children to clean their plates at lunch, then you should set the example. If you smoke, do it in a private place away from the children. If you want children to stop biting their fingernails, be sure you don't bite yours.

Sometimes a story can help motivate the desired behavior. *The Quitting Deal* (Tobia, 1975) is a well-written, contemporary story about Jennifer, who wants to break her thumb-sucking habit, and her mother, who wants to quit smoking. Although written for 6- and 7-year-olds, the book is appropriate for younger children and should stimulate discussion about breaking unhealthy and even dangerous habits.

PROVIDES AND USES MATERIALS TO INSURE CHILDREN'S HEALTH AND CLEANLINESS

The classroom environment must be clean and sanitary. Even if a janitorial staff does the cleaning, it is your responsibility to make sure the job is done properly and that the center remains in good condition throughout the day. Floors, tabletops, and food-serving areas should be kept clean. Food should be stored properly and garbage disposed of promptly. You can prevent the spread of infectious diseases by keeping your classroom clean and sanitized. To disinfect toys and surfaces the children have touched, wash or wipe them with a solution of 1/4 cup bleach to 1 gallon water, prepared fresh each day.

Use a Classroom Cleanliness Checklist, shown in Table 2.1, each day to make sure your center is clean and sanitary.

Light, heat, and ventilation should be kept at healthy levels. Children and their parents need to be informed about the type of clothing children should wear at the center. If an extra sweater is necessary and the parents cannot provide one, you may have to seek other sources. Keep a supply of clean clothing items on hand in case children have spills or accidents, or they lose clothing items, such as mittens.

Your outside playground should also be kept clean and free of debris. If you have a sandbox, keep it covered so that animals cannot get into it. If you have tire swings or climbers, have holes punched in them so that they will not collect water and become a breeding place for germ-carrying mosquitoes.

Your classroom also needs a basic supply of tissues, paper towels, paper cups, and liquid soap. If you use sheets or blankets for napping, they must be individually labeled and washed periodically. Also, make sure eating utensils are washed at appropriately hot temperatures and then properly stored.

TABLE 2.1 Classroom Cleanliness Checklist

_____	Classroom floors and rugs clean
_____	Table and counter surfaces clean and disinfected
_____	Trash containers empty
_____	Bathroom floor clean and disinfected
_____	Sinks and toilets clean and disinfected
_____	Food stored properly
_____	Eating utensils washed and stored properly
_____	Garbage disposed of
_____	Paper towels available
_____	Paper tissues available
_____	Liquid soap available
_____	Paper drinking cups available
_____	Toothbrushes available in individual holders
_____	Individual toothpaste available
_____	Toys clean and disinfected
_____	Stuffed animals clean
_____	Pet cages, boxes clean
_____	Blankets, mats, cots clean

Permission is granted by the publisher to reproduce this checklist for evaluation and record keeping.

Toothbrushing after meals is an important habit for your children to learn. Each child needs an individual brush marked with a name or symbol that the child can recognize. Also, mark the area where children store their brushes. You might use upside-down egg cartons, or you could ask a parent to make a wooden toothbrush holder. Using only one tube of toothpaste increases the possibility of passing germs from one child to the next. You should consider having small individual tubes for each child. Some centers turn small individual paper cups upside down and place a blob of toothpaste on the bottom of each cup. The child then uses the toothbrush to lift the paste off the bottom of the cup and onto the brush. After brushing, the child can rinse with the cup and then throw it away. However you prefer to do it, make sure children brush hygienically after each meal.

RECOGNIZES UNUSUAL BEHAVIOR OR SYMPTOMS OF CHILDREN WHO MAY BE ILL, AND PROVIDES FOR THEM

Sick days for the children in your program are inevitable, and you need to be prepared. Can you recognize when children are ill? Does your center have the space and staff to provide for them? If not, have you made arrangements with parents for alternate caregivers?

You need to discuss policies about caring for sick children with your staff and communicate these policies to parents so that everyone is familiar with the procedures. First of all, you must make sure that all children are immunized against diphtheria, typhoid, whooping cough, measles, mumps, rubella, and polio. The booklet *Sick Child Care Book for Parents and Child Care Providers* (Bananas, Child Care Information & Referral, 1980) gives helpful hints on common childhood illnesses, when to call a doctor, and comfort measures for sick children.

You must also check on children when they arrive each day. Any of the following symptoms may indicate the child is ill and needs attention:

Unusual paleness	Unusual tiredness	Fever, chills
Skin rash	Abdominal pain	Sore throat
Red, watery eyes	Nausea, vomiting	Earache
Swollen neck glands	Diarrhea	Headache

Child caregivers also need to know general information about the seriousness of children's illnesses. For instance, a child with a runny nose, slight cough, slight headache, or slight stomachache may remain in the classroom if this is your policy. But a child with a fever, vomiting, an earache, a congested cough, a severe headache, or a sore throat should be sent home or to the alternate caregiver. In the meantime, the child needs to be isolated from other children, with an adult on hand to offer help and comfort. The center and the parents should set up these arrangements ahead of time.

You should be familiar with children's health needs. Are any of the children on medication? Do any of them have allergies? Having a classroom pet may aggravate an allergy. Have any children been exposed to a communicable disease? What about physical limitations? Some children become fatigued more easily than others. Whether or not you are responsible for keeping the children's health records, you should familiarize yourself with them, and be prepared to respond to individual needs.

Abused Children

Abused children are children whose parents or caregivers have mistreated, neglected, or intentionally injured them. As a teacher or child care worker, it is your responsibility to report suspected cases of child abuse. This type of mistreatment of children includes physical, emotional, verbal, and sexual abuse, as well as physical and emotional neglect. Physical abuse is usually easiest to recognize because of its visible signs, but it is possible for you to identify other forms of abuse as well.

Physically abused children may display repeated or unexplained injuries, burns, bruises, welts, or missing patches of hair. They may complain of harsh treatment or be unusually fearful of adults, including parents. Sometimes they may appear to be malnourished or dehydrated. They may also be withdrawn or disruptive at times. Physically neglected children are often unclean and may have bad odors, or they may wear shoes and clothing of the wrong size. They may have untreated illnesses or injuries. They may be chronically hungry or tired and may spend much time alone.

Emotionally abused or neglected children are more difficult to identify, but they are generally unhappy and seldom smile. Sometimes they, too, are withdrawn or disruptive. Often they react without emotion to unpleasant statements or situations. They may appear apathetic and seldom participate in classroom activities.

Sexually abused children may have underclothing that is torn or stained. They may complain of pain or itching in the genital area or may have difficulty urinating. They may also be withdrawn or have trouble getting along with others.

Abused children need help of two kinds. First, you must accept them as worthy human beings in your classroom and let them know you accept them. They need to experience success and be praised for it. At the same time, the abuse must be stopped.

The law requires that child caregivers report cases of child abuse. Most states have toll-free "hot" lines you may call 24 hours a day. You must follow up the telephoned report with a written report within 24 hours. The state then contacts the local Department of Social Services, which sends caseworkers to investigate and take action with the family involved.

If you suspect that a child is the victim of abuse or neglect, you should contact your center director, your principal, or the health specialist to evaluate the situation. You should also know the policy your center or school has adopted for reporting child abuse. If you do not, ask to have an in-service program to outline policies for dealing with abuse and neglect.

Children with Handicapping Conditions

Many children with handicapping conditions have special health needs. They may need special medication or a special diet. They may become fatigued more easily than other children and thus need more rest and fewer strenuous activities. Your center or school health specialist should help you determine these needs. You should also arrange parent conferences to determine how best to serve the child with special needs. It is important to maintain close contact with parents of these children so they can let you know their expectations and concerns.

Be aware, however, that many parents may not have fully accepted their child's handicapping condition. You may need to discuss your concerns with the parents and a health or mental health specialist and provide parents with information, resources, and referrals to help their child.

Can the child move freely, easily, and safely in the classroom? You may have to rearrange furniture, widen walkways, or make activity areas more accessible. What about special toys, equipment, and activities? Books such as *Including All of Us: An Early Childhood Curriculum about Disability* (Froschi, Colon, Rubin, & Sprung, 1984), *Mainstreaming Young Children* (Spodek, Saracho, & Lee, 1984), and *Young Children with Special Needs* (Fallen & Umansky, 1985) offer many suggestions.

Do the children in your program accept children with handicapping conditions as a matter of fact? If you treat all children with the same care and concern, then the youngsters should model this behavior with one another. You may also want to include story books in your library area featuring children with handicapping conditions as main characters—whether or not your classroom contains such children. Eloise Greenfield's *Darlene* (1980) presents a story about an African American girl in a wheelchair playing with her cousin and uncle while waiting for her mother to return. Jeanne Peterson's *I Have a Sister My Sister Is Deaf* (1977) is a sensitive story of a young Asian girl telling about her very special deaf sister's accomplishments. *A Button in Her Ear* (Litchfield, 1976) is Angela Perkin's own story about how she came to wear a hearing aid.

SUMMARY

After reading this chapter, you should be able to set up and maintain a healthy classroom that promotes good health and nutrition and is free from factors contributing to illness. You will be providing daily opportunities for children to exercise both indoors and out, whether or not a large space is available. The balance of active and quiet activities you set up will include rest periods as a natural follow-up to exertion, although you will accommodate individual needs for children who no longer nap during the day.

Washing hands and brushing teeth will be an important part of your program, with care taken to prevent the transfer of germs during toothbrushing. You can meet the nutritional needs of your children through snacks and meals. In addition, they will learn good food habits through their own fun experiences with nutritious foods.

they
You will know how to prepare children to take medical tests and examinations through preliminary classroom activities that you or a health specialist set up. You will be able to recognize symptoms of illness in children and know how to deal with them. You will also be familiar with the characteristics of abused children and with the ways that you and your program must respond. You will also be able to recognize and accommodate the health needs of children with handicapping conditions in your classroom.
the

LEARNING ACTIVITIES

1. Read Chapter 2, "Maintaining a Healthy Classroom," and answer Question Sheet 2–A.

2. Read one or more of the books listed under Suggested Readings. Make 10 file cards with ideas for promoting health and nutrition in your classroom. Include the reference source on the back of each card.

3. Use the Classroom Cleanliness Checklist for a week, making any corrections necessary to keep the room clean and sanitary.

4. Make a card for each child in your class on which you can record information about general health, weight and height, energy level, napping habits, eating habits, any special health concerns, and, where necessary, suggestions for health improvement.

5. Do a large motor exercise in the classroom with your children, such as a body action chant.

6. Use ideas from this chapter to help a small group of children learn a particular health or nutrition practice. (Trainer can observe.)

7. Celebrate a child's birthday with one of the nutritious food ideas described in the chapter. (Trainer can observe.)

8. Make a list of health facilities or human resources in your community that children and families can use for dealing with injuries, illness, dental health, mental health, abuse, and handicapping conditions.

9. Complete the Chapter 2 Evaluation Sheet and return it to your trainer or college supervisor.

QUESTION SHEET 2–A

(Based on Chapter 2, "Maintaining a Healthy Classroom")

1. How are good health practices best taught to young children?

2. How should you provide for large muscle exercise?

3. When should children have rest time in the classroom? What can you do to encourage children to rest or nap?

4. How can children best be encouraged to keep clean?

5. How can children learn what foods are the best for them?

6. What kinds of foods besides cookies and cake can you provide for a birthday celebration?

7. How can you prepare children for an eye examination?

8. What can you do to keep the classroom and playground clean and sanitary?

9. How can you recognize whether a child is ill, and what should you do about it?

10. How can you recognize child abuse, and what should you do about it?

SUGGESTED READINGS

Bailey, D. B., Jr., & Wolery, M. (1992). *Teaching infants and preschoolers with handicaps* (2nd ed.). Columbus, OH: Merrill.

Bananas, Child Care Information & Referral. (1980). *Sick child care book for parents and child care providers.* Oakland, CA: Bananas.

Cherry, C. (1981). *Think of something quiet.* Belmont, CA: Pitman Learning.

Cook, R. E., & Tessier, A. (1992). *Adapting early childhood curricula for children with special needs* (3rd ed.). Columbus, OH: Merrill.

Endres, J. B., & Rockwell, R. S. (1990). *Food, nutrition, and the young child* (3rd ed.). Columbus, OH: Merrill.

Fallen, N. H. (Ed.), & Umansky, W. (1985). *Young children with special needs* (2nd ed.). Columbus, OH: Merrill.

Froschi, M., Colon, L., Rubin, E., & Sprung, B. (1984). *Including all of us: An early childhood curriculum about disability.* New York: Educational Equity Concepts.

Hart-Rossi, J. (1984). *Protect your child from sexual abuse.* Seattle, WA: Parenting Press.

Kendrick, A. S., Kaurmann, K., & Messger, K. P. (1990). *Healthy young children: A manual for programs.* Washington, DC: NAEYC.

Learning Institute of North Carolina. (1976). *Good times with good foods.* Greensboro, NC: LINC.

Marotz, L., Rush, J., & Cross, M. (1985). *Health, safety, and nutrition for the young child.* Albany: Delmar.

McClenahan, P., & Jaqua, I. (1976). *Cool Cooking for Kids.* Belmont, CA: Fearon.

Moukaddem, V. (1990). Preventing infectious diseases in your child care setting. *Young Children, 45* (2), 28–29.

Reinisch, E. H., & Minear R. E., Jr. (1978). *Health of the preschool child.* New York: John Wiley & Sons.

Rogers, C. S., & Morris, S. S. (1986). Reducing sugar in children's diets. *Young Children, 41,* (5), 11–16.

Rothlein, L. (1989). Nutrition tips revisited: On a daily basis, do we implement what we know? *Young Children, 44* (6), 30–36.

Spodek, B., Saracho, O. N., & Lee, R. C. (1984). *Mainstreaming young children.* Belmont, CA: Wadsworth.

Wanamaker, N., Hearn, K., & Richarz, S. (1979). *More than graham crackers.* Washington, DC: National Association for the Education of Young Children.

Wardle, F. (1990). Bunny ears and cupcakes for all: Are parties developmentally appropriate? *Child Care Information Exchange, 74,* 39–41.

CHILDREN'S BOOKS

Brown, M. W. (1947). *Goodnight moon.* New York: Harper & Row.

Greenfield, E. (1980). *Darlene.* New York: Methuen.

Kellogg, S. (1976). *Much bigger than Martin.* New York: Dial Press.

Litchfield, A. B. (1976). *A button in her ear.* Chicago: Albert Whitman.

Marzolla, J. (1978). *Close your eyes.* New York: The Dial Press.

Peterson, J. W. (1977). *I have a sister my sister is deaf.* New York: Harper & Row.

Rey, H. A. (1966). *Curious George goes to the hospital.* New York: Scholastic.

Rockwell, H. (1975). *My dentist.* New York: Mulberry Books.

Sharmat, M. (1980). *Gregory, the terrible eater.* New York: Scholastic.

Showers, P. (1980). *No measles, no mumps for me.* New York: Thomas Y. Crowell.

Tobia, T. (1975). *The quitting deal.* New York: Penguin.

Zion, G. (1956). *Harry the dirty dog.* New York: Harper & Row.

Zolotow, C. (1965). *Flocks of birds.* New York: Thomas Y. Crowell.

VIDEOTAPES

Health Professionals in Child Care (Producer). *Healthy child care: Is it really magic?* [videotape] St. Paul, MN: Toys 'n Things Press.

National Association for the Education of Young Children (Producer). (1990). *Building quality child care: Health & safety* [videotape]. Washington, DC: NAEYC.

**CHAPTER 2 EVALUATION SHEET
MAINTAINING A HEALTHY CLASSROOM**

1. Student _____

2. Trainer _____

3. Center where training occurred _____

4. Beginning date _____ Ending date _____

5. Describe what student did to accomplish General Objective

   _____

   _____

6. Describe what student did to accomplish Specific Objectives

   Objective 1 _____

   _____

   Objective 2 _____

   _____

   Objective 3 _____

   _____

7. Evaluation of student's Learning Activities
       (Trainer Check One)   (Student Check One)

   _____ Highly superior performance   _____

   _____ Superior performance   _____

   _____ Good performance   _____

   _____ Less than adequate performance   _____

Signature of Trainer: Signature of Student:

_____   _____

Comments:

3 Establishing a Learning Environment

General Objective

To be able to set up and arrange an early childhood classroom so that children will become self-directed in their learning.

Specific Objectives

☐ Determines what activity areas can and should be included in the classroom on the basis of program goals, space available, and number of children.
☐ Separates activity areas and places them in appropriate spaces.
☐ Arranges equipment and materials so children can make choices easily and independently.

I n early childhood classrooms, the physical arrangement of equipment and materials often determines what will happen. The physical arrangement conveys a message to the children, telling them what they may or may not do, and what we expect of them.

Wide-open spaces invite children to run and shout. Small, closed-in spaces indicate quiet and limited access for only a few children at a time. Carpeted areas invite children to sit on the floor. Pillows near bookshelves say, "Relax and look at a book."

Water tables full to the brim are asking to be spilled. An inch or two of water in the bottom gives children freedom to move it around without spilling.

Tall shelves stuffed with art materials say, "This is not for you to touch," to many children. To the adventurous ones, they say, "See if you can reach us!"

A table with four chairs invites four children to sit down. Only one puzzle on the table invites a squabble. Thus, how you arrange the classroom helps decide what will take place in it.

GOALS

What do we want to happen? The primary goal of many early childhood programs is to promote a child's positive self-image. If that is your goal, you will want to arrange your classroom in a way that will help children develop confidence, help them feel good about themselves as people, and help them become self-directed in learning activities.

The physical arrangement of the classroom can help you accomplish this goal if you keep the children in mind when you arrange the activity areas.

DETERMINES WHAT ACTIVITY AREAS CAN AND SHOULD BE INCLUDED IN THE CLASSROOM ON THE BASIS OF PROGRAM GOALS, SPACE AVAILABLE, AND NUMBER OF CHILDREN

Determining Activity Areas

Activity areas are known by different names in various programs or parts of the country: learning centers, stations, zones, or play units. Whatever you call yours, they are the areas in your classroom devoted to particular activities.

The number and kinds of activity areas your classroom should contain depends on program goals, space, and number of children. Many programs follow state or federal government regulations that require from 35 to 50 square feet of space per child.

Many early childhood programs follow a rule of having a ratio of 5 or 6 children to 1 adult. Using this ratio, if you employ a teacher, a teacher's aide, and a volunteer, you will be serving 15 to 18 children. Three- and 4-year-old children need such close adult support. On the other hand, as many as 20 five-year-old children work well in a classroom with 2 adults.

Many programs follow a rule of thumb that counts 4 children to an activity area. Young children often have difficulty working or playing in larger groups. Thus, if you serve 18 to 20 children, you will need a minimum of 5 permanent activity areas, or more if possible. What will they be?

Ideally, you will be able to include a permanent block-building area, book area, dramatic play area, manipulative area, art area, and science/math area. In addition, you may also be able to set up temporary areas for large motor activities, music, sand/water play, woodworking, and cooking.

Activity Area Checklist

Many teachers-in-training have profited from the use of a field-tested checklist to help them arrange the physical environment of the classroom. The Activity Area Checklist in Table 3.1 has proved helpful to many teachers in setting up their classrooms.

Using the Checklist

You can use the Activity Area Checklist as a guide to setting up your classroom from scratch, or as an assessment tool to help evaluate your present physical arrangement. From the 12 areas suggested by the checklist, you can determine how many areas you can accommodate in your own program according to the goals of the program, the number of children, the space available, and the children's interests and needs as well as your own.

It is important not only to set up these various areas, but also to know how to use them. Ways to use each of the 12 areas are discussed in this chapter.

TABLE 3.1 Activity Area Checklist

Student _____ Date _____

DIRECTIONS: Place a checkmark in the space before each item observed in the classroom.

1. Provide classroom areas for:
_____ Block building
_____ Books
_____ Dramatic play
_____ Large motor activities
_____ Manipulative activities
_____ Art
_____ Music
_____ Science/math
_____ Sand/water play
_____ Woodworking
_____ Cooking
_____ Child's private area

2. Organize block-building area to contain:
_____ Blocks in order on shelves
_____ Enough blocks for several children to build large buildings
_____ Room for children to build undisturbed
_____ Large and small figures and trucks

3. Organize book area to contain:
_____ Books appropriate for preschoolers
_____ Multi-ethnic books
_____ Books arranged at children's level
_____ Books in good condition
_____ Books arranged attractively
_____ A comfortable place to enjoy books
_____ A location away from noisy activities

4. Organize dramatic play area to contain:
_____ Appropriate equipment, furniture, accessories
_____ A full-length mirror
_____ Men's and women's dress-up clothes
_____ Clothes out where children can see them
_____ Materials neatly arranged for easy selection and return
_____ Dolls of different skin colors
_____ Language props such as two telephones

5. Locate large motor activities and equipment:
_____ To promote climbing, balancing, large movements
_____ In an area where children can use them freely and safely
_____ Away from quiet activities

TABLE 3.1 (continued)

6. **Arrange manipulative materials:**

_____ Close to the area where they will be used

_____ For easy selection and return by children

_____ With enough materials for several children at once

_____ With materials of varying levels of complexity

_____ So that necessary parts and pieces are not missing

7. **Have art materials for immediate use:**

_____ Located near tables or easels where they will be used

_____ Usable with minimum adult direction

_____ For easy selection and return by children

8. **Arrange music equipment and activities to:**

_____ Include sound- and rhythm-producing materials

_____ Include body movements

_____ Include songs with children

_____ Include record player and records

9. **Include in science/math corner:**

_____ Children's displays or collections

_____ Materials for sorting, counting

_____ Changing materials or displays

_____ Animal, fish, or insect pets

_____ Plants

_____ Appropriate books

_____ A computer

10. **Arrange sand and water activities:**

_____ With enough accessories for several to play with at once

_____ To be used with minimum adult direction

_____ Near source of water

_____ For easy clean-up

11. **Provide woodworking activities with:**

_____ Usable pounding, sawing equipment

_____ Enough equipment for more than one child

_____ Wood scraps, nails, etc.

_____ Safety limits to protect children

_____ Necessary adult supervision

_____ Minimum adult direction

12. **Include in cooking activities:**

_____ A variety of food preparation

_____ Use of real facilities

_____ Utensils such as knives, spoons, beaters

_____ Necessary adult supervision

_____ Minimum adult direction

TABLE 3.1 (continued)

---

13. Provide general room conditions with:

_____ A cubby, shelf, or box for each child's possessions

_____ Adequate storage space so room can be kept orderly

_____ Noisy activities separated from quiet activities

_____ Uncluttered space where children can move freely

_____ Any special arrangements for handicapped children

_____ Pictures, photos, displays at child's height

_____ Appropriate preventive measures for safety hazards

_____ Light, air, and heat conditions at best possible levels

---

Permission is granted by the publisher to reproduce this checklist for record keeping.

Child's Private Area

The child's private area is a place where a child can get away to be alone when the need arises. This is not an activity area as such, but a space you should provide on a permanent basis if your goal is to promote the child's positive self-image. If yours is an all-day program, such a location is a necessity. Three- and 4-year-olds find it especially overpowering to be with large groups of children for any length of time.

An overstuffed chair in a comfortable corner, away from noisy activities, may be all that you need. Some classrooms use a large cardboard carton with a cut-out door and window for a hut or playhouse. This can serve as the private area when dramatic play is finished. A packing crate or a card table covered with a blanket for the child to crawl under serves the same purpose. Some centers have a loft that can be used for a private retreat.

It is important to set up the private area in the classroom, not isolated in another part of the building. Children need to be by themselves, but at the same time they like to know what others are doing. Being isolated in another room is too much like punishment.

Block-Building Area

Wooden unit blocks have played an important role in early childhood programs since their introduction by Carolyn Pratt during the early years of the century (Koepke, 1989). Her units, half units, double units, arches, and ramps stimulate children's imaginations and creativity in constructing buildings of all sizes and shapes. The blocks help develop children's perceptual skills, such as eye-hand coordination, as they match sizes or balance one block on another when building towers and bridges. They promote counting and categorizing skills as children learn to sort shapes and sizes during pickup. The blocks help reinforce concepts learned on field trips when children use them to reconstruct a fire station or farm they have just visited.

2. Organize block-building area to contain:
_____ Blocks in order on shelves
_____ Enough blocks for several children to build large buildings
_____ Room for children to build undisturbed
_____ Large and small figures and trucks

Many prepackaged nursery school sets of unit blocks contain too few blocks for children to construct even a small number of moderate-size buildings at one time. It is better to order the blocks separately by size according to the amount of space available in the classroom.

Most teachers believe that unit blocks are well worth their expense. But if you have no money to buy them, you can make your own set of blocks using cardboard milk cartons, masking tape, and vinyl adhesive paper. Collect as many half-gallon, quart, pint, and half-pint containers as possible. Then cut, fold, and tape each top flat, and cover with plain contact paper. Bring parents together for a block-making bee to help equip the classroom.

Hollow cardboard blocks are also available commercially. They are similar to large hollow wooden blocks, and thus help to develop large motor skills in children. Both wooden and cardboard hollow blocks are popular with children for making child-size buildings that they can climb into. You may want to store the blocks in the large motor skills area, rather than in the unit block area.

It is important to store building accessories in the same area as the unit blocks, so children will know they are available and use them with the blocks. Small wooden figures of people and animals are popular if you want dramatic play to occur. Sometimes children prefer to play only with blocks, but often they want to pretend that people and animals are doing things in the block buildings. Small vehicles are also appropriate accessories. However, large wooden riding vehicles belong in the large motor area, not in an area where they can knock down unit block buildings. Other building accessories can include string for wires and plastic aquarium tubing for hoses, especially after children have taken field trips to a construction site or a fire station.

The block area is ideal for follow-up activities after a field trip. Be alert during the trip for ways to duplicate the experience in the block corner. Display a picture or book of the fire station, post office, or farm you have visited to stimulate building. (For more information on block building, see Chapter 9.)

Book Area

Early childhood specialists tell parents that reading to their preschool children is one of the most important things they can do to help their children's development. Preschool programs must go even further. You should not only read to the children, but also provide opportunities for children to spend time with books on their own. To

Cutouts or outlines of toys and blocks should be mounted on storage shelves so that children can choose toys and return them easily.

help children succeed in school and develop essential verbal skills, you need to introduce them to books in a pleasurable way as early as possible.

Because of its importance, the book area should be one of the most comfortable and inviting areas in your classroom. A soft throw rug, bright puffy pillows, and a bean bag or upholstered child-size chair may be the items you choose. Children enjoy taking part in furnishing the book corner. Bring in square rug samples and have the youngsters help carpet the floor.

Because the book area is a quiet one, it should be separated from noisy areas by room dividers, or placed next to other quiet activities, such as art or manipulatives.

Display books in the most inviting way possible. If book covers are torn or missing, repair or replace them. Torn books are not inviting to children; in fact, they communicate negative messages. Torn books imply that the teachers are not very concerned about keeping books in good condition. This further implies that books are not important, or someone would see that they were kept in shape. In addition, children may decide that it must be all right to tear a book, since someone already has.

3. Organize book area to contain:

_____ Books appropriate for preschoolers

_____ Multi-ethnic books

_____ Books arranged at children's eye level

_____ Books in good condition

_____ Books arranged attractively

_____ A comfortable place to enjoy books

_____ A location away from noisy activities

If you have a large book collection, consider displaying only part of it and changing the books from time to time. Putting out too many books at once tends to confuse young children. Be sure the books are displayed at children's eye level. If you have bookshelves made for older children, scale them down to your children's height.

Where do the books come from? A bookmobile? A library? Private donations? No matter what the source, you should be the one to choose the books for your classroom. Preschool children do not yet know how to select the best books. You need to acquire that knowledge, if you do not already have it, and put it to use. With the number of children's books presently being published, you must become familiar not only with the best books but also with selection techniques, so that you will be able to choose wisely from the many books available.

Some should be multi-ethnic books, showing children of different races and cultures as main characters. Whether or not your classroom has African American, Hispanic, or Native American children, you should have books that portray the multi-ethnicity of American life. There are excellent picture books available today showing children of almost every race or culture. From Eloise Greenfield's African American city children to Peter Parnell's American Indian children of the desert Southwest, modern picture books show boys and girls of every race doing interesting things in a setting any reader can respond to. (For more information on children's books, see Chapter 6.)

Dramatic Play Area

Young children live in a world of pretending. To adults, who often view fantasy with misgivings, this may seem unhealthy, but it is quite the contrary. In pretending, young children are not trying to escape from reality, they are trying to understand it. They are doing their best to deal with people and circumstances that sometimes confuse them. They are trying to bring some sense, order, and control into their world with dramatic play.

To assist children in their pretending, provide a classroom area that encourages imaginative play. Some programs call it the "housekeeping corner," "doll corner," or "dress-up corner." Others prefer the term "family corner" to eliminate sexist overtones.

---

4. Organize dramatic play area to contain:

_____ Appropriate equipment, furniture, accessories

_____ A full-length mirror

_____ Men's and women's dress-up clothes

_____ Materials neatly arranged for easy selection and return

_____ Dolls of different skin colors

_____ Language props such as two telephones

This area often contains kitchen furnishings, such as a stove, a refrigerator, a sink, cupboards, and a table, scaled down to child size. Some programs have a store with shelves of empty food packages. Some have a bedroom with a mirror, a dresser, and doll beds.

All these arrangements are familiar to children, and encourage them to dress up and play a variety of roles without teacher involvement: mother, father, uncle, aunt, grandmother, grandfather, sister, brother, baby, storekeeper. Playing these roles helps children experience life from another point of view. It helps them to understand these roles and, in many instances, to work out fears and frustrations in their own lives.

The little girl who dresses up as Mommy and then proceeds to beat a doll is not necessarily imitating a role she has witnessed at home. She is more likely expressing frustration with being in a helpless, powerless role as a child. Dramatic play allows children to express such frustrations in acceptable and harmless ways. Fears of going to the doctor can be played out ahead of time through such pretending. Dramatic play experiences help a child gain a healthy and positive self-concept.

You should provide both men's and women's clothes, hats, and shoes. Teenagers' clothes are just as appropriate and even fit the children better than adult sizes.

Dolls should be of different skin colors, whether or not your children are. Introduce children to the fascinating variety of Americans in a positive way as early as possible. Attitudes that develop in the early years last a lifetime.

Children learn much about themselves through dramatic play. They quickly learn how other children respond to them in the frank give and take of peer play. They should also be able to look at themselves in a full-length mirror, an item that needs to be a part of every dramatic play area. (For more information on dramatic play, see Chapter 9.)

Large Motor Area

If your program has a well-equipped outside playground, you may wonder why you should provide a large motor area inside. It is essential during the preschool years for children to practice large motor skills as often as possible every day, whether or not they go outside. In addition, some skills, such as walking on a balance beam, can be practiced more easily inside.

---

5. Locate large motor activities and equipment:

_____ To promote climbing, balancing, large movements

_____ In an area where children can use them freely and safely

_____ Away from quiet activities

An indoor wooden climber is perhaps the best single piece of equipment if you have room for only one piece. Molded plastic climbing and circular sliding equipment is popular in some programs. A homemade substitute could be a packing crate and a ladder, or a loft with a ladder and slide. Cardboard cartons with low doors cut out of both ends make fine tunnels to promote crawling skills. Commercial foam tunnels are also popular. Ordinary chairs and tables can serve as climbing, jumping, and crawling equipment when nothing else is available. Any teacher can make an indoor obstacle course out of ordinary classroom furnishings, masking tape, and imagination.

As you become more aware of how closely intellectual development is tied to motor control, you will want to provide many opportunities for children to practice control of their bodies in the classroom. Plan to include movement activities in the daily program and make sure that children have the opportunity to play outside whenever possible. (For more information on motor activities, see Chapter 4.)

Manipulative Area

Manipulative skill is the ability to use one's hands and fingers with dexterity. It is important for young children to develop such skills, not only so they can learn to button and zip clothes, tie shoes, and hold a pencil with ease, but also so they can later learn to read without difficulty. Eye-hand coordination is a prerequisite for developing the visual perception necessary to read from left to right.

Early childhood classrooms generally have many games and puzzles to promote small motor coordination. All puzzles provide good practice. Commercial wooden puzzles, in which each piece is a separate part of the picture, are best for unskilled 3-year-olds to start with. In the beginning, try out puzzles with the children to make sure they are not too difficult. Children may need help at first to experience success. Encourage them to stay with the puzzle until they finish it, and then praise them for a job well done. As the children's skills increase, you can add more challenging puzzles or games to the manipulative area.

An almost unlimited supply of commercial materials is available to fill your manipulative shelves: interlocking blocks, stacking toys, dominoes, snapping beads, stringing beads, pegboards, and table blocks. You may want to add teacher-made games to the area. Not only will you save money with homemade materials, but you can also provide directly for the children's particular needs.

---

6. Arrange manipulative materials:

_____ Close to the area where they will be used

_____ For easy selection and return by children

_____ With enough materials for several children at once

_____ With materials of varying degrees of complexity

_____ So that necessary parts and pieces are not missing

It is important to check the manipulative games frequently to see that parts and pieces are not missing. It is frustrating for a child to try to put together a puzzle with missing pieces. If pieces are missing, either replace them or discard the puzzle. Of course, it may be equally trying for you to keep track of all the parts. Some classrooms use plastic margarine containers with an outline of a part traced on the top to encourage children to put away pieces where they belong. Opening and closing these storage containers gives children additional practice in developing small motor coordination.

Being able to hold a pencil is another small motor skill children will eventually need to accomplish. Some children are ready now. You might try setting up a "writing table" in your manipulative area. It could contain primary-size pencils, crayons, and felt-tip markers, as well as paper and pads of various sizes to encourage scribbling and eventually printing. (For more information on manipulative activities, see Chapter 4.)

Art Area

Most early childhood programs use art activities almost every day. Unfortunately, however, adults seem to control art activity more often than almost any other activity. Teachers or aides usually get out the art supplies, pass out the paper, give instructions, and then remain in the area to make sure their instructions are carried out.

If we truly want to help a child develop a positive self-image, we should allow the child to be as independent in art activities as in dramatic play or block building. Giving a child the freedom to explore and experiment in art activities encourages and supports creativity. Direction and instructions are appropriate in certain art activities and at certain times, but we should also allow children the opportunity to try out paints of their own choosing with paper they select. To encourage independence, place art materials on child-level shelves near the tables or easels where they will be used; arrange materials for easy selection and return by the children; and allow and encourage children to participate in setting up and cleaning up art activities. When children become independent in art, they will happily choose this activity on their own during the daily work/play period.

---

7. Have art materials for immediate use:

_____ Located near tables or easels where they will be used

_____ Usable with minimum adult direction

_____ For easy selection and return by children

Art is a quiet activity, so the area should be removed from the more boisterous activities of the classroom. If you have a water source in the room, the art area should be nearby, if at all possible. With minimum direction, children can become entirely independent in set-up and clean-up when the necessary materials are close at hand. (For more information on art activities, see Chapter 7.)

Music Area

Music is important in the early childhood classroom. Young children are at a stage in their growth and development when they can and want to express themselves freely in all sorts of ways. Music is one of those ways. It is up to you to provide an atmosphere where music is as much a natural part of the day as conversation. Chanting, singing, dancing, moving to rhythm, playing records, tapes, and instruments should be a part of every day's activities for both children and adults.

---

8. Arrange music equipment and activities to:

_____ Include sound- and rhythm-producing materials

_____ Include body movements

_____ Include songs with children

_____ Include record player and records

Some music areas contain shelves to store rhythm instruments. You can also store instruments on hooks attached to a pegboard wall. Either way, it is a good idea to trace around each instrument with a magic marker to give children yet another opportunity to match shapes and return materials to their proper locations.

An inexpensive record player or tape recorder that children can learn to operate by themselves is a wise investment. Rules on an illustrated chart directing its use are easy for children to learn and satisfying for them to follow. Records and tapes, however, should not be the full extent of music in your classroom. Children also need opportunities to make their own music—singing, humming, or whistling, or playing a harmonica, drum, or keyboard. (For more information on music, see Chapter 7.)

Science/Math Area

In some programs, science and math activities are relegated to a side cupboard or window ledge. But teachers and aides who realize that such an area can be the most exciting spot in the classroom often reserve much more space: a cozy corner with a table for the daily "science object," shelves for children's collections, and space for the tools of science and math. These tools may include magnifying glasses and magnets of different sizes, tweezers, a tape measure or wind-up ruler, a balance, and a box of Cuisenaire rods, for starters.

---

9. Include in science/math corner:
   _____ Children's displays or collections
   _____ Materials for sorting, counting
   _____ Changing materials or displays
   _____ Animal, fish, or insect pets
   _____ Plants
   _____ Appropriate books
   _____ A computer

Some teachers make space for a terrarium full of ferns and moss and wintergreen gathered on a trip to the woods. Some have an aquarium for goldfish or tropical fish, with a book nearby to help children identify them. You might have a cage with a gerbil or guinea pig in residence. Shelves close to the window may contain bean sprouts in paper cups.

There will be something going on in the science corner every day in such a classroom. An egg carton full of a bean-seed-button mixture encourages children to sort and classify, or perhaps weigh the items with the balance. A chart to record how many inches each child's beans have grown invites all kinds of measuring with the wind-up ruler. A sealed box in the middle of a table will intrigue children with the sign, "Guess what's inside. Tell your guess to the tape recorder." The curious ones will ask what the sign says, shake the box, listen closely, and cautiously record their guesses. Another sign, "Bring something green tomorrow," sets off a babble of ideas.

Children in such a classroom expect to be challenged to find out something. They know they must use their five senses as well as the available science tools to discover "how much" or "what kind" or "how many." What's more, these children have learned on their own because of the arrangement of materials and the stimulating manner in which science objects are displayed.

Children will welcome the addition of a personal computer to the science area. More and more early childhood educators have come to realize that these powerful interactive learning tools can be used with great success by preschoolers. Many computers use the same exploring-through-play and trial-and-error style of learning young children use when they investigate new objects. This approach makes the computer an ideal vehicle to teach concepts such as symbolization, cause and effect, matching, and numbers, as well as skills such as learning to take turns, participating in conversation, and being creative with art programs.

Educators know that the best way for young children to learn to use these machines is not to be taught by adults but to experiment on their own with two children at a time in front of the computer. The book *The Computer as a Paintbrush* (Beaty & Tucker, 1987) tells how to set up and use a computer in an early childhood classroom. (For more information on science activities, see Chapter 5.)

Sand/Water Play

Water has an irresistible fascination for youngsters. Watch them wash their hands or get a drink. The splashing and squirting that often occur are part of the natural discovery process that children use to learn about new things.

---

10. Arrange sand and water activities:

_____ With enough accessories for several to play with at once

_____ To be used with minimum adult direction

_____ Near source of water

_____ For easy clean-up

Yet it is more than that. Water seems to have a mesmerizing quality. The smooth or bubbly feel of it . . . the gushing, gurgling sound of it . . . the way you can squirt it or spray it or pour it. Even children with short attention spans can play with water for hours. The hyperactive or unruly child often quiets down remarkably during water play. Its calming effect makes water play an excellent quiet activity, a wonderful change of pace after a hectic morning.

The physical arrangement of the water play area, just as with the rest of your classroom, determines whether children can enjoy playing on their own, or whether the area will invite squabbling and the need for close adult supervision.

If you have a water table, put only an inch or 2 of water in it. Children can have fun with this much, and still keep themselves and the floor fairly dry. Have equipment for use in the water table on nearby shelves or hanging from a pegboard rack in the area. To avoid arguments, be sure to have more than one of the children's favorite toys. Most children enjoy playing with large plastic basters and eggbeaters. A supply of empty plastic squeeze bottles of various sizes, as well as plastic pitchers, bottles, hoses, and eye droppers should be standard equipment. Plastic or wooden boats and figures of people are also popular.

To keep children's clothes dry, have aprons available, either hanging on hooks or folded on shelves nearby, so the children can get the aprons by themselves. A water table can usually accommodate a maximum of four children. Place the number 4 or four stick figures of children in the area, and let the children regulate themselves.

If you don't have a water table, use four plastic dishpans on any classroom table. The sink in the housekeeping corner also makes a good, if small, water play area for doing the dolls' dishes or laundering doll clothes.

Put a squirt of liquid detergent in the water at times and let children play with bubbles. They may want to blow through straws. Another day, let them use food coloring and droppers to mix colors.

Water tables can easily be converted to sand tables for another activity children really enjoy. The same directions apply. Two or 3 inches of sand is plenty. Keep sand accessories and clean-up equipment in the area. Help children understand a few simple rules: keep the sand in the table; no throwing sand; no more than four children at a time. Then enforce the rules with quiet, consistent firmness. If sand is spilled, children can help sweep it up.

Small containers, sifters, hoppers, scoops, shovels, small dump trucks, and figures of people are popular sand toys. Be sure to have enough toys so that four children can play without squabbles. Have the children wear safety goggles to keep sand out of their eyes.

Woodworking Area

Wood is another medium that children find especially attractive. You can see this by the way they handle wooden blocks. The fact that wood can be pounded and transformed into different shapes makes it as creative a medium as paint.

Both boys and girls love to pound. Thus, woodworking is an excellent channel for the acceptable venting of frustration. Children can pound wood and let off steam harmlessly.

---

11. **Provide woodworking activities with:**
    _____ Usable pounding, sawing equipment
    _____ Enough equipment for more than one child
    _____ Wood scraps, nails
    _____ Safety limits to protect children
    _____ Necessary adult supervision
    _____ Minimum adult direction

Not every early childhood program can afford a workbench. You may find that tree stumps make an excellent substitute and have even more suitable surfaces for pounding. Just for the fun of pounding, let children nail things onto the tops of tree stumps. A box with nails of many sizes and another with pine wood scraps are enough to keep your woodworking area going for many days. Children should wear safety goggles for this activity. Most children feel grown-up when they put on goggles and also like the looks of them.

Some teachers substitute ceiling tiles for wood because children have better control over hammers and nails with this softer substance. Building supply dealers will sometimes donate extra tiles. Children can also pound nails through leather scraps or Styrofoam boards more easily than wood at first.

Small adult tools are more effective than children's toolbox toys. You can store tools on shelves or hang them from pegboards with their outlines traced, so that children can match shapes and return the tools easily.

Cooking Area

Many adults misunderstand the intent of cooking in the preschool classroom. This activity in no way purports to teach a child to cook. Instead, cooking is an exceptional vehicle to promote growth and learning experiences, such as eye-hand coordination, small muscle strength, cause and effect, sequencing, one-to-one correspondence, measurement, and sensory exploration. For example, peeling shells from hard-boiled eggs offers unparalleled practice in small motor skills. Scraping carrots, dicing potatoes, mixing batter, and turning the handle of an eggbeater strengthen hand and arm muscles.

---

12. **Include in cooking activities:**

_____ A variety of food preparation

_____ Use of real facilities

_____ Utensils such as knives, spoons, beaters

_____ Necessary adult supervision

_____ Minimum adult direction

Cooking activities also present the opportunity to conduct science observations and experiments: showing how heat changes things; demonstrating how liquids dissolve things; illustrating the changes produced by freezing. You can promote understanding of math through weighing and measuring. Using illustrated recipe charts strengthens symbolization skills.

The intense interest of most children in food and food preparation provides the motivation for learning, and your ingenuity supplies the activities. There are virtually no limits to the learning possibilities of a cooking area. Cooking is fascinating to children because it is a real activity, not a pretend one—and they can eat the results!

Cooking can take place in the classroom at a table set up for it, on a counter near an electrical outlet, or in the center kitchen. A microwave oven, a toaster oven, or an electric fry pan can supply the heat if your safety and insurance regulations permit hot cooking. (For more information on cooking activities, see Chapter 2.)

SEPARATES ACTIVITY AREAS AND PLACES THEM IN APPROPRIATE SPACES

Separating Activities

Most classrooms use shelves, cubbies, or large pieces of equipment as dividers to separate activity areas from one another. Use your ingenuity to section off your classroom areas. Instead of placing bookshelves against the wall, use them as dividers between the book area and another learning center. Use block shelves the same way. The stove, refrigerator, and wooden sink can serve as dividers in the dramatic play area. Then children can see each activity area as a separate learning center and choose to use it with better understanding.

Dividers should not be so high that they conceal children from one another or from the teacher's view. The room should be open and cheerful, with spaces used effectively. In lieu of room dividers, you might consider permanently placed furniture to divide your areas. Section off particular areas with chairs, benches, or couches, and fasten colored corrugated cardboard to their backs. Some classrooms have a loft built to provide interesting extra space, not only to promote climbing but also to create activity areas both on top of and under the loft. Some teachers put pillows in the space under the wooden climber for a music listening center during quiet periods.

Use room walls and corners as the backs of activity areas, with these dividers forming the sides of the areas. The walls can serve as spaces for mounting photos, posters, and pictures appropriate to the various areas. In the block area, for example, mount pictures of buildings, bridges, and towers on the walls, to give the children motivation for block building. After a field trip, mount photos from the trip or cut out pictures from magazines. Various pictures, charts, and illustrations can be mounted on the walls of each activity area.

Before you begin rearranging the classroom, step back and watch how the children use it now. Do they all crowd together in one area? Do they mill around in the center of the room without much direction? Do they have to walk through the block area to get to the bathroom? Are your clothing cubbies somewhere other than near the door where children enter? Is the sink near the art area? Are certain areas more popular than others? What seems to make them this way? To arrange the activity areas so that children can move freely to each area and use it with ease, it is important to determine how the room works in its present arrangement.

Floor Planning

Make a floor plan of the present arrangement, and record directly on it as you observe children during the free-choice period for 10 minutes on 3 different days. Use some sort of symbol, such as x's and o's for girls and boys, to record on the plan the location and movement of the individual children in each area for the 10 minutes of your observation. Use arrows to show how children move from one area to another. This exercise will help you to step back and objectively evaluate the children's use of the classroom. Discuss your findings with members of your team. If movement, work, and play are not orderly or not even taking place in certain areas, you may want to make some changes.

How much empty space do you have? How much do you need? Large areas of empty space encourage children to run around wildly or aimlessly. Would your program be better served if you sectioned off some of that space into activity areas? You may feel you need large areas for circle time or whole group activities. Instead, you might consider using the block area for circle time after the blocks are put away. Whole group activities do not require permanent space when none is available, or when such space will reduce the number of necessary activity areas.

Some teachers place all the tables in a large area in the center of the room. Is this necessary? Wouldn't the room be more interesting if you divide the large central space into activity areas and move a table into each area?

Is there an activity area that few children use? Why do you think this is so? Some book areas consist merely of a shelf against the wall with one chair nearby. Few children may use such an area because it is not sectioned off for the privacy of looking at a book or because it is not inviting. Pull the bookshelf away from the wall and use it as a divider. Bring in some bright pillows, stuffed animals, or puppets that go with the books. Be sure that your books are appropriate for the age and interest of your children. Mount colorful book posters on the walls of the area at the children's eye level. Look for posters in children's book departments or order them from Children's Book Council, Inc., 350 Scotland Road, Orange, NJ, 07050.

Traffic Patterns

Now look at the traffic patterns in your classroom. Can children move freely from one area to another? They should not have to squeeze between tables and room dividers or step over someone's block structure to get a library book. On the other hand, you need to avoid having one long traffic lane that encourages running from one end of the room to the other. Simply move a room divider or a piece of equipment into the pathway to prevent this uncontrolled movement.

What happens when the children enter your classroom? If they remove their outer clothing inside the room, are their cubbies nearby or must they cross the room to find a clothes hook? Set up areas for quiet activities away from the entrance, for there will be much bustling in and out of any preschool classroom entrance.

Regulating Behavior

Do your observations indicate problems with regulating the number of children in any one area? Children can regulate themselves if you make it interesting for them. For example, you can mount pictures of four fish on the wall by the water table, six construction workers in the block area, or four books in the book area, with a hook under each picture. Then a child who wants to play in a particular area can hang a picture or tag on one of the hooks. When all the hooks are full, other children must either trade a place or play elsewhere.

The number of chairs at a table regulates how many children can play there. Some teachers section off the floor of the block area with masking tape to delineate building lots if children have been crowding one another. Give your children some options for this kind of regulation and ask them what they'd like to try. Some teachers prefer a color-coding method, making up a certain number of tags of one color for children to use in an area of the same color. You can keep the tags on a pegboard near the front of the room for the children to choose from. Others have a particular number of special necklaces in each activity area for children to wear when they want to play in the area.

Check your room after you have rearranged it to see if movement, work, and play are more orderly than before. If not, you may want to try another arrangement. Plan it on paper first and discuss it with your team and your children. It is their room as well as yours.

ARRANGES EQUIPMENT AND MATERIALS SO CHILDREN CAN MAKE CHOICES EASILY AND INDEPENDENTLY

Careful arrangement of equipment and materials can also help promote children's independence and self-direction. Place materials in the appropriate activity area where children need to use them and make them accessible to the children on low shelves or pegboards. Arrange materials so the children understand what is available and can make choices. There is no need to display all the toys at the same time; this makes it too difficult for young children to choose. Keep a closed storage cabinet for extra supplies and materials. Add a few new ones to each area from time to time.

Book Area

For example, your book area should display a moderate number of books arranged with the covers facing the children. Children can then see what is available and choose what to look at. If your shelves are not the type for displaying books with the covers showing, you might rather put books flat on the shelves or hang them on clotheslines with clothespins. Books crammed on a shelf with only the bindings showing are not inviting for children. They cannot see what is available, and they usually respond by avoiding the book area altogether.

You may not want to keep all the books in one area. To encourage young children to go to books for information on their own, you may want to place certain books in other activity areas. How about a paperback fish book from an aquarium store hanging from a cord next to the aquarium? Let your children have the fun of matching the fish in the aquarium to the pictures in the book. What about a gerbil or guinea pig book in your pet area? Books about farms or fire stations or post offices may inspire children playing in the block area. Fasten manila pocket folders to the wall in the various areas and place a book in each, featuring the subject you are currently investigating.

Your purpose should be to draw children and books together. You can do this by placing books where the children are, as well as by attracting children to the book area.

Dramatic Play Area

In the dramatic play area, the dress-up clothes should be hung on hooks, pegs, clothes trees, or hangers at child-height, so children can easily choose and later return their costumes. Clothes crammed into a box or drawer make it difficult for the children to see what is available and to make choices. Prop boxes can be stored on low shelves, with pictures on the outside indicating their contents, e.g., doctor's equipment or fire fighter's gear. Then children are free to select props on their own to play the role of barber, beautician, supermarket clerk, doctor, fire fighter, or police officer.

Keep this area neat if you want children to be attracted to it. When play is finished, have them help you get it back in order, with clothes on the dolls or on the hooks, a baby doll asleep in the crib, and the table set and ready for its next role-players.

Manipulative Area

Puzzles and table games should be stored on low shelves next to the table or floor area designated for manipulative play. Children can then choose the games they want to play with. When they are finished, they will have no difficulty returning them. Why should teachers make choices for the children? Allowing children to make their own choices strengthens their independence and self-concept. If they find a puzzle too difficult, they can return it and take another. Set up your classroom to give children this opportunity.

Block Area

Blocks should be on low shelves and stacked lengthwise so that children can decide easily what they need for building. A cutout or outline of the block at the back of the shelf enables children to return blocks to the proper shelves and stack them the right way during pickup. Every item of equipment in your classroom can be so designated. Draw or mount cutouts or outlines of woodworking tools, rhythm instruments, water table playthings, house corner dishes, cooking implements, and paint jars on their appropriate storage shelves so that children can easily choose and properly return the items. These signs not only help children find the place for their toys but also develop the cognitive skill of matching the blocks and toys to their cutout shapes. In addition, the process helps children develop symbolization skills, since the signs stand for or symbolize an object.

Evaluating Room Arrangement

Your children's behavior in the classroom will tell you whether you have planned and arranged well for them. Large groups of children milling around aimlessly may indicate too much open space or too few activity areas. A great deal of running may mean that open areas need to be sectioned off with room dividers. On the other hand, your room may be too cluttered, so that children, especially 3-year-olds, have difficulty making choices and settling down; perhaps they are suffering from "sensory overload." Make the environment simpler by putting away some of the materials or taking unnecessary pictures off the walls. When most of the children become engrossed in activities, you will realize your arrangement is working as it should.

During the year, you may want to rearrange the room for variety or for new challenges. It is best to change only one or two areas at once. Abrupt changes can easily upset young children. Allow them to participate in the planning and rearranging, since it is their room as much as yours.

SUMMARY

This chapter has provided ideas for setting up and arranging an early childhood classroom so that children will become self-directed in their learning. You will need to articulate your program's goals to decide what activity areas to include in your classroom. Using the Activity Area Checklist should help you understand how each activity area can promote your program's goals for young children. Since the physical arrangement of a preschool classroom is the structure for an open and flexible curriculum, you will want to arrange your room carefully based on ideas from this chapter. Separating one area from another by pulling shelves away from the walls and using them as dividers is a simple, effective way to make the areas obvious to the children. Mounting the outlines of blocks, toys, and utensils on their shelf locations makes the use of each area and its materials meaningful to the children. Self-regulating devices, such as hooks and tags or charts and necklaces, help children become independent in the use of their environment.

LEARNING ACTIVITIES

1. Read Chapter 3, "Establishing a Learning Environment," and answer Question Sheet 3–A.
2. View Videopak A, "Setting Up the Classroom," and answer Question Sheet 3–B.
3. Read one or more of the books listed under Suggested Readings. Add 10 cards to your file with specific ideas for setting up the classroom. Include the reference source on the back of each card.
4. Use the Activity Area Checklist to assess your room arrangement. Set up a new activity area or rearrange an old one based on the results and ideas gained from this chapter. (Trainer can visit.)
5. Visit another early childhood classroom and make a floor plan showing the areas children were using during your visit. Record on file cards at least three new ideas for classroom arrangement gained from this visit.
6. Set up and implement a children's self-regulating method for choosing activity areas in your classroom. (Trainer can observe.)
7. Make outlines of materials and equipment and mount them on their particular shelves and hook-boards. Observe how children use the materials afterwards.

8. Bring in new games, books, pictures, or props that illustrate a field trip you have taken, and add them to one or more activity areas. Observe how children use them.

9. Complete the Chapter 3 Evaluation Sheet and return it to your trainer or college supervisor.

QUESTION SHEET 3–A

(Based on Chapter 3, "Establishing a Learning Environment")

1. In what way does the physical arrangement of the classroom control the children's behavior?
2. What is one way your room arrangement can promote the children's positive self-image?
3. How can you determine what activity areas to establish in your room?
4. Why should you have a child's private area? What should it consist of?
5. How can the arrangement of your block building area prevent squabbles?
6. How can you set up the classroom for children to regulate their own numbers in the various areas?
7. What are two different ways for separating one area from another?
8. What equipment might your dramatic play area contain after a field trip?
9. How can you set up a particular area so that the children can use it independently?
10. When should you rearrange your classroom, and how should you go about it?

QUESTION SHEET 3–B

(Based on Videopak A, "Setting Up the Classroom")

1. What is one way you can arrange your classroom so that children become more self-directed in their learning?
2. What can you do specifically to help children make choices in the room?
3. How will you decide what block building accessories to provide?
4. How can you provide for both boys and girls in dramatic play?
5. How should you arrange your dramatic play area to help children make choices?
6. How can children develop independence in the art area?
7. Why is it important to display children's art products attractively? How can you do this?
8. Where should children's manipulative materials be located? What should they consist of?
9. How can your arrangement of the water play area promote children's independence?
10. How can you tell whether your room arrangement is successful?

SUGGESTED READINGS

Beaty, J. J., & Tucker, W. H. (1987). *The computer as a paintbrush: Creative uses for the personal computer in the preschool classroom.* Columbus, OH: Merrill.

Greenman, J. (1988). *Caring spaces, learning places: children's environments that work.* Redmond, WA: Exchange Press.

Hill, D. M. (1977). *Mud, sand, and water.* Washington, DC: National Association for the Education of Young Children.

Koepke, M. (1989, December). Learning by the block. *Teacher,* pp. 52–60.

Kritchevsky, S., & Prescott, E. (1969). *Planning environments for young children: Physical space.* Washington, DC: National Association for the Education of Young Children.

Lindberg, L., & Swedlow, R. (1985). *Young children exploring and learning.* Boston: Allyn & Bacon.

Loughlin, C. E., & Suina J. H. (1982). *The learning environment: An instructional strategy.* New York: Teachers College Press.

Manwaring, S. (1977). *Room arrangement and materials.* Ypsilanti, MI: High/Scope Press.

Provenzo, E. F., Jr., & Brett, A. (1983). *The complete block book.* Syracuse, NY: Syracuse University Press.

Skeen, P., Garner, A. P., & Cartwright, S. (1985). *Woodworking with young children.* Washington, DC: National Association for the Education of Young Children.

Vergeront, J. (1989). *Places and spaces for preschool and primary (Indoors).* Washington, DC: National Association for the Education of Young Children.

CHILDREN'S BOOKS

Barton, B. (1981). *Building a house.* New York: Puffin Books.

Browne, A. (1989). *Things I like.* New York: Alfred A. Knopf.

Gibbons, G. (1982). *Tool book.* New York: Holiday House.

Gibson, G. (1986). *Up goes the skyscraper.* New York: Macmillan.

Magorian, M. (1990). *Who's going to take care of me?* New York: Harper & Row.

Rey, M., & H. A. (1985). *Curious George at the fire station.* Boston: Houghton Mifflin.

Rockwell, H. (1984). *My nursery school.* New York: Puffin Books.

Stevenson, R. L. (1988). *Block City.* New York: E. P. Dutton.

Stinson, K., & Collins, H. (1990). *The dressed-up book.* Willowdale, Ontario, Canada: Annick Press.

Weiss, L. (1984). *My teacher sleeps in school.* New York: Frederick Warne.

VIDEOTAPES

Beaty, J. J. (Producer). (1979). Setting up the classroom (Videopak A), *Skills for preschool teachers* [Videotape]. Elmira, NY: McGraw Bookstore, Elmira College.

Berlfein, J. (Producer). *A classroom with blocks* [Videotape]. Washington, DC: National Association for the Education of Young Children.

Space to grow [Videotape]. Portland, OR: Educational Productions.

Greenman, J. (Producer). (1990). *My kind of place* [Videotape]. Minneapolis, MN: Greater Minneapolis Day Care Association.

South Carolina Educational TV (Producer). Room arrangement and scheduling: Getting it all together, *Calico Pie* [Videotape]. Columbia, SC: SCETV.

CHAPTER 3 EVALUATION SHEET
ESTABLISHING A LEARNING ENVIRONMENT

1. Student _____

2. Trainer _____

3. Center where training occurred _____

4. Beginning date _____ Ending date _____

5. Describe what student did to accomplish General Objective

   _____

   _____

6. Describe what student did to accomplish Specific Objectives

   Objective 1 _____

   _____

   Objective 2 _____

   _____

   Objective 3 _____

   _____

7. Evaluation of student's Learning Activities
   (Trainer Check One)   (Student Check One)

   _____ Highly superior performance   _____

   _____ Superior performance   _____

   _____ Good performance   _____

   _____ Less than adequate performance   _____

Signature of Trainer: Signature of Student:

_____   _____

Comments:

4 Advancing Physical Skills

General Objective

To promote children's physical development by determining their needs and providing appropriate materials and activities.

Specific Objectives

- ☐ Assesses physical needs of individual children and makes appropriate plans to promote their development.
- ☐ Provides equipment and activities to promote large and small motor skills in and out of the classroom.
- ☐ Provides opportunities for children to move their bodies in a variety of ways.

T he physical growth and development of young children during their preschool years is such an obvious occurrence that we sometimes take it entirely for granted. Children will of course grow bigger, stronger, more agile, and more coordinated in their movements without outside help. It is part of their natural development. But at times, we are suddenly caught up short by the 4-year-old who cannot run without stumbling, has trouble holding a paintbrush, or cannot walk up and down stairs easily.

We realize that individual differences in development account for many such lags. Some children are slower than others in developing coordination. Neurological problems or even lack of opportunity to practice skills may account for others. But no matter what the cause of developmental lags, classroom workers can help young children improve both large and small motor coordination by providing activities, materials, and equipment that will give them practice with basic movements.

ASSESSES PHYSICAL NEEDS OF INDIVIDUAL CHILDREN AND MAKES APPROPRIATE PLANS TO PROMOTE THEIR DEVELOPMENT

All children pass through the same sequence of stages in their physical growth, but some do it more quickly or evenly than others. Since individual children in a single classroom will be at many different levels of physical development, the teacher will want to determine at the outset each child's physical capacities to provide appropriate activities to promote growth. To provide relevant help for your children, you should determine the large motor skills they already possess, as well as the skills they need to strengthen. It is best to avoid a formal evaluation with each child attempting the activities as you watch and record, since this tends to create a win-or-lose situation that makes children become self-conscious and less free in their movements.

Instead, make an informal assessment while children play in the large motor area, on the playground, or in the block corner. Observe the children as they go up the steps and into the building. You will soon learn which children move with confidence and which have difficulty. Take a bean bag out on the playground and toss it back and forth to individuals. Put out tricycles for them to ride. You will soon have a comprehensive survey of each child's large muscle development.

You will plan activities as a result of this assessment; however, be sure not to single out a particular individual. There is no need to focus attention on an awkward child. All the children can benefit from practice with large body movements. But you will want to be sure to involve children who need special help in such activities.

Large Motor Assessment

The checklist in Table 4.1 includes the large motor skills you will want your children to perform. Copy it onto a 5-by-7-inch card for each individual and check off items as they are accomplished. Add the date after each skill to keep a running record.

Walking

Uncoordinated children may still have trouble walking; they need as much practice as you can give them. By playing walking games with small groups of children, you can make this practice fun for all. Play Follow the Leader with different kinds of walking, for example, tramping, striding, tiptoeing, strolling, shuffling, marching, and waddling. You might say aloud the kind of steps you are making as you walk: "Tramp, tramp, tramp, shuffle, shuffle, shuffle," and so forth.

TABLE 4.1   Large Motor Checklist

_____	Walks up and down stairs easily
_____	Walks across a balance beam
_____	Balances on one foot
_____	Jumps with both feet over a low object
_____	Runs without falling
_____	Climbs up and down a piece of climbing equipment
_____	Crawls, creeps, or scoots across the floor
_____	Picks up and carries a large object
_____	Throws a beanbag/ball
_____	Catches a beanbag/ball
_____	Rides wheeled equipment

Permission is granted by the publisher to reproduce this checklist for evaluation and record keeping.

The children can also try to walk like certain animals—a duck, an elephant, a cat, or a mouse—and let the others try to guess what they are. This activity is especially appropriate after you have read to a small group of children the book *Pretend You're a Cat* (Marzollo & Pinkney, 1990). Full-page illustrations show children making motions like cats and dogs or birds and bees.

Another walking activity involves cutting out vinyl adhesive paper and mounting a trail of stepping-stones on the floor, and having the children step from one to another. Some teachers prefer to use stepping-stones made of floor tile squares instead.

Walking up and down stairs calls for coordination and balance. A piece of commercial equipment that promotes this skill is the Rocking Boat, which becomes steps when turned upside down. Children also like to make their own steps with large hollow blocks pushed together.

Balancing

To make any kind of movement with confidence and stability, children must be able to balance themselves. They must maintain body stability while stationary as well as during movement. To promote stationary balance, you can play Follow the Leader in the classroom, having the children stand on one foot while holding the other, then shift to the opposite foot. If you have large hollow blocks, have children try to stand on a horizontal block and then on top of a vertically placed block.

In another stationary balancing activity, children pretend to be various animals and birds, as suggested in the book *Pretend You're a Cat* (Marzollo & Pinkney, 1990). Large pictures of animals placed around the room at the children's eye level will help them choose which animal to mimic. They might choose to be a bird dog pointing, a heron standing on one leg, or a frog getting ready to hop. Have one child pretend to be an animal or a bird in one of the pictures, and let the others guess which one.

Children with physical handicaps can practice stationary balancing. The book *The Balancing Girl* (Rabe, 1981) shows Margaret balancing a book on her head while moving in a wheelchair. Then she balances herself on crutches. Read this book to your class whether or not you have children with handicapping conditions. Then have children try out their balancing skills in a wheelchair and/or on crutches.

Activities to promote balance while moving involve the traditional balance beam. You can purchase a balance beam from a school equipment company, or make one by placing blocks in a row. Children can practice walking across the wide side of the beam and then the narrow edge. They can first learn to balance while walking forward, and later while walking sideways and backwards. For a permanent balance beam on the outside playground, anchor railroad ties to the ground.

For another walking balance activity, the teacher can cut out vinyl adhesive paper footprints and handprints and fasten them on the classroom floor in a series of "baby steps," "giant steps," "frog hops" (i.e., both hand and footprints), and "tiptoes" for the children to follow during Follow the Leader games. Also include "crutch marks," "cane marks," and "wheelchair tracks" with contact paper for

Balance beams can be made by placing blocks in a row.

children to follow while using this equipment. Don't limit this activity to children with handicapping conditions—all of the children should try it.

Still another piece of balancing equipment is the commercially available "balance board," which is flat on top and curved underneath for a child to stand on and rock back and forth.

Hopping, Jumping, and Leaping

Once children have learned to balance on one foot, they can try hopping. The hopping movement is done on one leg. At first, children can practice hopping in place on one leg and then the other. Then they can move forward with their hops. Make a hopping contact paper trail just as you did for balancing. Place several single footprint cutouts in a row on the right side of the trail, and then more single footprints in a row on the left side. When children come to these, they will have to hop first on the right foot and then on the left. Make a hopscotch game with masking tape and cutout vinyl adhesive paper symbols of geometric designs or colors. Children can call out the symbol when they hop on the design, or you can call out a symbol and see if children can hop to it.

Jumping is the same as hopping, only with both feet together. Children can jump in place, to move forward, to get over something, or to get down from a height. Children can try to jump over a "river" you create on the classroom floor with two strips of masking tape for the "river banks." Keep the banks close together at first, but widen them as the children improve their jumping skills. Encourage them to jump with both feet together and not merely leap across with one foot. Once children develop the skill of jumping over lines, let them try jumping over a unit block with both feet together.

Children also enjoy jumping down from a height. You may want to use a mat for a landing pad. Jumping off a low chair is high enough for 3- and 4-year-olds. One teacher found that her children liked to measure and record their jumps. She planned a "jumping jack period" once a week in which each child in a small group jumped off a low wooden box; another child marked the landing spot; and together, they measured the length of the jump. This was recorded on a "jumping jack chart." The children tried to better their previous record every time they jumped.

Preschool-size trampolines are also available commercially for practicing the skill of jumping in place. To prevent falls the best equipment has a safety bar for the child to hold while jumping.

Children can also pretend to be various jumping creatures, such as rabbits, grasshoppers, frogs, or kangaroos. They can jump to music or the beat of a tambourine. Your "footprint trail" can encourage jumping by mounting pairs of vinyl adhesive paper footprints placed together with a space in between the next pair. You can also read a book about jumping to a small group of children, and have them jump at the proper time in the story. *Jump, Frog, Jump* (Kalan, 1981) lends itself well to such an activity.

Leaping is easier than jumping for most children. It is done on one foot and can carry the child farther than a jump. Children can pretend to be deer leaping through a forest or runners leaping over hurdles.

Running, Galloping, and Skipping

Children who can run well spend a great deal of time doing so. It is the uncoordinated child who needs special practice running. When you plan running games for small groups, be sure to include all the children and encourage all to run. Games on the playground or in the gymnasium can include Follow the Leader, relay races, and simple circle games. Avoid placing emphasis on competition with winners and losers by praising the efforts of each child. If someone is declared the "winner," it may very well discourage the slower child, who will not want to participate in an activity for fear of being a sure "loser." Yet this is the child who needs the practice.

Inside the classroom, running skills can be promoted with action chants that encourage running in place:

Trains

Huff, huff,	(Run slowly in place)
Puff, puff,	
Watch me go!	
I'm a locomotive	
Going slow;	
Chug, chug,	(Run slightly faster)
Tug, tug,	
Watch me pull!	
I'm a diesel engine,	
Pulling up the hill;	
Zip, zip,	(Run as fast as you can)
Click, click,	
Watch me come back!	
I'm a string of subway cars	
Zipping down the track;	
Whoa!	(Slow down)
Slow!	
Stop!	(Come to a halt with a jump)

The galloping motion is a combination of a walk and a leap. The child takes a step with one foot, then brings the other one up behind it and leads off with the first foot again. In other words, one foot always leads. Children enjoy pretending to be horses and galloping around the room to music or tambourine beats.

Skipping is a much more complex skill than running or galloping. Preschool programs should not be concerned with teaching children to skip. Most children do not master this skill before age 5 or 6, nor should they be expected to do so.

Climbing

Climbing can be done with legs or arms or both. To ensure the safety of the children because of the height involved, you will want to purchase commercial climbing materials from reliable firms. Any homemade climbing equipment needs to be tested carefully before children use it.

Indoor climbing equipment includes wooden jungle gyms, rung ladders, and the climbing house. Many indoor climbers include metal nesting climbers of different heights that can stand alone or be used to support a walking board, a horizontal crossing ladder, a wooden sliding board, or even a teeter-totter. Indoor climbers are usually movable rather than anchored to the ground as those on outdoor playgrounds. For safety's sake, classroom workers need to stand nearby when children are using indoor climbers. Pads or mats should be placed underneath in case of falls.

Outdoor climbing equipment includes metal dome climbers, satellite climbers, jungle gyms, rung ladders, rope ladders, link chain ladders, cargo nets, and tires, to mention a few. The equipment your children use outside should be designed for preschoolers. You should not have large-size playground pieces. Not only is large equipment dangerous for 3- and 4-year-olds because of its size, but the movements and skill required are beyond the capacity of most young children.

Commercial climbing equipment is expensive. You can substitute your own outdoor equipment through donations, such as tree stumps, truck tires, cable spools, or an old rowboat for climbing and dramatic play. Be sure that the wooden equipment is free of splinters and that paint is free of lead. Drill holes in any tires that you use, so that water will not collect and serve as a breeding place for mosquitoes.

Outside climbing equipment should be anchored firmly to the ground and cushioned underneath with sawdust, wood chips, bark, sand, or other soft materials. (See Videopak H, "Outdoor Play Equipment.")

Crawling, Creeping, and Scooting

The crawling movement is made with the body flat out on the floor, with arms pulling and legs pushing. Children can pretend they are worms, snakes, lizards, beetles, caterpillars, or alligators. They can also pretend to be swimmers who are swimming across a river or lake. You can read or tell the class a story about some creature, and ask the children to move like the creature. You might play music while they are moving. They can crawl to spooky music played on a tape or record player, or to tambourine or drumbeats that the teacher makes.

Creeping, on the other hand, is done on hands and knees with the body raised above the floor. Some children have difficulty creeping in a cross-pattern, that is, moving the opposite arm and leg in unison. If this is the case with any of your children, give them many opportunities to practice.

Children can pretend to be any one of a number of animals as they creep: a dog, cat, horse, tiger, elephant, or dinosaur. They can creep to music or drumbeats. They can creep through tunnels made from cardboard boxes, card tables, or two chairs tipped forward with their backs joined together. Commercial creeping equipment includes barrels, fabric, and foam tunnels. You can create an obstacle course around the room for creeping only, with the path marked out by masking tape. Children can pretend to be an animal or a mountain climber as they creep through the course.

Scooting is done by sitting, kneeling, or standing on a movable piece of equipment and pushing it along with one foot or both feet. Children can sit on a piece of cardboard and push themselves backwards across a polished floor with their feet. Commercial scooter boards are designed for children to sit on and move with the caster wheels on the bottom. Young children, in fact, do better by sitting than by standing on skateboards. The scooter vehicle, operated by standing and steering while pushing with one foot, is beyond most 3- and many 4-year-olds, but they enjoy walking it around. Some tricycles are propelled by the movement of children's feet on the floor rather than by pedals. Children also like to push themselves around on large wooden vehicles. This equipment should be kept in the large motor area for daily use.

Picking Up/Carrying

Use a stack of hollow blocks or something similar for the children to pick up and carry one by one. When all the blocks have been moved in one direction, reverse the course. Children can also carry large pillows, empty cartons, chairs, mats, and large toys.

Throwing/Catching

A great deal of practice is necessary for young children to become skilled at the arm movements of throwing and catching. Catching is the more difficult of the two. For children to experience success in your classroom, start with something large, for example, a large bean bag, a foam ball, a beach ball, a small soccer ball, or a basketball. Children can throw to one another, to the teacher, up in the air, or at a target such as a carton or a preschool-size basketball basket.

Children can perfect their underhand throwing skills with other objects, such as rings and ring-toss targets. Beanbags can be thrown into a wastebasket or a cardboard carton with a clown's face on it.

Young children usually catch with both hands and their body. To develop catching skills, you can throw children objects like yarn balls, Nerf balls, beach balls, and beanbags at first.

Riding Wheeled Equipment

Tricycles and Big Wheels help young children learn the skills of pedaling and steering. Some centers have halls that can be used for riding activities, and others have sidewalks outside. If you do not have such a hard surface, consider asking an industry or shipping firm to donate an old conveyer belt to be used as a tricycle path across the lawn.

Making Plans for Individuals

Once your assessment is complete, you should begin planning for the child's continued physical development. As previously mentioned, you should not single out a child who has a particular need, but instead plan a small group activity that will address that need and include the child. If the activity can focus on a skill that the child possesses, all the better. Whenever possible, you should begin with the strengths of a child to help him develop in an area of need. For example, 5-year-old Andrew's Large Motor Checklist, prepared by his teacher on a 5-by-7-inch card, is shown in Table 4.3.

Large Motor Checklist

____√____	Walks up and down stairs easily
____√____	Walks across a balance beam
____√____	Balances on one foot
____√____	Jumps with both feet over a low object
____√____	Runs without falling
_____	Climbs up and down a piece of climbing equipment
_____	Crawls, creeps, or scoots across the floor
_____	Picks up and carries a large object
_____	Throws a beanbag/ball
_____	Catches a beanbag/ball
____√____	Rides wheeled equipment

The teacher was surprised at the throwing/catching results, since Andrew's running and jumping skills were better than average and he was an active boy. He seemed to love balls and would try hard to throw and catch, but without much success. It seemed strange that his arms were not as strong or coordinated as the rest of his body. A conference with his parents revealed that Andrew's right arm had been injured in a car accident, and, although it had healed, he did not use it as well as he should be able to. It embarrassed him not to be able to keep up with his friends in ball games.

The teacher decided to find a physical activity that would help strengthen Andrew's arm. She discussed the problem with a physical education teacher, who suggested playing tetherball with a small ball on a short tether. It worked very well because Andrew enjoyed any kind of ball game. This activity was so new to the whole class that no one excelled at it. As the teacher noted on the back of Andrew's card, he spent a great deal of time playing tetherball and his arm became much stronger.

Small Motor Assessment

You can assess small motor abilities in much the same way as large motor skills. Copy the list in Table 4.2 onto a card for each child.

Small motor coordination involves using the fingers with dexterity to manipulate objects. This is also known as eye-hand, visual-manual, fine motor, or perceptual-motor coordination. It is an important skill for young children to develop as a prerequisite for learning to read and write. Children who experience difficulty in these checklist areas often exhibit a lack of small motor coordination. Young boys frequently show less dexterity with their fingers than do girls of the same age. As with girls and large motor skills, the lag may result from inherent genetic differences, but encouragement and practice in small motor activities nevertheless benefits both boys and girls.

TABLE 4.2   Small Motor Checklist

_____	Inserts pegs
_____	Zips a zipper
_____	Laces a shoe
_____	Twists a nut onto a bolt
_____	Pours a liquid without spilling
_____	Cuts with scissors
_____	Cuts with a knife
_____	Pounds a nail with a hammer
_____	Paints with a brush
_____	Traces objects with crayon, felt-tip pen
_____	Writes with an implement

Permission is granted by the publisher to reproduce this checklist for evaluation and record keeping.

Games for each of the small motor skills should be put out separately on different days. It is otherwise confusing for young children to have to perform more than one skill at a time.

Inserting

Small motor activities help establish handedness in young children. Most of the children will already have exhibited a preference for either right- or left-handedness by the time they enter a preschool program. You should note which hand each child uses most frequently, and help them strengthen handedness through manipulative games. Do not try to change a left-handed child. You can help the child best by providing opportunities to become proficient with the left hand.

Picking up small objects with the preferred hand helps children develop and strengthen their handedness. This activity also promotes eye-hand coordination, which allows children to manipulate the object they are viewing. It further helps strengthen finger muscles that will eventually be needed for grasping a writing implement.

Teacher-made sorting games are especially helpful in this area. In addition to promoting manual skills, sorting games help children develop cognitive concepts, such as sorting and matching according to size, shape, or color.

Shoe boxes and plastic margarine containers are handy accessories for these games. Each shoe box can contain a separate game. Label each empty margarine container with the picture and name of the item it should contain. Then cut a hole in the top just large enough to permit the item to be dropped in. Have one extra container to hold the entire assortment of items. Label the outside of the shoe box with an illustration of the items so children can identify separate games.

The idea of the game is to sort a collection of items by putting each one in the container where it belongs. Each shoe box game will contain a different collection. One can be a collection of beans of different kinds; another, a collection of different seeds large enough to be picked up; others, a collection of pasta of different shapes, or a collection of nuts, bolts, and screws, buttons, poker chips of different colors, golf tees, seashells, nuts, and so forth.

To begin, the children should pour the collection of items into the top of the shoe box for ease in sorting. Once they have finished the task of dropping the items through the holes in the tops of the proper containers, they will want to remove the plastic tops to see how accurate they were in their sorting. If the game has captured their interest, they will want to pour the items back into the top of the shoe box and sort them over and over.

You can also use egg cartons for sorting. Either keep the top closed and puncture holes over every egg section, or let the children play with the carton open. Labels of the items can be pasted on the different sections or next to the holes. All of these games can be kept on the shelves of your manipulative area near the tables where they will be used.

Many commercial games also promote finger dexterity: wooden puzzles with knobs on each piece, Legos, pegboards, lacing boards, stringing beads, Bristle Blocks, slotted wheels, Montessori cylinder blocks, and shape inlays.

You can make your own pegboards by acquiring scraps of pegboard material from a lumber company and using colored golf tees as pegs. Another teacher-made board for promoting finger dexterity is the geoboard. Pound headless nails equidistant (e.g., 1 inch apart) in rows on a 12-inch-square board. Children can then stretch colored rubber bands over the nails to make various designs.

Puzzles require the same skill: picking up and inserting an item into a space. The first puzzles for young children are the large wooden ones, with only a few pieces to be inserted into a cutout wooden frame. Children who have never assembled a puzzle are more successful when each puzzle piece represents a whole item rather than a part of an item in the picture. Check your puzzles carefully. You will need a wide selection because of the children's range of abilities.

It is especially important at the beginning of the year to have puzzles that children new to the program can complete successfully. If some children have had no previous experience with puzzles, you may need to sit with them for encouragement or even to help them continue until the puzzle is completed.

A wide range of commercial puzzles is available, but you can also make your own. Enlarged photographs of each child can be glued and laminated on cardboard and cut with a modeler's knife or a jigsaw. Make no more than four pieces for each puzzle. Store the pieces in separate manila envelopes with picture labels on the front. Do not put out the puzzles for use until pictures of everyone are ready. It is distressing for a child to be left out.

Zipping

You can observe and record how children zip their own clothing, or you can make or purchase a zipper board. Cut the zipper and enough cloth around it from an old skirt and staple or tack the two sides to a board. Don't forget to sand the wood so there are no sharp edges.

Twisting/Turning

Different small muscles must be developed to accomplish the skills of twisting or turning something with the hands. You can help by giving the children opportunities to use tools like eggbeaters, food mills, or can openers in their cooking activities or water play.

Start collecting small plastic bottles with screw-on tops. When you have several, wash them out and put tops and bottles separately in a shoe box for the children to try to put together. They must practice the additional skill of matching sizes before they can screw on the tops successfully.

You can also make a board with bolts of different sizes protruding through the surface, with a container of nuts the children can screw onto the bolts. These boards can also be purchased commercially. Squeezing oranges for orange juice is another activity that promotes the twisting, turning skill.

Pouring

Children need the practice of pouring liquids. Do not deprive them of the opportunity by doing all the pouring yourself. Use small pitchers for snack or lunch, and the children will be able to pour their own juice and milk. Even programs using pint or half-pint milk cartons should consider emptying these into small pitchers for the children to use on their own. You may also want children to experience pouring something other than a liquid. Let them pour rice from a pitcher to a bowl and back again. Salt, sugar, and sand present other possibilities to practice pouring.

Cutting with Scissors

There are several ways to help children who have not yet learned to cut with scissors. Show them how to hold the scissors with their favored hand. If a child is left-handed, provide left-handed scissors. Then hold a narrow strip of paper stretched taut between your two hands for the child to practice cutting in two. Once the child can do so without difficulty, have another hold the paper and let them take turns holding and cutting. Another day, show how to hold the paper in one hand and cut with the other. Let the child practice on different kinds and sizes of paper, including construction paper, typing paper, and pages from old magazines. Finally, draw a line on a sheet of paper and let the child practice cutting along a line.

For fun as well as practice, let children cut up colored ribbon into small pieces for confetti. Small adult scissors work better than blunt or dull children's toy scissors. Preschool youngsters can learn to use sharp scissors safely.

Cutting with a Knife

Young children can also learn to handle knives safely. Not only does cutting with a knife provide excellent small motor coordination practice, but it is a highly satisfying adult-type skill for young children to accomplish. You can start with table knives and soft items. Children can learn to hold the knife in one hand with the sharp edge of the blade down, while holding a peeled, hard-boiled egg, a cooked potato or carrot, or a peach or pear with the other hand. Some children may have to make a sawing motion to get started. After learning to control a table knife, they can begin learning to use a sharp paring knife for the same kind of cutting. Eventually they should be able to help prepare food for snacks, such as raw carrots, apples, and celery.

Using a vegetable scraper is another satisfying skill to learn. Carrots are best to begin with, but children will eventually be able to peel potatoes successfully. These are real experiences rather than games or simulations, and children understand the value of such skills because they have seen grown-ups use them. It gives children great satisfaction to realize that they can take part in and contribute to the adult world. Their teachers can feel satisfaction, too, knowing what an excellent opportunity cooking experiences provide for developing children's small motor control. Other cooking tools such as shredders, graters, grinders, and melon ballers are valuable in this respect.

Holding and Pounding

To pound a nail with a hammer takes well-developed eye-hand coordination, even for an adult. At first, let children practice at the woodworking table with soft materials, such as plasterboard or ceiling tiles and large-headed nails. They can pound pieces of tile or wood together, or they can pound objects such as Styrofoam onto a board. Bring in several tree stumps and let them pound nails into them just for the fun of pounding.

Holding and Printing/Tracing/Painting

Many children have already learned to hold and use pencils, crayons, and paintbrushes before they enter preschool. For those who have, let them continue their practice; for those who have not, allow them the opportunity to learn.

Many teachers set up a writing table in the manipulative area with a variety of writing or drawing tools and paper for children to experiment with. The youngsters especially like felt-tip markers and fat crayons as well as primary-size pencils and regular pens and pencils.

Let them practice scribbling and eventually tracing and writing some letters. Some children may want to try printing their names. Give all the children name cards to copy if they want.

The paintbrushes in the art area should be large enough for preschoolers to be able to grip them well. Easel brushes that are fat enough are often too long for 3- and 4-year-olds to handle well. Simply cut off and sand down the ends to a manageable length.

Planning for Individuals

Once you have completed the small motor assessment, you and your classroom team will have a better idea of the activities you should provide. Although you will be planning for individuals, be sure not to single them out as being deficient in these skills. Because a classroom of children will exhibit a wide range of motor abilities, all children should be accepted as they are. If one child's development seems to lag behind another's, simply involve that youngster in activities to strengthen a particular skill. As with large motor activities, all the children can benefit from the small motor games you provide for certain children.

Children with Handicapping Conditions

Mentally impaired or physically handicapped youngsters should be encouraged to accomplish as many large and small motor activities as they can. Once you have assessed what they are able to do, you will be ready to make appropriate individual plans to challenge them, just as you do for all the children.

PROVIDES EQUIPMENT AND ACTIVITIES TO PROMOTE LARGE AND SMALL MOTOR SKILLS IN AND OUT OF THE CLASSROOM

We have described how to assess children's large and small motor skills. The same activities used for assessment can also promote motor skills on a daily basis. Remember that the children will gain the most through individual and small group activities. Large group games with rules are not appropriate until the children are older.

Remember also when you purchase or construct equipment, try to make it serve several purposes at once. For example, one program invented what it called a "Swiss Cheese Board" for climbing on and throwing beanbags through, to be used both indoors and out. It was made from sturdy pressboard with a frame around it and struts at the bottom to hold it upright. Holes of various sizes were cut through it to serve as hand- and footholds for climbing, windows for dramatic play, and targets for beanbags. The board was so popular with the children that three more similar boards were constructed, thus making walls for a playhouse as well as for room dividers.

Although many of the activities described can take place in the classroom, some should also be pursued out-of-doors. Young children need opportunities to run and play in the fresh air. Small motor as well as large motor skills can be pursued outdoors. Bring your paints and puzzles out on the sidewalk, for a change, and see what renewed interest occurs on the part of the children.

The following motor activities and equipment discussed in this chapter can be used to promote motor skills both in and out of the classroom.

Walking	*Throwing/Catching*
Follow the Leader	Beanbags
Walk like an animal	Ring toss
Rocking boat	Sponge balls
Walking trail	Yarn balls
	Beach balls
	Rubber balls

Balancing
Follow the Leader
Hollow blocks
Be an animal
Balance beam
Block beam
Contact paper footprints
Balance board

Hopping, Jumping, Leaping
Footprint trail
Hopscotch
Jump over the river
Jumping jack period

Running, Galloping, Skipping
Follow the Leader
Relay race
Action chants

Climbing
Jungle gym
Rung ladder
Nesting climber
Dome climber
Tires
Swiss Cheese Board
Rowboat
Tree stumps
Cable spools

Crawling, Creeping, Scooting
Spooky music
Tambourine
Tunnels of cardboard
Barrels
Styrofoam tunnel
Masking tape obstacle
    course
Scooter
Wooden vehicles

Picking Up/Carrying
Large hollow blocks
Boxes
Furniture
Large toys

Wheeled Equipment
Tricycle
Big Wheel
Large wooden vehicles
Scooter
Conveyer belt trike path

Inserting
Shoe box collections
Egg carton
Wooden-knob puzzles
Legos
Pegboards
Golf tees
Geoboard
Frame puzzles
Photo puzzles

Zipping
Clothing with zippers
Zipper board

Twisting/Turning
Eggbeaters
Food mills
Can openers
Bottle and screw tops
Bolt boards
Orange squeezer

Pouring
Small pitchers
Rice, salt, sand

Cutting
Table knife and
    cooked vegetables
Paring knife and
    raw vegetables
Shredder
Grater
Melon baller

Holding and Printing/Tracing/Painting
Pencil, crayon
Felt-tip pen

PROVIDES OPPORTUNITIES FOR CHILDREN TO MOVE THEIR BODIES IN A VARIETY OF WAYS

Preschool classrooms in the United States seem to make less use of body movement than those in Europe, perhaps because we as adults are less inclined to express ourselves through our bodies. Perhaps we are more inhibited and uncomfortable with our bodies.

Children do not need to grow up feeling this way if you help them to be comfortable with creative movement activities. Until they can control their body motions, they will not feel free to move creatively. Some of the activities already described will help them to loosen up. Here are some other suggestions.

Imitating Animals

Begin by giving children something familiar to imitate. Let them move like familiar animals. Display pictures of dogs, cats, birds, rabbits, mice, guinea pigs, snakes, beetles, and spiders around the room at the children's eye level. Let them try to move on all fours like one of the animals. Do it to appropriate music or a chant you make up, such as:

> I am a bunny,
> Watch me hop,
> Here I go
> And never stop.

Encourage your children to watch how classroom pets move. Take the group to a pet store, a farm, or a zoo.

Perhaps one or two children will want to demonstrate their own movement while the rest clap a rhythm. You may want to tap on a tambourine or drum as children move like animals. They may want to try certain kinds of movements, such as crawling like snakes or worms, leaping like cats or tigers, or waddling like ducks. Picture books such as the previously mentioned *Pretend You're a Cat* (Marzollo & Pinkney, 1990) can also motivate children to move like real animals.

Other picture books feature animals dressed up as humans. In *Mama Don't Allow* (Hurd, 1984) the Swamp Band, composed of a possum, a parrot, a lizard, and a rat, play music so loudly that the animal residents of Swampville send them off to the swamp to play for the alligators. Your children can participate in the Alligator Ball on the Swamp Queen Riverboat by singing the tune "Mama don't allow no music playin' 'round here" as they stomp and sway like the alligators, and later move around to keep from getting snapped up by hungry 'gators!

Other Motions

You can often entice an awkward or shy child to engage in movement activities with the right equipment: ribbons, scarves, paper streamers, hula hoops, balloons, or giant bubble hoops.

Soon children will feel free enough to move like trees in the wind, ocean waves, or lightning in a thunder storm. They can learn to move silently, heavily, slowly, or rapidly. They can be a plane moving down a runway, an eagle soaring through the sky, or a skier going downhill. Eventually, they will be able to express emotions such as happiness, sadness, anger, and surprise in their movements. Accompanying mood music can help.

Do not force children who are not ready to join the group. The activity should always be fun for individuals, not an embarrassment. Leaving movement pictures and props in the music corner encourages individuals to try out body movements on their own.

Body Action Chants

Body action chants are like finger plays for the entire body. Teachers can lead children in all kinds of whole body motions while chanting. They can pretend to be carpenters standing on tiptoe to pound a nail in the ceiling, or elevator operators going up or down.

You Can Be a Carpenter

You can be a carpenter	(Stand, stretch arm above head)
Pounding in nails;	
Get them out of boxes,	(Bend over, reach down with right hand)
Get them out of pails;	(Reach down with left hand)
Pound them in the ceiling,	(Stretch arm above head)
Pound them in the floor,	(Stretch arm down to floor)
Put them in your pocket,	(Hands in pocket)
And walk out the door.	(March in place)

Elevator Operator

Elevator operator	(Stand in place)
Going down, please;	(Squat down)
Down to the basement	
To look for the keys;	
Up to the first floor	(Straighten up halfway)
To let out the cat;	
Up to the second floor	(Straighten up all the way)
To take a nap;	
Up to the third floor	(Raise arms above head)
To find a friend;	
Up to the top floor	(Jump up and sink down in squat)
And back down again.	

A teacher should lead the chanting. Do each one several times together if the children like them, and they will soon have them memorized. Body action verses like these are especially good to use as transitions between time blocks or while waiting for lunch or for the bus.

Let children make up their own chants and follow them. They can choose an animal with distinctive motions, or a worker such as a house painter. Then have them tell you the names or sounds of the motions that painters make: "Splash, drip, step, stir, reach, bend." Have them think of rhymes for these words: "Splash-dash, drip-trip, step-hep, stir-whir, reach-teach, bend-send." Finally, try to put together some verses of your own with body action in them:

> Joshua is a painter,
> Stir, stir, stir;
> Likes to slap the paint on,
> Whir, whir, whir;
> Likes to climb the ladder,
> Step, step, step;
> Likes to carry buckets,
> Hep, hep, hep;
> Likes to mix the colors,
> Splash, splash, splash;
> Hopes he never spills them,
> Or he'll have to dash!

Children can make up the motions they want to use for every other line. There may not be room for every suggested motion in a single verse, but have the children make up more verses if they want. They will be more interested in acting out body action chants that they have invented themselves. Post the words in the classroom so that parents and volunteers can join in the fun when they visit.

These particular movements are, of course, highly structured. You can begin with such movements and then move to more abstract motions as your children show ability and enthusiasm in moving. Play records or tapes with words calling for particular movements at first. Then play music without words and let the children create their own movement to the music. Children from different cultures or ethnic groups may also want to bring in records or tapes of their own special music. Perhaps a parent could be invited to demonstrate or teach the children a dance from another culture.

SUMMARY

To promote children's physical development, you should determine their needs and then provide appropriate materials and activities. Using a checklist of large and small motor skills for informal observation of children helps the classroom worker assess clearly where each child stands in the motor ability area. Then the teacher can make individual plans based on the child's needs, using the child's strengths as a starting place.

A child with a particular developmental need should not be singled out for special help, but should be included in small group activities designed for that child but worthwhile for others as well. Getting children involved in creative movement activities is also important, with special focus on imitating animals, using books to motivate movement, using props, moving to music, doing body action chants, and making up movements.

LEARNING ACTIVITIES

1. Read Chapter 4, "Advancing Physical Skills," and answer Question Sheet 4–A.
2. View Videopak H "Outdoor Play Equipment" and answer Question Sheet 4–B.
3. Read one or more of the books listed under Suggested Readings, and add 10 cards to your file with specific ideas for helping children develop large and small motor skills. Include the reference source on the back of each card.
4. Assess each child's large motor skills, using the checklist on page 85. Record the results.
5. On the basis of your results, construct a game, bring in materials, or conduct an activity to promote the large motor skills of children who need help. (Trainer can observe.)
6. Assess each child's small motor skills, using the checklist on page 86. Record the results.
7. On the basis of your results, construct a game, bring in materials, or conduct an activity to promote the small motor skills of children who need help. (Trainer can observe.)
8. Lead the children in a creative movement activity as described in the chapter.
9. Complete the Chapter 4 Evaluation Sheet and return it to your trainer or college supervisor.

QUESTION SHEET 4–A

(Based on Chapter 4, "Advancing Physical Skills")

1. How can you provide for children who seem awkward when they walk or have difficulty balancing?
2. What should you do about children who have difficulty skipping?
3. How can you help your children develop the skills of throwing and catching?
4. If only one child in your classroom has difficulty throwing and catching, what should you do?
5. How can you best help a left-handed child?
6. How would you help a child learn to cut with scissors?
7. How do cooking activities promote small motor development? Be specific.
8. Describe a beginning activity to encourage creative movement with children.
9. How might you engage a shy child in creative movement activities?
10. What should you do if children refuse to join in a movement activity?

QUESTION SHEET 4-B

(Based on Videopak H, "Outdoor Play Equipment")

1. What pieces of equipment would you choose for your outdoor play area? Why?
2. If you could choose only one piece of equipment, what would it be? Why?
3. If you have little money to spend, how could you provide climbing equipment?
4. How can you provide for digging in sand on your playground?
5. What different large motor skills can be promoted through the use of slides?
6. In what different ways can the skill of swinging be promoted in an outdoor playground?
7. In what different ways can old tires be used on a preschool playground?
8. How can the skills of creeping and crawling be promoted in the outdoor play area?
9. In what ways can balancing be promoted?
10. What kinds of large motor skills can be promoted on a concrete or blacktop surface?

SUGGESTED READINGS

Beaty, J. J. (1990). *Observing development of the young child* (2nd ed.). Columbus, OH: Merrill.

Benzwie, T. (1987). *A moving experience.* Tucson, AZ: Zephyr Press.

Cherry, C. (1971). *Creative movement for the developing child.* Belmont, CA: Fearon.

Curtis, S. (1982). *The joy of movement.* New York: Teachers College Press.

DiMartino, E. C. (1989). Understanding children from other cultures. *Childhood Education, 66*(1), 30–32.

Frost, J. L., & Klein, B. L. (1979). *Children's play and playgrounds.* Austin, TX: Playgrounds International.

Gallahue, D. L. (1982). *Developmental movement experiences for children.* New York: John Wiley.

Hoppert, R. (1985). *Rings, swings, and climbing things: Easy-to-make play equipment.* Chicago: Contemporary Books.

Javernick, E. (1988). Johnny's not jumping: Can we help obese children? *Young Children, 43*(2), 18–23.

Poest, C. A., Williams, J. R., Witt, D. W., & Atwood, M. E. (1990). Challenge me to move: Large muscle development in young children. *Young Children, 45*(5), 4–10.

Sullivan, M. (1982). *Feeling strong, feeling free: Movement exploration for young children.* Washington, DC: National Association for the Education of Young Children.

Thompson, D. (1981). *Easy woodstuff for kids.* Mount Rainier, MD: Gryphon House.

Weikart, P. (1987). *Round the circle: Key experiences in movement for children ages 3 to 5.* Ypsilanti, MI: High/Scope Press.

CHILDREN'S BOOKS

Hurd, T. (1984). *Mama don't allow.* New York: Harper & Row.

Kalan, R. (1981). *Jump, frog, jump!* New York: Mulberry Books.

Marzollo, J., & Pinkney, J. (1990). *Pretend you're a cat.* New York: Dial Books for Young Readers.

Rabe, B. (1981). *The balancing girl.* New York: E.P. Dutton.

VIDEOTAPES

Beaty, J. J. (Producer). (1979). Outdoor play equipment (Videopak H), *Skills for preschool teachers.* Elmira, NY: McGraw Bookstore, Elmira College.

South Carolina Educational TV (Producer). Music movement with young children, *Calico pie,* Columbia, SC: SCETV.

Tennessee Technological University (Producer). (1986). *Stepping stones: Pathways to early development.* Bloomington, IN: Agency for Instructional Technology.

CHAPTER 4 EVALUATION SHEET
ADVANCING PHYSICAL SKILLS

1. Student _____

2. Trainer _____

3. Center where training occurred _____

4. Beginning date _____ Ending date _____

5. Describe what student did to accomplish General Objective

   _____

   _____

6. Describe what student did to accomplish Specific Objectives

   Objective 1 _____

   _____

   Objective 2 _____

   _____

   Objective 3 _____

   _____

7. Evaluation of student's Learning Activities
   (Trainer Check One)   (Student Check One)

   _____ Highly superior performance   _____

   _____ Superior performance   _____

   _____ Good performance   _____

   _____ Less than adequate performance   _____

Signature of Trainer: Signature of Student:

_____   _____

Comments:

5 Advancing Cognitive Skills

General Objective

To promote children's questioning, exploring, and problem-solving skills in order to develop their thinking ability.

Specific Objectives

- ☐ Helps children use all of their senses to explore their world.
- ☐ Helps children develop such concepts as shape, color, size, classification, seriation, number.
- ☐ Interacts with children in ways that encourage them to think and solve problems.

Advancing cognitive skills in young children involves helping them develop their intellectual or thinking abilities. Many preschool programs have overlooked or downplayed this important area of development. Somehow we have the notion that we should not teach children to learn until they enter public school at age 5 or 6. The preschool, we declare, should be concerned with play.

We seem to have overlooked the fact that young children are progressing in their intellectual development with or without our help. Cognitive development is just as important as physical or language development. In fact, they go hand in hand. Cognitive development occurs at the same time and is integrated into every other aspect of the child's development.

We also seem to have forgotten that the principal direction of play for young children is not entertainment or recreation, as it is for adults, but learning. It is therefore essential that teachers of young children understand how cognitive abilities develop and how they can utilize play in their classrooms to promote cognitive development and give it direction.

HELPS CHILDREN USE ALL OF THEIR SENSES TO EXPLORE THEIR WORLD

Preschool children are born explorers. Even as infants and toddlers, they come with all the necessary equipment to be great discoverers: eyes, nose, mouth, tongue, lips, ears, fingers, toes. In addition to this array of sensory apparatus, each child starts out with a strong natural drive or curiosity to put this equipment to good use. Children are forever trying to poke, pry, bite, chew, lick, rub, pinch, sniff, stare at, listen to, or examine in great detail any object, person, or situation that gets in the way.

This is how children learn about themselves and their world. They have to try everything. They have to touch and test and pull things apart. (Putting them back together, however, is not really a part of this initial investigation!) They may also drop or throw breakable objects, not to be naughty but to find out what happens when objects hit the floor. They are true scientific explorers of their environment. Thus, cognitive development for preschoolers involves the use of their senses to examine things and explore their surroundings.

Yet some 3- and 4-year-olds seem to make no use of their sensory equipment in exploring the world around them. They don't seem to notice anything new or different in the classroom. In fact they show little interest of any kind in their surroundings. Since we know most children possess a great natural curiosity, we can only surmise that somewhere along the way they lost it. Perhaps their curiosity was mistaken for mischief by the adults in their lives, and they were punished for it. Perhaps there were never adults around who took the time to answer their questions or support their exploratory activities. Whatever the reason, it is up to you—teachers, aides, and volunteers in preschool classrooms—to re-awaken the children's sense of curiosity and wonder if they have lost it, or to help direct it toward exploring their environment if they have not.

Re-awakening Curiosity

What about the children in your classroom? Do they still retain their natural sense of curiosity? Take a moment to observe their actions when they first enter your new environment. Listen also to the questions they ask. You should soon be able to identify the children with a drive to explore and those who seem to have little interest in the new things around them.

Your job, of course, is to re-awaken this curiosity and encourage them to find things out for themselves. To do so, you will need to serve as a behavior model and help them learn how to explore with their senses through the interesting play activities you provide. You will need to put forth special effort to show your own interest in every new and different thing you see both in and out of the classroom.

Field Trips

The immediate environment of the center offers unlimited opportunities for children to explore and discover. Take the children on a walk outside around the building. Give them each a paper bag to collect anything that strikes their fancy. Take a tape recorder with you to record the sounds of the environment. Take an instant-print camera to record the scenes.

What will you find out? First of all, you will learn who are the curious children. Second, you will find out whether you yourself are tuned in to children and their interests. Was it a child who pointed out the dandelion growing from the crack in the sidewalk, or was it you? Perhaps you will have to get down on your knees to look at the world from the perspective of a 3-year-old before you can become a behavior model for exploring.

Field trips need not be elaborate, all-day, long-distance affairs. Brief ventures outside or around the building are best, because this is the environment the children are involved with and want to find out about. Their own personal environment is always more meaningful to children than a visit to a remote spot they may never see again. Sometimes adults do not understand the young child's point of view when it comes to field trips. A trip to the basement of your building may be more exciting than a trip to the zoo. After all, a basement is more immediate—and more mysterious! Most adults have little interest in basements, but think what young children can learn about heat and water and electricity!

One class made exciting discoveries all year long on their weekly "field trip to a tree." They chose a maple tree on the playground to visit once a week throughout the fall, winter, and spring. They took photographs, made bark rubbings, pressed leaves, collected and grew seeds, and recorded on tape the sound of wind in the leaves. They learned about the birds that nested in the tree and the insects that lived there.

A city location may not have trees in the vicinity, but surely many other objects await the examination of young explorers. One city class visited a used car lot across the street. While such locations may not hold much interest for adults, they represent new worlds for young children to explore. The teachers were surprised to find that the children showed less interest in the cars themselves than in their wheels. This should not have been surprising, since young children tend to focus on things at their own eye level. Back in the classroom, the children found circle blocks to use as wheels for the block cars they were building. This led to a search for other circles in the classroom.

Sensory Questions

What do you do on a field trip? You can start by asking exploratory questions involving the senses, if the children have not already begun to do so. "Close your eyes and what do you hear?" or "Does anyone smell anything different?" or "Put your hand on this. What does it feel like to you?"

When possible, take your lead from the children. Follow the direction of their interests. When they display little interest, you may need to lead them. Look around you for things to explore with the senses. How do these objects look, sound, feel? Is there another one like the first? They may want to compare two objects. How are they the same? How are they different? Take a photo. Make a rubbing. Make a tape recording of sounds. Take something back with you to the classroom to help children clarify and understand what they have seen and explored.

Materials in the Classroom

For children's curiosity to be aroused, there has to be something for them to be curious about. Children will often bring an interesting item from home or something they have picked up on the way to the center. This can be the beginning of their exploration, especially if you display the item attractively to focus attention on it.

In the beginning, however, it is often up to the adult classroom worker to bring new material to stimulate children's curiosity. Set up a special table or counter top area to feature new or unusual items you or the children bring, and label it the "What's New?" table. To feature the new item of the week, you can place a piece of colored contact paper or construction paper on the table underneath the item.

Bring an interesting piece of tree bark if you want to arouse the children's sense of touch, or if you plan to explore living trees by touch, or if you hope to do bark rubbings. Bring a piece of driftwood or a seashell—but only if your community is near a river, lake, or ocean, where such items are common. It is essential to begin with something familiar to the children.

One teacher brought a yellow fire-hydrant top and displayed it on a bright red piece of construction paper on her "What's New?" table. She had arranged to get it from a hydrant foundry near the children's homes, where many of their parents worked. The children were already used to the unusual items that appeared weekly on this table. Almost immediately some of the more aggressive children began talking about it and touching it. The teacher listened to their conversations to see how much they knew about it and whether they could discover more through their own senses. One boy tried to lift it and was surprised to find how heavy it was. Then they all had to try.

But it was Christina, a shy girl who rarely played with the others, who finally identified the item. Her father worked in the foundry, and she was pleased to be able to share her knowledge about its products. This one item led to many weeks of sensory discovery in that particular classroom. The children explored colors, especially the use of red and yellow as warning colors. Christina's father came to the class to talk about his job in the foundry. The children visited the foundry's shipping department—the only area safe for visitors—to see rows of new fire hydrants ready for shipment around the world. They explored more deeply the concept of metal and began looking for and identifying other metal objects.

You and your co-workers must decide in what directions you want the children to go during the year, what simple concepts you want them to explore. It is much more appropriate in preschool programs to start with the simplest and most basic kinds of things, then follow the children's interests as far as they will lead you.

For example, if your children are learning to identify colors in their art activities, you might ask the children to bring something green for the "What's New?" table. If several children bring green items, display them all. If nobody brings anything, be prepared to bring something yourself, or have the children choose something green from the classroom to display there, for example, a plant—making sure it is nonpoisonous.

Exploring plants can, of course, take you in many directions. Children might eventually discover that it takes sunlight to make a plant green. If you are still concerned with colors, you might feature a new one every few weeks until all the colors are thoroughly familiar to your children. It is up to you and your co-workers, however, to plan for something to happen.

You will want your children to explore their surroundings. Again, start with something simple. For instance, we all need water to live. One teacher brought in bottled water from the supermarket for her display table. This stimulated the children to wonder and talk about other kinds of water. They filled a glass with water from the tap and visually compared the bottled water with the glass of water. They looked the same. The teacher then asked the small group who had gathered around the display table, "How else can we tell if there is any difference between bottled water and tap water?"

After one child suggested smelling the two types of water, everyone wanted a turn. All decided there was a difference that was hard to put into words, but they agreed that the tap water smelled stronger. Next, of course, everyone decided they had to taste the two. Most of the children liked the tap water better. The teacher recorded the results on newsprint after each child's name.

The simple display led to more activities than the teachers had anticipated. One child brought in muddy river water. Another brought a jar of greenish pond water. The word *pollution* became meaningful to preschoolers. The class traced the building water pipes to the meter in the basement, and had fun watching the numbers change when water was turned on. The class eventually took a field trip to the city filter plant and reservoir. All these activities resulted from just one bottle of water.

This example points out the need for you and your co-workers to plan for something to happen. Then you should extend the activity according to your children's interests and needs. To determine their interests, listen closely to their comments and questions. Ask questions yourself about the activity to stimulate their thinking. Use your imagination to plan follow-up activities that will strengthen and extend their learning.

Other items relevant to the children and their surroundings that you might bring in to display on your "What's New?" table from time to time might include:

A sealed bottle of brown liquid (vanilla)
An open box of maple seeds
A brick
A hard-boiled egg
A sealed margarine cup full of navy beans
A baby's shoe
A cup of brown powder (chocolate drink mix)
A house painter's roller
An onion and a tulip bulb
A carpenter's level

To prepare for the children's possible questions and avenues of direction, you and your co-workers should make a list of free-association ideas for whatever object you display. For instance, whatever comes to your mind when you see an egg should be included in your list, no matter how improbable. This will help prepare you for possible areas your children may want to explore. Nevertheless, be prepared to be "out-associated" by the children! Unfettered children's minds are often more imaginative than those of adults, once the children are turned on to wondering.

One classroom team came up with this list of free-association ideas for an egg:

shell	yellow	nest	smell
chicken	smooth	sticks	Easter
hatch	round	fry	grass
warm	bird	omelet	hunt

These words will give you and your co-workers clues to possible directions for exploring activities involving eggs. Perhaps the children will want to hatch eggs in an incubator. On the other hand, they may want to start exploring eggs by cooking them in different ways and eating them. Since Easter was one of the free-association words, this may tell you to save the egg experience until the Easter season. But whenever you do it, listen to what the children are asking about the egg on your "What's New?" table. This will tell you the direction your egg study should take. Your free-associating has merely prepared you for possible directions.

As you may have noticed, each of the 10 items listed above can be explored with one or more of the senses. Let the children try out the items in their own way before you start with questions. Then go in whatever direction seems profitable for you and the class. If an item doesn't arouse interest, try a new item another day. Your own modeling behavior should, in fact, stimulate the children to (a) bring in their own items, (b) ask questions about them, and (c) test them with their five senses.

Using the Senses to Examine Materials

Seeing, hearing, smelling, tasting, touching—these are the natural tools children use to explore and try things out. Even babies depend upon them. Taste seems to be one of the first senses developed. Babies almost always begin exploring new items by putting the items in their mouths. Three- and 4-year-olds do a great deal of touching, yet they are not beyond tasting when the occasion arises.

How do you as a classroom worker help children use their sensory abilities? You may want to start with the items on a science table. First, observe how the children themselves handle the items. Are they doing sensory exploration, that is, picking up the items, shaking them, smelling them? If so, you need to support and encourage this by giving positive reinforcement. "Look what Joel's doing with the maple seeds. How did you discover they would fly, Joel?" or "You've discovered that the brown liquid has a smell, haven't you, Shirley? What can you tell us about it?"

If you find your children are not using their senses to explore new things, you will want to encourage them by serving as a model. You can start by touching the item yourself, picking it up and rubbing it for instance, all the while describing your actions verbally. Or, you can start by covering your eyes with your hand or a blindfold, then try to find out as much as possible about a new item without using the sense of sight. This can become a fascinating game for children in a small group around the science table. The children take turns being blindfolded and try to discover as much as possible about the secret items you have brought in a bag, for example, a hairbrush, a tennis ball, or an hour-glass egg timer. Be sure children feel comfortable about using a blindfold. It can be a frightening experience for some preschoolers, and these children would be better off covering their eyes with their hands.

Where else besides the science table can the children practice their new-found tools of discovery? Hopefully, they will extend them to exploring the environment of the classroom, the center, and the surrounding grounds or neighborhood. Once the children are familiar with their classroom, they may want to branch out by exploring the rest of the building. You should make arrangements or get permission ahead of time, if necessary.

It may be overwhelming for 3- and 4-year-olds to try to explore a large building all at once. It is better to concentrate on one room or area at a time. If you have a kitchen or food preparation space separate from the classroom, this may be a good place to begin.

Collecting, Comparing, Recording

To find out as much as possible about an object or idea under scrutiny, adult scientists collect similar things, compare and contrast them, and record their findings. Preschool children can do the same. In fact, once they are deeply involved in wondering about things, your children will want to follow up with collecting, comparing, and recording information.

For instance, children can bring in seeds they find on field trips, or they can save fruit seeds from their snacks or lunches. They may soon have a collection of maple seeds, catalpa pods, acorns, orange seeds, grapefruit seeds, apple seeds, and even horse chestnuts or buckeyes if these are available where they live. This can be an individual or group effort. With very young children who may eat the seeds, aim your collecting towards nuts of different kinds.

How will you display them? One easy way is to use the sectioned half of an egg carton and cover it with clear food wrap. The seeds in each section can be labeled before the wrapping is put on. Each collector can fill his own carton. Or seeds can be displayed separately in clear sandwich bags next to a copy-machine picture of the tree they came from. Identification guides about birds, flowers, trees, insects, and minerals should be part of your classroom library.

How can children's collections contribute to the sensory exploration methods they are developing? This practice can help them to develop the thinking ability they need to view things logically. They will begin to understand how things are alike and how they are different. Does this seed look like the one in the book? How are they alike? How are they different?

Suppose a child named Bernie brings in stones he has collected on the way to the center. You might ask, "What is it about all of these stones that makes them alike?" He may have to examine them closely, using his senses carefully to determine why they are alike. It is not their color. Some are gray, but different shades of gray. One is blackish, two are whitish, and one is sort of pink. Neither is it their size or shape that makes them alike. Some are large and round, some small and round, and some angular. So it must be the way they feel. They all feel hard; they are all some kind of stone.

Next you can talk with Bernie about how he will display them. Posing this problem means he will have to determine how individual stones are different from one another. The ability to sort and classify according to a particular attribute is another facet of thinking. He may sort his collection on the basis of one of its most obvious attributes, color. Once he has arranged the stones in groups according to color, you might ask, "How else could you sort out your stones if they were all the same color?" Will he be able to do it by size or shape? Maybe not at first. The more ways Bernie can find to classify objects, the more sophisticated his sensory exploration will become. He is developing not only his cognitive abilities but a scientific mode of inquiry.

Scientists keep records of whatever they are investigating. They must record information such as where, when, how often, and how much. If we are serious about re-awakening our children's sense of wonder and curiosity, we will want our preschool scientists to keep records as well. If they are making collections, they may want to record where or when they found the different items. It will be up to the adult classroom workers to do the actual writing. The record of a collection can be kept in an individual scrapbook with a page devoted to each item, or it can be kept on a wall chart.

For example, Bernie may want to keep a file card record for each of his stones. You might set up the following kind of record for him:

Large White Stone

Where found: _____

When found: _____

What it looks like: _____

Let Bernie tell you the words to write on the card. Under "What it looks like," he may want to trace around the stone and color in the tracing with white chalk.

Some children may be far enough along in scientific inquiry to identify rocks. But for most preschoolers, it is not necessary or even appropriate to identify quartz or sandstone or limestone. The importance of recording lies in its impact on helping the children develop a more focused, in-depth kind of observation, as well as motivating them to continue to find out all they can about the things.

If your children are not collectors, start a simple collection yourself to get them started. Don't let it turn into a competition over who has the most or best; keep it strictly scientific. Later you can extend the activity by bringing a simple science book with pictures to help the collectors identify some items. Again the collector must compare and contrast the pictures with the real items. You can help by asking questions such as, "What makes your stone like the one in the picture?"

Other kinds of records might include simple graphs to show how much the children's plants have grown each week. Set aside a special time for every child to measure and record his plant's growth. A ruler or a strip of construction paper can be used for measuring. Have the child cut it to the height of the plant and paste it on the chart. Graphs can be individual or group projects.

Children's height and weight can be measured and recorded if the class is involved with examining the growth of living things. Classroom pets can be weighed monthly and the results recorded. Seasonal changes in leaves, plants, and trees can be observed and recorded with words, graphs, or even photographs. Daily weather records can be kept with colorful symbols for the sun, rain, clouds, snow, and wind. Once a few children start making records or scrapbooks about interesting things in the world around them, others will be motivated to begin their own scientific recording.

HELPS CHILDREN DEVELOP SUCH CONCEPTS AS SHAPE, COLOR, SIZE, CLASSIFICATION, SERIATION, NUMBER

As young children begin to perceive the world around them, they need some direction in organizing their perceptions to enable them to make sense of things and begin to think with clarity. Helping them develop certain simple concepts or ideas is an important way preschool programs can encourage this mental process.

Shape

Research shows that children develop concepts in a certain sequence. Shape is one of the earliest concepts to be formed. That is, young children can begin to discriminate objects on the basis of their shape quite early.

It is best to present activities around only one concept at a time, and then give children plenty of time and opportunity to make that concept a part of their thinking process. In every instance, activities should involve familiar objects at first, and should be presented as games or play.

It is true that young children learn through exploring with their senses, but the way they do so is far different from adult scrutiny of a new object. Children learn through play. They try out a new object or new concept in a playful way to see what it will do or what they can do with it. Take, for example, a rattle. Adults know from past experience that a rattle should be picked up and shaken and that it will make a noise. Babies and toddlers who have never had experience with a rattle do not know how it is supposed to be used. They will experiment playfully with this new item, putting it in the mouth, hitting it on a surface, perhaps even throwing it, until they discover its most interesting aspect: the noise it makes when you shake it.

This is how young children learn concepts, as well. Your classroom concept activities should provide children with all kinds of play opportunities for learning. For children to learn about circles, squares, and triangles, they will need to play circle games, sing square songs, make triangle hats, and have shape-hunting contests, lotto games, and puzzles. They can sort and pick up unit blocks on the basis of their shapes, cut out cookies or mold clay circles and squares, and saw wood into different shapes.

Color

Although young children seem to talk about colors first, research shows that they develop the color concept shortly after that of shape, reflecting the fact that people around them make more reference to color than to shape. Children can often name colors before truly understanding what they mean. You can help them clarify color concepts by starting with one color at a time and providing them with all kinds of games and activities relating to that color. Start with the primary colors of red, yellow, and blue, since young children seem to recognize these most easily. Then introduce secondary colors: green, and then orange when Halloween comes.

Color songs, guessing games, pegboards, color lotto, food colors in water, paint mixing, and cutting colored construction paper are a few of the activities you can use. Have children do a "color dance" with filmy capes of the primary colors, red, yellow, and blue, as in the children's book *Color Dance* (Jonas, 1989). Dancing children can swish together red and yellow capes to make orange, or blue and yellow capes to make green.

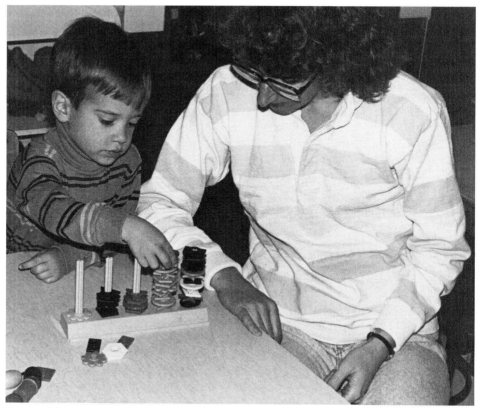

Young children can learn to discriminate objects on the basis of shape, color, and size.

Children with handicapping conditions can learn color concepts along with the other children. Set up color-related activities as you do everything in your classroom, so that children with physical and mental disabilities can participate. A child in a wheelchair, for instance, may not be able to do a "color dance" on his feet, but he could do a "color dance" with his hands shining flashlights covered with colored cellophane. Shining a flashlight covered with yellow cellophane and one covered with blue cellophane will make a spot of green where the two beams converge. Children can act out the story *Little Blue and Little Yellow* (Lionni, 1959) by shining flashlights in this manner while the teacher reads the story.

Feature color concept books in the book area as you introduce each color. *Red Is Best* (Stinson, 1982) makes a fine introduction to the color *red*. Use the book *Is it Red? Is it Yellow? Is it Blue?* (Hoban, 1978) after introducing the three primary colors. *Brown Bear, Brown Bear, What Do You See?* (Carle, 1983) includes an array of birds and animals decked out in their particular colors.

Size

As young children construct their own knowledge by interacting with the objects and people in their environment, their brains seem to pay special attention to the relationships between things. Size is one of those relationships. Children must understand the property of size, as with the properties of shape and color, to make sense of their world.

There are various orders of size, usually thought of in terms of opposites: big-little, large-small, tall-short, wide-narrow, thick-thin, deep-shallow, loud-soft. Direct comparison of objects based on one of these aspects seems to be the best way for young children to learn size.

Yet most children can only relate to one aspect of an object at a time when they are comparing, contrasting, or categorizing. First they must learn the single concept, say, of *big,* through many games and concrete activities—never work sheets! Next they can contrast that concept with *little*. But don't confuse them by bringing in examples of thick and thin, or short and tall, all at the same time. Give them plenty of time to learn the concept *big* through all sorts of materials, games, and concept books before moving on to *little*.

Classification

After learning simple concepts, children need to be able to apply them. Classification has to do with sorting or separating objects into groups or sets on the basis of a common characteristic, such as shape or color or size. This ability is a necessary component of cognitive development for the brain to sort out and process the wealth of incoming data obtained through the child's sensory activities. Sorting objects and materials in the classroom gives children practice in this skill, and involves identifying the similarities of objects as well as understanding relationships between them.

Piaget and other researchers have noted that children progress through a sequence of sorting skills, and that each step is more complex than the previous one as the youngsters' cognitive abilities develop (Wadsworth, 1989, pp. 103–104).

Bring collections of items for children to sort out according to one attribute at a time. A box of buttons, for instance, can be sorted by size into margarine containers with holes in the lids. Another time, the children can sort the buttons on the basis of color. Still another time, they can sort on the basis of the number of holes in the buttons. Other collections for sorting can include sea shells, nuts, toy cars, pasta shapes, and of course the children's own science collections.

Seriation

Seriation involves arranging a set of objects in a certain order according to a certain rule, for example, from short to tall, from light to heavy, from loud to soft, or from light to dark. Both commercial games and teacher-made materials help children learn such arrangements. Much Montessori equipment involves the self-teaching of seriation skills.

Young children are usually able to form a series if they are provided with cues. Montessori size-cylinders, for instance, are to be arranged in a board into graded holes in a sequence of sizes. Children fit the cylinders from large to small in the increasingly smaller holes in this self-correcting activity. The youngsters match the size of the cylinders with the size of the holes, and find out by trial-and-error which cylinders do or do not fit. Once they have learned the concept, many children are able to line up the cylinders on the table in the proper order without cues from the board.

Stacking blocks and rings work on the same principle of arranging items in a series from the largest to the smallest. Even toddlers soon learn that the largest item will not fit into a smaller one, and that if one item is left over, they need to start over to find their mistake. Children should be allowed to play these learning games without your help, to learn such concepts on their own, a necessary skill in their development of logical thought.

Number

Children encounter the spoken form of numbers long before they understand the meaning. Many can count accurately to 10 or even 20 without having the slightest idea of what 6 or 13 means. Nursery rhymes such as "One Two, Buckle My Shoe," and counting books such as *The Very Hungry Caterpillar* (Carle, 1971) encourage this skill. Counting in other languages is fun for young children, too. Whether or not you have bilingual children, have everyone learn number names in another language. Perhaps a parent or relative can visit the class and help them chant the numbers in another language. The picture book *Moja Means One* (Feelings, 1971) introduces the numbers *1* through *10* in Swahili.

Next, children need to learn about number concepts: that *1* means one object; that *2* means two things. They can begin to count people, dolls, toys, or any other three-dimensional object that is meaningful to them. Don't start out with number symbols; they are still too abstract. Instead, use stick figures or geometric shapes such as triangles or circles. Once the children have truly learned what oneness and twoness are all about, you can begin writing number symbols. Counting books such as *Demi's*

Count the Animals 1*2*3 (Demi, 1986) present large colorful animal illustrations showing different animals in numbers from *1* to *20* on double-spread pages.

The children may want to count their collections. You or they can record the amount in symbols of stones, nuts, or whatever. They may want to keep count of something, such as the number of cars or people that pass the center. Give them a file card and a paper punch, and let them punch one hole for every car or truck they see. You may want to paste a picture of a car on one card and a truck on another. Another day, use pictures of people.

Once you have introduced number symbols, be sure you give children many opportunities to play with them using concrete, three-dimensional materials and number symbols themselves. At this time you may want to change the signs in the activity areas that regulate the number of children allowed in each. Switch from stick figures to number symbols. Let the children demonstrate by their presence what these number symbols mean in each area.

INTERACTS WITH CHILDREN IN WAYS THAT ENCOURAGE THEM TO THINK AND SOLVE PROBLEMS

Your modeling behavior can be your most important contribution to this skill. If you demonstrate to children by your actions how interested and excited you are about the world around you, you will ignite their interest as well. It makes no difference whether you have any previous knowledge of plants, insects, or numbers. What makes the difference is that you show children that you also want to find out, just as they do. Show your enthusiasm by your tone of voice, the sparkle in your eye, and the questions you pose.

Questions: Open-ended and Closed

What kinds of questions are your children already asking? Get into the habit of writing them down so you'll have a concrete and specific take-off point in activities. Place some 3-by-5-inch cards and pencils around your room on top of shelves or room dividers, so you and your co-workers can record a child's question when you hear it.

Joel asks, "Why do we always have to have orange juice for a snack?" Later he wants to know, "Where is Mrs. Appleton? Isn't she coming to our room any more?" And still later, "Is that a piece of tree? It looks like the one in my back yard."

From your record of Joel's questions, you begin to realize that he is a curious boy who notices when things are repeated as well as when they are not. He is even able to make comparisons. You will want to provide Joel with new opportunities to explore.

Shelley, on the other hand, asks only, "Can I play with the baby buggy now?" This is a permission question, not a *why* or *how* question. She doesn't seem to notice the tree bark displayed on the science table, nor does she comment on the new arrangement of the dramatic play corner.

The questions children ask tell us many things about them. First of all, they tell us whether children are curious. Children who are not curious ask few *how*, *why*, or *where* questions. If we keep a record, we will soon know which children are not curious. Then it is up to us to help these children start thinking in terms of questions.

We often have to be the ones to start the questioning process. Children closely imitate the adults around them. If we are successful in our questioning, many of the children will soon be copying us.

What kinds of questions should we ask? Open-ended questions seem the most valuable. These are questions that can be answered in many ways. They require the child to think and imagine and explore in order to come up with an answer. The answers to open-ended questions are never right or wrong, they are merely possibilities. Thus, such questions are not threatening to the child.

For example, Joel evidently discovered the piece of bark the teacher had displayed on the science table. If the teacher wanted to interest Joel more deeply in this item, she might ask an open-ended question, "What can you tell me about this?" This kind of question could result in many answers. On the other hand, a closed question such as, "What is this?" usually calls for only one answer that is either right or wrong. In this case, the teacher's closed question usually cuts off further discussion. Either children are right, and that's the end of it, or they are wrong and will seldom make further attempts to answer.

An alert teacher might notice that Shelley was preoccupied with wheeling the doll buggy around and around in the dramatic play corner. The teacher might try to stimulate Shelley's consideration of other possibilities, with one of the following open-ended questions: "What else can you do with your baby buggy?" or "How else could you give your baby a ride if you didn't have a buggy?" or "What do you suppose your neighbors in the play corner are thinking when they see you go by with your buggy?"

Open-ended questions like these are provocative. They ask the child to look at an ordinary situation from a new perspective.

But, first of all, the teacher or aide needs to see things from a new perspective: the point of view of a scientist trying out and testing the self and the environment. It is not easy for most adults to pose open-ended questions. For example, what might you ask a child who has painted vertical red squiggles all over his paper? The questions we more frequently revert to are closed: "What is that?" or "Is your painting about rain?" Instead, the classroom worker aware of the value of open-ended questions might ask, "What can you tell me about those interesting red squiggles?"

Test yourself on your ability to pose open-ended questions. Suppose one of your children found a woolly bear caterpillar on the way to the center and brought it to class. What could you ask the child to stimulate curiosity about the creature?

1. Do you know what it is? (A closed question that cuts off further discussion or thinking, especially if the answer is "no.")
2. What do you call a caterpillar like that? (A closed question that ends with the answer.)

3. What can you tell me about that fuzzy little creature? (An open-ended question that allows for all sorts of possibilities.)
4. Look how fast he crawls! Where do you suppose he is going? (Open-ended and unlimited.)

Follow-Up

Your children may not be able to answer your open-ended questions any more accurately than you can, but what fun it will be to find the answers together. If you have involved the children in the sensory exploration and concept development activities described, then you have at your fingertips the means to find answers together.

"Why is our aquarium getting all dirty on the glass inside?" From this question, what can you find out together about the growth of algae? You might discover that the algae is green and needs light to grow, or that it also needs food to grow. You might find out the food source is waste matter from the fish—maybe you have too many fish; maybe you feed them too much; or maybe you need to clean the filter. You may also learn that you need to remove excessive algae to have a healthy fish tank; that certain creatures such as snails and algae-eating fish will remove the algae; and that too much algae is a sign of pollution in rivers, ponds, and lakes, as well as in fish tanks. This may lead a child to say, "Let's find out if our river is polluted!" Be alert to comments like this. When your children pose such problems, help them become involved in solving them by modeling your own interest and enthusiasm: "Yes, let's!"

SUMMARY

This chapter has looked at ways to promote children's questioning, exploring, and problem-solving skills to develop their thinking skills. Early childhood classroom workers need to be aware of how children use their sensory apparatus to explore the world around them, and need to set up classroom activities to promote such exploration. Using children's natural curiosity or re-awakening it if they seem to have lost it should be the classroom worker's goals in the cognitive development of young children. Bring in new materials, pose questions about them, take children on nearby field trips, and be sure to record the questions the children are asking so that you will know what direction to take in planning cognitive activities.

Help children develop cognitive concepts such as shape, color, size, classification, seriation, and number through real activities in the classroom. Then they can apply these concepts to the exploration they are already doing as they collect, compare, and record interesting materials in their environment.

Interact with the children yourself to stimulate their curiosity and encourage them to think and solve problems. Ask open-ended questions and listen to the way the children answer them. This should give you clues as to what direction you should take with individuals and the group in providing them with new cognitive activities or extending the present ones.

LEARNING ACTIVITIES

1. Read Chapter 5, "Advancing Cognitive Skills," and answer Question Sheet 5–A.
2. View Videopak G, "Preschool Science Experience," and answer Question Sheet 5–B.
3. Read one or more of the Suggested Readings and add 10 cards to your file with specific ideas for helping children develop cognitive skills. Include the reference source on each card.
4. Take some or all of your children on a brief field trip to a nearby area. Follow up with a classroom activity to clarify concepts or support learning. (The trainer can go along.) Prepare a lesson plan for this activity.
5. Set up a "What's New?" table and record how you or the children use or explore the materials, including any questions they ask.
6. Help the children learn a new concept using ideas from this chapter. (The trainer can observe.) Prepare a lesson plan and record results.
7. Help children start a collection or record information about their scientific explorations.
8. Bring in several children's books and use them to support the activities described in this chapter. Record the results.
9. Complete the Chapter 5 Evaluation Sheet and return it to your trainer or college supervisor.

QUESTION SHEET 5–A

(Based on Chapter 5, "Advancing Cognitive Skills")

1. Why is it important to help children develop cognitive skills during the preschool years?
2. How do children use their senses to explore the world around them?
3. What can we do to re-awaken the curiosity of children who seem to have lost their sense of wonder?
4. How can field trips promote cognitive development?
5. How can you follow up on the children's interests with materials in the classroom? Give specific examples.
6. How can you use collections to promote cognitive development?
7. How would you help children to learn a new concept such as *circle?*
8. How can children in your classroom learn the meaning of numbers?
9. Give two examples of open-ended questions about a guinea pig.
10. Why is it important for children to learn classification skills? How can they do it in your classroom?

QUESTION SHEET 5–B

(Based on Videopak G, "Preschool Science Experience")

1. What are three important goals for science in the preschool program?
2. Give an example of a broad science concept you might follow throughout the year.
3. How would you involve your children in your science planning?
4. How do children learn original information?
5. What form should your science activities take to insure that real learning takes place?
6. What is the most important aspect for children in their scientific exploration of a guinea pig?
7. How would you begin planning a study of the concept, "we use water?" Why?
8. How can a cooking activity promote scientific exploration?
9. Would you have allowed your class to study plants when your plans called for a study of animal pets? Why or why not?
10. How can you re-motivate your children once their interest in a science project begins to lag?

SUGGESTED READINGS

Beaty, J. J. (1990). *Observing development of the young child* (2nd ed.). Columbus, OH: Merrill.

Brown, S. (Ed.). (1981). *Bubbles, rainbows & worms.* Mount Rainier, MD: Gryphon House.

Bauch, J. P., & Huei-hsin, J. H. (1988). Montessori: Right or wrong about number concepts? *Arithmetic Teacher, 35,* 8–11.

Harsh, A. (1987). Teach mathematics with children's literature. *Young Children, 42*(6), 24–29.

Kramer, D. C. (1989). *Animals in the Classroom.* Menlo Park, CA: Addison-Wesley.

Price, G. G. (1989). Mathematics in early childhood. *Young Children, 44*(4), 53–58.

McIntyre, M. (1984). *Early childhood and science.* Washington, DC: National Science Teachers Association.

Redleaf, R. (1983). *Open the door, let's explore.* St. Paul, MN: Toys 'n Things Press.

Rockwell, R. E., Sherwood, E. A., & Williams, R. A. (1983). *Hug a tree, and other things to do outdoors with young children.* Mt. Rainier, MD: Gryphon House.

Saunders, R., & Bingham-Newman, A. M. (1984). *Piagetian perspective for preschools: A thinking book for teachers.* Englewood Cliffs, NJ: Prentice-Hall.

Simon, S. (1975). *Pets in a jar: collecting and caring for small wild animals.* New York: The Viking Press.

Smith, R. F. (1987). Theoretical framework for preschool science experiences. *Young Children, 42*(2), 34–40.

Tudge, J., & Caruso, D. (1988). Cooperative problem solving in the classroom: Enhancing young children's cognitive development. *Young Children, 44*(1), 46–52.

Wadsworth, B. J. (1989). *Piaget's theory of cognitive and affective development.* New York: Longman.

Ziemer, M. (1987). Science and the early childhood curriculum: One thing leads to another. *Young Children, 42*(6), 44–51.

CHILDREN'S BOOKS

Carle, E. (1983). *Brown bear, brown bear, what do you see?* New York: Holt, Rinehart, & Winston.

Carle, E. (1971). *The very hungry caterpillar.* New York: Thomas Y. Crowell.

Coxe, M. (1990). *Whose footprints?* New York: Thomas Y. Crowell.

Demi. (1986). *Demi's count the animals 1*2*3.* New York: Grosset & Dunlap.

Ehlert, L. (1988). *Planting a rainbow.* San Diego, CA: Harcourt, Brace, & Jovanovich.

Feelings, M. (1971). *Moja means one.* New York: Dial Press.

Hoban, T. (1978). *Is it red? Is it yellow? Is it blue?* New York: Greenwillow Books.

Jonas, A. (1989). *Color dance.* New York: Greenwillow Books.

Lionni, L. (1959). *Little blue and little yellow.* New York: Astor-Honor.

Stinson, K. (1982). *Red is best.* Toronto, Canada: Annick Press.

Titherington, J. (1986). *Pumpkin pumpkin.* New York: Mulberry Books.

VIDEOTAPES

Beaty, J. (Producer). (1979). Preschool science experience (Videopak G) *Skills for preschool teachers.* Elmira, NY: McGraw Bookstore, Elmira College.

CHAPTER 5 EVALUATION SHEET
ADVANCING COGNITIVE SKILLS

1. Student _____

2. Trainer _____

3. Center where training occurred _____

4. Beginning date _____ Ending date _____

5. Describe what student did to accomplish General Objective

   _____

   _____

6. Describe what student did to accomplish Specific Objectives

   Objective 1 _____

   _____

   Objective 2 _____

   _____

   Objective 3 _____

   _____

7. Evaluation of student's Learning Activities
      (Trainer Check One)   (Student Check One)

   _____ Highly superior performance   _____

   _____ Superior performance   _____

   _____ Good performance   _____

   _____ Less than adequate performance   _____

Signature of Trainer: Signature of Student:

_____   _____

Comments:

6 Advancing Communication Skills

General Objective

To promote children's verbal skills to help them communicate their thoughts and feelings.

Specific Objectives

- [ ] Interacts with children in ways that encourage them to communicate their thoughts and feelings verbally.
- [ ] Provides materials and activities to promote language development.
- [ ] Uses books and stories with children to motivate listening and speaking.

Most people now agree that the early childhood years, from birth to the time of entering school, are among the most important years of development. At no other time does development advance so rapidly in so short a time. Surely one of the most remarkable aspects of this period is the process of acquiring a native language. From being totally non-verbal at birth, the young child develops the ability to think and speak in a native language by the time of entering school. If the family is bilingual, the child may learn two languages.

How does this happen? Although psycholinguists advance several theories, the process is still something of a mystery. But we do know certain facts. We know that the drive to communicate is inherent in all human beings. We also know that children will strive endlessly to accomplish this goal of communication unless impaired, totally thwarted, or frustrated by circumstances. And we know that the failure to develop verbal ability during these crucial early years can affect a child's thinking and learning abilities throughout life.

Physical or mental disability may prevent language development from occurring at a typical time or rate. Abusive or uncaring home environments may discourage children from trying to express themselves verbally. The opposite may also be true. If a child has every need fulfilled without having to utter a word, language is sometimes delayed. Some twins satisfy each other's communication drive by developing their own verbal or non-verbal communication system, thus delaying native language development.

We also know that modeling behavior is as important here as in other aspects of development. Children from highly verbal homes seem to speak early and well, while children from homes where non-verbal communication is the norm often experience a delay in learning to speak fluently. Young children need to hear language spoken to learn to speak it themselves.

It is your role as a teacher or aide in a preschool program to promote language development in some of the following ways.

INTERACTS WITH CHILDREN IN WAYS THAT ENCOURAGE THEM TO COMMUNICATE THEIR THOUGHTS AND FEELINGS VERBALLY

For verbal communication to occur with preschool children, two factors seem essential, the appropriate environment and the necessity. First, there must be a stress-free environment that allows children to communicate, but does not force them. Children need to feel support from people around them to express themselves in their very personal but still imperfect mode of communication, language. Second, children must have the need to communicate in the classroom.

Stress-Free Environment

For many children, verbalizing is a new and untried skill outside their home. They need not only opportunities to become proficient, but also encouragement to continue. Children usually respond well to anything closely associated with themselves. Try playing name games to put them at ease and pique their interest:

> Bobby, Bobby, dressed in blue,
> Tell us what you like to do
> On the playground.

> Jennifer, Jennifer, dressed in red,
> Tell us what your good friend said
> In the house corner.

Play a follow-the-leader naming game in your classroom in which the leader touches and names items in the room and everyone who follows does the same. As children become proficient with one-word names, use two-word and three-word names (e.g., brown table, glass aquarium, little white telephone).

Praise children for their verbal accomplishments just as you would for a block building or a painting. "I like the way you said my name, Sharon. Sharon is such a nice sounding name, too."

A stress-free environment also means that you accept the children as they are—for themselves. This means you accept their language, no matter how poorly pronounced or how ungrammatical. Language is a very personal thing. It reflects not only the child's early stage of development, but also his or her family. Therefore, you must be especially careful not to correct a child's language. Telling them they are saying a word wrong is a put-down. Then how, you may ask, are they going to learn the "correct" pronunciation? They will learn it by hearing you use words and by practicing new words in the many interesting language activities you provide.

A stress-free environment also means that your classroom is free from stressful situations for young children. They should not be put on the spot and forced to perform verbally, creatively, or in any other way. Offer them interesting opportunities and warm encouragement, but do not force shy or unsure children to speak.

Necessity

Do children have the need to communicate in your classroom? For what reason? You may want to list some of the reasons. If you are not sure, take time to observe and listen for communication opportunities. Your list may read something like this:

> Giving a greeting
> Asking a question
> Giving a direction
> Asking for permission
> Telling what is happening
> Inviting someone to participate
> Reporting someone else's communication
> Expressing an emotion
> Relating an incident
> Calling for attention
> Expressing an inner thought, an idea
> Pretending to be someone
> Wondering about something
> Saying thanks

Next you need to provide opportunities for these types of communication to take place. Remember, you are the role model. You need to communicate verbally yourself whenever possible. Referring to your list, begin setting up opportunities for children to participate in talking.

Set aside a time of day when you greet the children and they greet one another. Have a small group or circle time in which the children have a chance to tell about something. A shy child might talk through a hand puppet at first. You can demonstrate how. Give your children a chance to pretend in the dramatic play area or with blocks or water. Ask one child to help another with a new tool or piece of equipment. Give children oral messages to carry to someone else in the room. Have them ask someone a question and return to you with the answer. Sit with the children at snack or lunchtime and start a conversation about something of interest to them.

Children need to hear words and how they are used in order to use the words themselves. Make sure your classroom is full of talking. You can take the lead if no one else does. Describe in positive terms, for instance, what one of the children is doing. "Jill, I see you painting with bright red paint at the easel." Then ask that child to describe what you are doing. "What do you see me doing?" Play games in which you give verbal directions to one child at a time to see if children can remember and carry out the directions. Start with one simple direction and add to it as the children become adept at playing: "Jeffrey, can you go to the window, turn around in place, pick up a block, and give it to Kay?" Soon your children will want to take over your role as the leader.

Verbalizing Feelings

Children also need to verbalize feelings. Whenever an emotional experience occurs in your classroom, take time out to talk about it with the individuals involved. Talk about feelings—yours and the children's. If something nice has happened to a child or his family, get him to tell how he feels about it. If someone is angry or upset, help him express his emotion in words.

Books can promote discussions about feelings. *Let's Be Enemies* (Udry, 1961) and *The Hating Book* (Zolotow, 1969) can stimulate a discussion about how a child feels when his best friend gets mad at him. *The Tenth Good Thing About Barney* (Viorst, 1971) explores feelings of grief when a pet dies. *Sometimes I Like to Cry* (Stanton & Stanton, 1978) is a simple but effective display of times that call for tears. *Grownups-Cry Too* (Hazen, 1973) shows that a person can express his emotions no matter how old he is. (This book is published in both English and Spanish.)

You might want to mount pictures of children laughing, crying, or feeling lonely in the area where you gather for group discussions. In the dramatic play area, you might photocopy and display some illustrations from the books mentioned to motivate children to talk about feelings on their own.

Child-Adult Communication

To promote good adult-child and child-adult communication, you need to be an active communicator. This means you need to be a person the children are able and willing to approach. You must therefore be accessible to them. You may have to take the initiative with children whom you have assessed as needing language practice. They may lack the confidence to approach you on their own. Try stationing yourself in a particular classroom activity area near these children and create opportunities for conversation. If the children do not respond, you may need to talk for a while at first until the children accept your presence and realize that you accept them.

Observers of teacher behavior note that teachers usually respond to the children who talk the most. The quiet or inarticulate children, those who truly need conversational practice, are frequently ignored. You must therefore make a special effort not to overlook such children. Remember that patience, not pressure, should govern your approach.

What will you say in your conversations with individual children? Things of interest to them about themselves, the clothes they're wearing, the other children, their family, things they like to do, and classroom activities, are always appropriate topics. Do not "talk down" to children in private conversations. They understand many more words than they use themselves. Instead, you should carry on a conversation just as you would with your own friends. Speak slowly and clearly, for in addition to stimulating the children to speak, you will be serving as a language model for them.

Bilingual Children

Bilingual children are fortunate to attend a preschool program that recognizes their native language as well as English, because they will have the opportunity to become fluent in both languages during this period of natural language acquisition. At no other time will they be able to acquire another language so easily.

To learn a second language, children must hear and practice it, and you must provide opportunities for them to do so. These should not be formal teaching situations. Young children from birth to age five acquire native and second languages in a most informal and spontaneous way: by hearing it spoken around them, by trial and error in speaking it themselves, and by extracting the rules of the language naturally—not through formal grammar teaching. This means you or your co-workers should speak the second language, for example, Spanish, as if it is the primary native language. Spend an hour a day, or a half hour in a half-day program, speaking nothing but Spanish. Those children who speak Spanish will respond naturally. Those children whose native language is English will pick up a great deal of Spanish not by being taught formally, but by hearing it around them.

Read children's books in Spanish, sing songs in Spanish, do painting or build with blocks making comments in Spanish, and have a wonderful time during your "Spanish hour" every day. By the end of the year, you may have many so-called "Anglo" children responding in Spanish as fluently as your native-Spanish speakers. Everyone will feel good about it: the Hispanic children because you have recognized their language by using it in school, and the non-Hispanic children because they have learned to say and understand simple phrases in a new language.

It is not the same to have a second-language person come into your classroom and teach the children to count to 10 and to say "hello," "goodbye," and "how are you?" Instead, if you are not a second-language speaker, ask such a person to come into your classroom to spend a half hour each day with the children, speaking nothing but the second language. Don't use a translator. The children will be able to pick up enough non-verbal cues to understand—perhaps even better than you do! Eventually, they will be able to reply in the second language. You may want to start by sharing picture books in the second language with the children. (See page 140 for books featuring language diversity.)

Adults tend to think about learning a new language in adult terms: that it is difficult for most people, and because it is so difficult for adults, what must it be for a little child! Just the opposite is true, however, for the young child. It is much easier for a preschooler to learn a new language than it is for an adult, because the brain of the preschooler is programmed to learn a native language, no matter what it is. Thus, young children can learn a second language just as easily as they learn their native tongue.

It is much more difficult for most adults to acquire a second language because they have passed the stage of natural acquisition, which ends at puberty, and thus have to learn the language formally. In addition, adults must overcome the set language patterns of native speech—something not entirely successful for most adult speakers who consequently speak the second language with an accent.

You or a co-worker should be fluent in the second language. If this is not possible, ask for a volunteer from the community to visit regularly so that the children will hear the language informally and practice using it. Perhaps one of the children's parents or relatives could be a volunteer. If you cannot find a native speaker to come in on a regular basis, locate a speaker somewhere and help by making audio-tape cassettes using the second language. The speaker can tell a story or ask the children questions in the second language, and you can tape the story or the children's answers and play the tape later for the class. If you have no children's books in the second language, record the speaker using the second language to tell the picture story of one of your wordless books (see page 150 for wordless books) for the children to follow when you play back the tape in the classroom.

Besides the many English-language activities you provide for your children, you should plan specific activities using the second language, such as name chants and songs. The children can speak daily on a toy telephone with another second-language speaker. A bilingual puppet can be part of your daily activities, talking to individuals and groups in both languages. Children can also learn to greet one another and say good-bye in the second language.

Dramatic play is one of the best vehicles for children's language development, no matter what the language, because natural conversation occurs. Be sure you allow enough time in your daily schedule for bilingual children to become involved in pretend play. If they seem shy, help them take on a role by playing alongside such children yourself until they feel comfortable with the other youngsters.

Child-Child Communication

An important but frequently overlooked element in promoting and stimulating children's language in early childhood classrooms is the mix of children. Is your classroom composed of a single age group, such as all 3-year-olds or all 4-year-olds? Or are these groups combined? Because children learn so much of their language through imitation of those around them, it is helpful for them to be around children a bit more advanced than themselves. The language of 3-year-olds will develop so much faster with 4-year-olds in the same classroom. The same is true when deprived and affluent children are mixed together in a single classroom. The children with limited language skills will soon expand and improve their own speech.

There is one instance, however, where child-child communication, may be detrimental to the speaker's language development. In the phenomenon known as *twin talk,* young twins sometimes find a way to satisfy the drive to communicate by developing their own private language, a jargon only they and occasionally another close sibling seem to understand. Once a youngster is communicating easily with another human being, the motivation to continue learning a new language is sharply reduced. Ordinarily, twin talk is a passing phase because other speakers in the home talk to and encourage the twins to respond normally. However, when twins are left to themselves too much or other family members accommodate them by learning enough twin talk to satisfy their needs, the twins will not develop their native language as rapidly or fluently as they should.

You can help twins who have delayed speech problems by placing each in a different classroom, or by having them come to the same classroom at different times. When this is not possible, make a special effort to involve each of them in different activities. Do not learn their twin talk yourself, but encourage them to learn normal language in the same manner you do with the others—by giving them a chance to listen to normal speech, providing them with incentives and opportunities for speaking, and involving them in experiences that give them something to talk about.

PROVIDES MATERIALS AND ACTIVITIES TO PROMOTE LANGUAGE DEVELOPMENT

To provide materials and activities that will promote children's language development, you need to know each child's level of language ability at the outset. As in every other aspect of development, the children in your preschool classroom will vary widely in speaking ability. These variations reflect their individual, physical, and intellectual development, the support they have received at home, the importance of verbal communication in their homes, the amount of practice they have had in speaking, and their own particular temperament.

The Language Assessment Checklist in Table 6.1 is a list of behaviors that most children with no physical or mental disability should be able to accomplish during the preschool years. Although it is important to know the speaking and listening abilities of all the children in your classroom, you or your staff may want to begin this informal language assessment with children who appear at the outset to need special help with language. They may be the children who seldom speak or those you are unable to understand. By taking time to listen, observe, and talk with each child while she is involved in normal classroom activities, you should be able to complete the checklist for one child in 1 or 2 days.

Then you need to interpret the results. We find it best to begin by looking for three areas of strength for each child and listing them. Then you can look for three areas needing strengthening, and list them also. Finally, use the child's strengths to plan activities to help with the areas needing strengthening.

TABLE 6.1 Language Assessment Checklist

Child's Name _____

Time _____ Date _____

Observer _____

(Check items you see child performing. Use "N" to mean "No opportunity to observe.")

1. Confidence

_____ Is confident enough to speak freely in surroundings other than home

_____ Speaks in normal tone of voice so others can easily hear

_____ Identifies himself/herself verbally by name

_____ Starts conversations sometimes

2. Articulation

_____ Speech is clear to other children

_____ Speech is clear to adults

3. Language production

_____ Speaks in simple sentences

_____ Asks questions; makes requests

_____ Converses informally at play or meals

_____ Responds to questions with more than one word

_____ Takes part in conversation

4. Vocabulary

_____ Uses names of people and things around him/her

_____ Uses simple verbs (come, go, see)

_____ Uses simple pronouns (me, him, her)

_____ Uses simple adjectives (big, little, red)

_____ Uses simple prepositions (in, out, up)

5. Communication

_____ Communicates wants and needs with words

_____ Talks with adults

_____ Talks with children

_____ Talks to animals, dolls, toys

6. Language understanding

_____ Follows teacher's simple directions

_____ Responds appropriately to another child's question or request

7. Word play

_____ Makes up nonsense words

_____ Enjoys doing finger plays; can repeat words

_____ Enjoys playing word and sound games

_____ Has favorite stories or songs he/she wants repeated

8. Listening skills

_____ Sits still and listens to someone talking or reading stories
_____ Can identify words and sounds that are alike or different
_____ Can find teacher when he/she calls from another room
_____ Can remember words and sounds when they are repeated

Permission is granted by the publisher to reproduce the Language Assessment Checklist for evaluation and record keeping.

A Learning Prescription for Sharon might read as follows:

Learning Prescription for _Sharon K._   Date _9/26_

Areas of Strength and Confidence

1. _Talks with adults_

2. _Follows teacher's simple directions_

3. _Talks to animals, dolls, toys_

Areas Needing Strengthening

1. _Confidence in speaking freely_

2. _Talking with other children_

3. _Taking part in conversations_

Activities to Help

1. _Involve her with toy telephone and another child_

2. _She could tell a newcomer how to use a toy_

3. _She could tell about guinea pig to another child_

Sharon's prescription seems to be telling us that she is comfortable and confident in talking with adults and to animals, dolls, and toys. She is not yet all that confident in talking to other children. The teacher will want to plan activities for Sharon that can help to involve her with perhaps one other child at first. Because she likes to play with toys, she might be willing to talk first to the teacher and then to another child on the toy telephone. The teacher might also ask her to tell a new child how to use a toy or a piece of equipment such as the tape recorder or a computer program. Because she likes the guinea pig and talks to it every day, the teacher could ask her if she would tell a guinea pig story to one of the other children that she seems to get along with. In this way, Sharon's language strengths can be used as the focus for improving the areas she needs to strengthen.

If, however, the activities seem to create pressure rather than pleasure, it may mean that Sharon is not yet confident enough to interact with another child. In that case, the teacher should concentrate on helping Sharon feel good about herself by setting up activities she can succeed in and by praising her for tasks accomplished. Language activities can come when the teacher feels they are appropriate. A discussion of each of the checklist items follows.

Confidence

The order of each numbered item or area on the checklist is worth noting. *Confidence* comes first, because preschool children must feel at ease in the strangeness of the classroom environment and among their peers before they can speak at all. The so-called non-verbal child is frequently one who lacks confidence to speak outside the confines of the home. You may want to talk with the parents to learn how much their child communicates verbally at home to assure yourself of the child's verbal ability. It is not good practice to tell parents that their child is not speaking in school. This might cause the parents to put pressure on the child to speak in school, thus producing the opposite of the desired effect.

Your principal task with shy or uncommunicative children, then, is to help them feel comfortable in the classroom. All classroom workers need to be aware that overt efforts to get such children to speak before they are at ease in the classroom may well be counterproductive. Instead, classroom workers should direct their efforts toward accepting the children as they are, using smiles, nods, and words of praise for positive accomplishments when appropriate and leaving the children alone when necessary.

It takes a great deal of patience and forbearance on the part of an early childhood classroom staff to allow shy children to become at ease in their own good time, but this is often the only successful method. Weeks and even months are sometimes necessary for the extremely sensitive child to open up. If you have persisted in your *support-without-pressure* approach, you will be rewarded one day by a smile and even a whispered sentence.

Articulation

Articulation, the second area on the checklist, is difficult for the lay person to evaluate. Mispronouncing words is a common speech disorder. Nevertheless, articulation problems with young preschool children tend to be developmental lags rather than disorders. After all, at 3 ½ years, many children have mastered only six consonants. What seems to you to be a disorder because you cannot understand the child, may be merely a delay in the child's language development. Certain speech sounds such as /l/ may still be impossible for them to pronounce, so they come as close as they can with /w/ instead of /l/, for example, saying, "Biwwy" instead of "Billy." Many children also know how to form past tense by adding *ed,* so they over-apply the rule to every verb, regular or not, saying, "I goed home" or "Baby taked her nap."

Preschoolers' language develops in a distinct sequence at a definite pace. Modern linguists now realize that it is pointless for adults to try to correct a preschooler's speech by making him repeat sentences according to an adult pattern that he is not yet ready to use. "Correcting" like this is a negative response that tends to reinforce the unwanted behavior and makes the child feel there is something wrong with him. Instead of improving a child's language, this technique often makes the child avoid speaking at all in the presence of the person who corrected him.

Instead, preschool classroom workers need to follow the positive reinforcement techniques used naturally by many parents and other adult caregivers in the home. They need to serve as good language models themselves, using clear words and simple sentences when they are around children. They need to support and encourage children's speaking efforts with smiles and praise, and by repeating words that children use correctly. They need to provide opportunities for young children to practice their speaking and listening skills.

If the other children in your classroom can understand the child speaker, you should be encouraged. It may take longer for you, as an adult with set speech and hearing patterns, to become comfortable with a child's speech idiosyncracies. Try hard to understand the inarticulate child without making her repeat everything. If you can pick up even one word that she says, repeat that word to encourage her to continue. With practice and patience, you will find yourself able to understand the child as well as the other children do.

Again, your role is to be supportive, to be a good language model yourself, to provide opportunities for children to practice speech sounds, and to give children positive reinforcement in the form of smiles and praise when they are successful.

A warning is necessary for preschool classroom workers in dealing with children's speech difficulties. Do not single out a child for special treatment. This may only accentuate the "problem." Instead, praise all the children for language accomplishments just as you do for their block buildings or paintings. Give special help where necessary, but as unobtrusively as possible.

A classic example of the difficulty adults can cause by calling attention to so-called "speech problems" involves stuttering. Some children, especially boys, go through a phase at about 3 or 4 years of age when their speaking seems to be out of synchronization with their thinking. Hesitations at the beginning of a word cause them to repeat the first consonant in a stuttering manner. Parents sometimes believe they must force the child to slow down or he will become a permanent stutterer. However, this is exactly what the parents should *not* do. Their efforts in this direction may only accentuate the "problem" and may actually cause the child to develop a real stutter.

This nonfluent speech phase will usually correct itself *if left alone.* What the child really needs from the adults around him is a demonstration of love and acceptance.

Language Production

The third area of the checklist, language production, will help you recognize whether a child is producing sentences and taking part in conversations. It is necessary to check on this area to make sure the opportunity to produce language occurs daily for each child. Do you or your co-workers initiate conversations with individual children on topics of interest to them to which they can respond in answers of more than one word? Are you asking open-ended questions that require thoughtful answers, questions that begin with "how" or "why" or "what do you like about—" ?

An interesting classroom activity that almost always stimulates language production is puppetry. Young children use hand puppets differently from older children and adults. They seem to perceive puppets as extensions of themselves, rather than as separate doll-like toys. Notice how many times preschool children use a hand puppet as a "biter." We need to redirect this energy into using hand puppets as "talkers" too.

Rather than putting on a puppet show, preschool children should be encouraged to talk to one another and you through puppets. Again, you can serve as a model for this behavior. Put a puppet on your hand and talk to a child or small group through the puppet. Use your own voice, or even better, make a squeaky or deep voice, depending on the puppet character you are portraying.

You could have a boy character, Sammy, for instance, who comes to your classroom for the first time and wants to be introduced to the children. He could tell them how scared he feels coming there for the first time without knowing anybody. Maybe they will talk to Sammy individually to help him feel better.

Or, you might have a bunny puppet who wants to meet your classroom animal pets and talk about how to care for rabbits or gerbils. The puppet might ask each of the children what pets are their favorites and why.

When young children put a puppet on their hand, they tend to think in terms of becoming the puppet. They will get deeply involved in the pretend situation—almost as if it were real. It offers the shy child an opportunity to talk through a "not-shy" character, and it offers all children an unparalleled opportunity for language production.

Children with special needs can be involved in language through puppets with special needs. Have a puppet who speaks a language other than English visit your class. Motivation for this activity might come from the book *Maria Teresa* (Atkinson, 1979), in which Maria Teresa's Spanish-speaking puppet speaks to the American children in Maria Teresa's class and helps her make friends. You might even use a non-verbal puppet who can only point, and ask the children to help the puppet learn to speak.

Vocabulary

A deficient vocabulary, the fourth area in the checklist, may cause language delay in children. Some children have not been around other children or adults who have used many words or encouraged them to do so. Their first words are usually nouns, or naming words. If they are not also using simple verbs, pronouns, adjectives, and prepositions, you may want to get them involved in small-group games such as homemade lotto, which shows pictures of actions or qualities (e.g., a child running, a child sleeping, a small house, a big building).

Children also learn many new words through imitation while interacting with peers. You can promote interaction by arranging classroom areas to encourage small group activities. Dramatic play opportunities also promote language interchange among youngsters, better than almost any other activity. Be sure to allow time for everyone to pretend and take on roles. Even the onlookers and listeners learn new words from the speakers.

You can also encourage vocabulary development by playing team language games with small groups. Secret Box Whisper is an example of such a game. Pair off children into teams. In this game you secretly show one member of the team an object you have hidden in a shoe box. This team member then whispers through a cardboard tube to her partner, telling her about the object in the box. The partner then says the name aloud, and they get to put the item in their own shoe box if they are correct. You can use picture post cards in the secret box as the children's ability to describe things increases.

Communication

Communication, the fifth checklist area, is closely connected with confidence. If children feel good about themselves, they will probably communicate with words. If they feel more comfortable with adults than with other children—as many preschoolers do—the communication problem may be one of socialization rather than language. The child who talks only to "animals, dolls, toys" may be the shy, uncommunicative youngster already described under "confidence." Besides giving support without pressure, your task will also involve easing the child into social situations with one or two other children, perhaps through role-playing or another activity that seems to attract the child. You may need to be nearby in the beginning, but you can withdraw when you see the child playing comfortably with others.

Toy telephones can help promote communication. Be sure to have at least two phones: one for the caller and one for the listener. For children who need special practice in speaking, you should put in a pretend call yourself, and talk with them every day. Other children will see you doing this and soon begin calling on their own. To make it more interesting, keep an old telephone directory in the area and pretend to look up the number.

Language Understanding

The sixth checklist area, language understanding, relates to listening skills and vocabulary. To respond with understanding, children must be able to hear and know the words they are exposed to. If you have not been able to check off either item for a child, you may want to test for hearing problems.

A teacher-made game that has proved a successful stimulus for language understanding uses a deck of playing cards. The teacher laminates pictures of children or objects cut out of magazines or catalogs to the cards, and then covers them with clear contact paper to keep them slick enough for shuffling and dealing. In this Talking Cards game, the teacher deals out a card to each child at the small table. Each must name the picture aloud. A child who can name the picture gets to keep the card. The teacher deals again, and the naming continues until all the cards are gone. More advanced forms of this game require the child to tell one thing, and later two things, about the picture to keep the card.

Word Play

We often forget that learning through play for young children applies to language as well as to blocks and dolls. Early childhood classrooms need to encourage this exploratory play type of learning by providing opportunities for word and sound games, finger plays, chants, songs, stories, and dramatic play. Encourage children to play with sounds and make up nonsense words on the tape recorder. If you don't have a tape recorder, you can jot down children's nonsense words and use a puppet to repeat them in a chant at circle time.

Play with words is featured in collections of finger plays, action verses, and funny rhymes such as those found in *Move Over, Mother Goose: Finger Plays, Action Verses and Funny Rhymes* (Dowell, 1987). A jump-rope rhyme that has found its way into a hilarious book, *The Lady with the Alligator Purse* (Westcott, 1988) is another source of word play and chanting.

Certain picture books stimulate children to have fun with words. They enjoy funny sounds in words like "mush" from *Goodnight Moon* (Brown, 1947), and sound words like "plink, plank, plunk" from *Blueberries for Sal* (McCloskey, 1948), or the raindrop sound of "bon polo, bon polo" from *Umbrella,* (Yashima, 1958). Another favorite is sure to be *Mert the Blurt* (Kraus, 1980), who blurts out funny family secrets to a colorful horde of animal characters.

Author Pat Hutchins focuses on humorous word play in two of her books. In *The Surprise Party* (1969), each of the animals passes along to the next a whispered secret about Rabbit having a party, in a most distorted fashion as in the game of Gossip. *Don't Forget the Bacon!* (1976) is about a little girl with four things to buy at the store who not only forgets the bacon, but garbles the rest of the directions as well, almost ending up with some surprising items.

Listening Skills

To learn to speak, young children need to be able to listen and to hear. If you have reason to believe any of your children have a hearing impairment, their hearing should be tested. Parents may want to attend to the problem, but in some communities both auditory and visual screening are available for preschool programs through community agencies. The earlier such impairments are detected, the sooner the child can be helped to overcome them.

If you notice a child's attention span needs strengthening because the child cannot sit still long enough to hear, you may want to devise activities of progressive lengths. In this way, you will first focus the child's attention and then help to extend it. Games and stories that use the child's name are always a good place to begin. Include the names of each one of the small group of listeners sitting close to you as you relate the story of the boy or girl who did everything backwards for one day, including getting up, getting dressed, eating breakfast, and coming to school.

Good listening is a skill that adults seldom take time to develop themselves. You need to become a good listening model yourself if you want to promote listening skills among your children. Listen with interest to each child every day, especially those you have trouble understanding. To understand a child's speech, you need to listen carefully with focused attention. At the snack table or book corner, seek out the child with articulation problems and encourage his conversation. Your good listening will promote listening on the child's part, just as a good language model promotes speaking.

To listen, you will need to stop speaking yourself. The child's utterances should be the focus of your attention. To encourage a child to continue, you should respond with smiles and nods. You need to make eye contact and concentrate on what the child is saying. With the inarticulate child, try to pick up a word or two that you can understand, rather than asking the child to repeat the communication. If you must ask questions, ask as a friend would, not as a teacher who requires a correct answer.

The children will want to play listening games if you present them in fun ways. At circle time, have the children listen quietly to the sounds around them. You may want to set a kitchen timer for one minute. What different sounds will they hear before the buzzer sounds? The furnace rumbling, typing in a nearby office, the air conditioning, the bubbling of an aquarium pump, or the cars on the street outside may be some of their answers. Tape-record familiar sounds such as a car door slamming, a kitten purring, the front door opening and closing, and the pouring of milk into a glass, and play them back for children to identify.

Once children are on the alert for sounds, they are likely to point out environmental noises and sounds you may not be aware of yourself. Adults take for granted so many things that children find new and intriguing. Give your youngsters the lead and see where it takes all of you!

Most of us are not used to verbalizing the simple, everyday actions we perform. Yet linguists have found this so-called "self-talk" to be an extremely helpful activity for preschool children during the long and complex process of learning a native language. Self-talk calls for you to put into words the actions you are performing so that the child hears and sees at the same time, and thus learns what words mean.

For instance, as you prepare one of the classroom areas for a cooking experience with the children around you, you might say: "I'm getting out a big bowl to use for making gelatin. I'm putting it right here in the middle of the table. Let's see. We'll need a spoon to stir with. Here it is—a big spoon, a ladle. I'm putting the ladle on the table next to the bowl. We'll need hot water. Where is our teakettle? Oh, here it is. Joel, will you fill the teakettle with water over at the sink? There, Joel is turning on the water to fill the kettle. Now I'm putting the kettle on the hot plate to heat the water for our gelatin-making. Tell me when you hear the teakettle whistle. Then it will be hot enough.''

Parallel talk, in which adults verbalize the children's actions as they occur, also helps children learn to listen and understand the meaning of words by the way they are used. During the same cooking experience, you might make a running commentary on the children's actions by saying: ''Joel is stirring the gelatin with a big spoon—a ladle. See how smoothly Joel stirs the gelatin, around and around. Joel gives the ladle to Sherry and lets her have the next turn. Thanks, Joel. Now Sherry has the ladle and is stirring.''

USES BOOKS AND STORIES WITH CHILDREN TO MOTIVATE LISTENING AND SPEAKING

One of the most important experiences a preschool child can have is a happy experience with storybooks. To meet with later success in learning to read and enjoying it, a preschooler needs to have a pleasant encounter with books at the outset. Hopefully, a child's acquaintance with books has begun in the home, long before the child enters your classroom. The books and activities you provide will then be a follow-up and expansion of the story reading that occurs at home. But for some children, the experience in your classroom will be their initiation into the exciting world of books and reading. You will want to make it a joyful one.

Children need to encounter books early in life for a number of reasons. Experiences with books help strengthen and reinforce children's experiences with language. As they learn their native tongue orally, they will also be hearing and seeing words written in books, used in both familiar and new ways. They will eventually become aware of the concept of symbolization as they look at written letters that stand for sounds—the same sounds they are picking up in their oral vocabulary. They will also learn new words themselves, and new uses for familiar words as they listen to favorite stories read over and over.

When children see their parents and other adults reading, they begin to internalize the idea that reading is something that people around them like to do, that it seems to be important and worthwhile. It is something they themselves will want to learn to do as soon as they can.

The adult who reads to a preschool child is saying something else very important: ''I like you enough to take time out of a busy day to share something that I like with you.'' It creates a good feeling for all concerned.

Characteristics of Preschool Children Useful for Book Selection

To bring children and books together successfully, you will need to know a great deal about both. Only a small number of the vast array of children's books published annually are really suitable for your 3-, 4-, and 5-year-olds. How will you know which ones to choose?

Plan your daily schedule to allow children to choose and look at books on their own sometime during the day.

One of the simplest ways to choose suitable books is to focus on the principal characteristics of preschool children themselves, and then select books that speak to the needs of the children based on these traits.

An outstanding characteristic of preschool children is their egocentrism, their self-centeredness. They are very much concerned with themselves, their homes, their families, their friends, and anything that happens to them. Thus, their favorite books will often be those in which they can readily identify with the main character, or in which the plot or the setting is familiar.

Another characteristic common to young children is that, because they are involved with learning a language, they are fascinated with words and their sounds. At no other time will words and speech sounds be so new and so much fun for them. This means that the books you choose to use with your children will be more enjoyable and meaningful if the words are fun and distinctive. They like to hear rhyming words, sound words, and nonsense words, as well as the repetition of words and phrases. Sometimes their attraction to a particular book is based entirely on one funny word in the story.

A third characteristic is their involvement with pretending and imaginative play. Young children spend a great deal of their time pretending to be someone else, and trying out roles they see enacted around them or on television. They are therefore in tune with books that feature fantasy or imaginative situations or characters. Books with talking animals, for instance, are more appealing to children of this age than any other age.

Children of preschool age are also dependent upon parents or the adults around them. Thus they seek security at home. For this reason, books that feature warm family stories appeal to preschoolers. But no matter what the story, it should end happily and satisfactorily. Unhappy or unsettling endings are not suitable for this age. Unpleasant experiences with books can cause preschoolers to form negative attitudes that last a lifetime.

A fifth characteristic of young children is their short attention span. Books for preschoolers must be completed at a single sitting. Moreover, the story should have only a few words per page and a great deal of action. You will soon lose a preschooler's attention if the story is too long. A child who misbehaves and is reprimanded during storytelling will soon begin to form a negative feeling for the book experience altogether.

Because books for young children are picture books, their illustrations are another feature to consider in light of the children's characteristics and needs. Young children seem to be attracted to bold, bright, primary colors. The younger the child, the simpler and less cluttered the illustrations should be—with one prominent exception. Preschoolers are also attracted to large pictures that show scenes in intricate detail. The *Madeline* books of Ludwig Bemelmans (1977), with their detailed paintings of Paris parks and squares, and Margaret Graham's line drawings of the city in Gene Zion's *Dear Garbage Man* (1957) or the inside of the house in *The Plant Sitter* (Zion, 1959), with all the tiny bugs, birds, and butterflies, provide examples of the kind of detail that seems to intrigue many young children.

Young children also seem to prefer realistic illustrations to those of an abstract nature. Adults usually select books for children and often do so on the basis of adult sensibilities, but we must remember that children will use the books. We should not overlook their tastes if we are to bring children and books together successfully. The illustrations and the text of a storybook should combine to help children identify with the characters, the situations, and the settings.

Choosing Books for Preschool Children

Every year between 2,000 and 3,000 new books are published for children. Book stores display dozens of them. Library shelves are crowded with them. But it is up to the staff of the preschool classroom to decide which ones are most appropriate for their children.

Once you know your children and understand their needs, you will want to learn a great deal about the available books to make the best selections. The following checklist, based on the characteristics of preschool children, has proved effective in helping teachers evaluate individual books. Although one book may not meet all the criteria listed, it should meet most of them to be acceptable for use with preschoolers. For example, many of the *Curious George* books (Rey, 1973) are long for preschoolers, but their exciting action along with the strong sense of identification that children feel for the mischievous monkey George make up for their length.

You can start your own card file of books to use with your children. If you duplicate the Book Selection Checklist in Table 6.2 and paste it on the front of a file card, you can fill in the blanks with an example for each appropriate item, as well as including other comments you or the children have about the book on the back of the card. Under the last item, "Use by children," you can include information on how many children have looked at the book, or how frequently it has been lent out to parents.

Because the book experience is so important for preschoolers, you need to guarantee its success at the outset. It is too important to be left to chance. Like every successful enterprise, it requires time and planning on the part of the preschool staff to review the books to be used. Use the Book Selection Checklist to assess the books you presently have in your classroom. Do you find them all suitable? If not, replace inappropriate books with a better selection. You will need to look over and read each of the books personally to determine their suitability.

Here are a few recent preschool picture books you might consider:

Browne, A. (1989). *Things I like.* New York: Alfred A. Knopf.
This is the simplest of the books discussed here. The "I" in the book is a little monkey dressed like a boy. Each page features a full-color picture of the plump monkey doing the things he likes against a white background, with a word or line of text at the bottom of the page.

King, D. (1989). *Cloudy.* New York: Philomel Books.
The gray cat Cloudy prowls through pages of murky weather or stalks in the shadows of this beautifully illustrated story done in muted colors on double-spread pages with a line or two of text somewhere on each page.

TABLE 6.2 Book Selection Checklist

Title _____ Author _____

Illustrator _____ Publisher _____

_____ Character children identify with _____
_____ Situation familiar to children _____
_____ Setting familiar to children _____
_____ Illustration attractive to children _____
_____ Words with distinctive sounds _____
_____ Action exciting, understandable _____
_____ Ending satisfying _____
_____ Story read in single sitting _____
_____ Use by children _____

Permission is granted by the publisher to reproduce this checklist for record keeping.

Kovalski, M. (1987). *The wheels on the bus.* Boston: Little, Brown.
Two girls and their grandma wait on a busy street for a bright red double-decker bus, but get so carried away with the words to this traditional nursery school song that they end up missing the bus and having to take a taxi!

Maris, R. (1986). *I wish I could fly.* New York: Greenwillow Books.
This is another simple book, with seashore drawings of a turtle who confronts a gull, a frog, a squirrel, and a rabbit with his wishes to fly, dive, climb, and run. But all his efforts only land him on his face, making wonderful sound words such as "wallop" and "wibble" in large bold-face type.

Matura, M. (1988). *Moon jump.* New York: Alfred A. Knopf.
Cayal, who loves to jump, spends the pages of this book jumping—out of bed, into the tub, into his clothes, and all the way to school. But one night he jumps so high that he lands on the moon. Large crayon-like illustrations of spread-armed Cayal fill each page with a line or so of text at the bottom.

Rounds, G. (illus.). *Old MacDonald had a farm.* (1989). New York: Holiday House.
Uniquely illustrated farm animals outlined in black almost jump off *every* other page with their *neighs* and *oinks,* while the words of the traditional song practically pop off the opposite page in variable-size, bold-face style.

Stinson, K., & Collins, H. (1990). *The dressed-up book.* Toronto, Canada: Annick Press.
Five children invade a closet full of dress-up clothes and romp through the pages of this book, trying on scary and funny wigs, wings, ears, and noses, with a text verse of questions on each page.

Yolen, J. (1987). *Owl moon.* New York: Philomel Books.
This powerful story follows a little girl and her father as they tramp through a moonlit winter woods to call up an owl. It is a prose poem of snow and shadows and silence, with the little girl telling what you have to do when you go owling, till at last a huge owl flares up and is caught in the glare of Pa's flashlight as the reader turns the last page.

Books for Children of Cultural and Language Diversity

Whether or not you have children from different cultural and language backgrounds, you will want to invite family members and neighborhood volunteers to visit your classroom who can tell stories from different cultures. You will also want to include appropriate picture books in your book area for children to look at and for you to read. More and more books for preschoolers feature a second language as well as English. In *Maria Teresa* (Atkinson, 1979), a Spanish-speaking puppet helps Maria Teresa make friends in her American class. *My Aunt Otilia's Spirits* (Garcia, 1978), in English and Spanish, tells of a mysterious Puerto Rican aunt who comes to visit her nephew every summer. In *What Does the Rooster Say, Yoshio?* (Battles, 1978), a Japanese boy and an American girl tell each other the sounds that different animals make in

[handwritten annotation: To attractive to chidren could be use words with distinctive sounds.]

[handwritten annotation: Wordless picture books are xcellet resource for use with bilingual children, because they can read in any language. You can record one of your child reading of a wordless book in french or English or chinese, so that children can enjoy listening to the story in a different language]

their two languages...the wonderful story of a day in t..., told in both Japanese and Engl...

The Litt...1977) tells the story in both Engli...comes to the United States. Alth...ations and its Vietnamese words ...People's Ears (Aardema, 1975) h...nimals. *Jambo Means Hello: Swal*...ords and their meanings for each ...ed not be of Spanish, Japanese ...to words and sounds in these lan...multi-cultural and multilinguistic heritage that the United States offers them.

[handwritten pronunciation: bɑɪˈlɪŋgwəl] Wordless picture books are another excellent resource for use with bilingual children because they can be read in any language. You, your children, and your bilingual visitors can make up stories in any language to go with the pictures in the books. You may want to record one of your visitors reading of a wordless book in Spanish or Navajo or Japanese, so that children can enjoy listening to the story in a different language on another day.

For children whose native language is English but whose heritage is a special ethnic or racial group, there are many new picture books featuring such children. We have come a long way since the 1960s when Ezra Jack Keats' wonderful books were the only ones featuring African American children. Today a whole new generation of writers presents us with a marvelous menu of books from which to choose. Eloise Greenfield continues to produce sensitive family stories about African American children, such as *The First Pink Light* (1976), *Me and Nessie* (1975), and *Grandpa's Face* (1988). Mary Stolz looks at the warm relationship between a little boy and his grandfather in the blues and blacks of *Storm in the Night* (1988). The *Jamaica* (1989) books of Juanita Havill and her illustrator Anne Sibley O'Brien bring another wonderful character to life, just as Keats did with Peter and Archie. The beautifully written and illustrated *Half a Moon and One Whole Star* by Crescent Dragonwagon and illustrator Jerry Pinkney (1986) takes Susan and a whole nightful of creatures and people through a warm summer night and into the day.

A good source of information for other multi-cultural books is The Council on Interracial Books for Children, Inc., 1841 Broadway, New York, NY 10023. For information on other cultures, see *Cultural Awareness: A Resource Bibliography* (Schmidt & McNeill, 1978). The children's books mentioned here, as well as others are listed by culture and language at the end of the chapter.

Books for Children with Handicapping Conditions

[handwritten pronunciation: n. hændɪ kæpɪŋ] Picture books that show acceptance of children with handicapping conditions by other children and adults can help your own children to be more accepting. Be sure that the books you select show the story characters as normal human beings, rather than

focusing on their handicap. For example, *Darlene* (Greenfield, 1980) shows that a little girl in a wheelchair can have the same kind of fun as the others in her family. It is an especially good book about not making such a child seem different. *A Button in Her Ear* (Litchfield, 1976) is a story about Angela and how she came to wear a hearing aid. *Arnie and the New Kid* (Carlson, 1990) has personified animal characters learning to accept the new kid in a wheel chair.

Reading Books to Children

Plan your daily schedule to allow children to choose and look at books on their own sometime during the day. But you or one of your co-workers will be responsible for reading at least once a day to the children.

You may choose to read to an individual child or a small group at a time while the rest of the children engage in another interesting activity. If so, be sure the others also have their turn to hear a story later on. Children need to sit as close as possible to the reader to see the pictures, to become personally involved in the story, and just because it feels good to sit close to someone you like. A small group makes it easier to accomplish this closeness. Don't read to the whole class at once. Make story reading a personal experience for your children by reading to individuals or small groups.

The reader should sit at the children's level rather than on a chair above them while they sit on the floor. You may want to invite a guest story reader from time to time. Parents, grandparents, teachers, and librarians are good possibilities.

Although individual children will readily come to you on their own with books to be read, you may also want to approach a particular child with a book you have picked out especially for her to hear. A child whom you have previously identified as needing help in language can benefit by having stories read on an individual basis.

To be a successful story reader, you will want to keep these hints in mind:

1. Know your book well.
2. Start with an attention-getting device.
3. Make your voice as interesting as possible.
4. Help children get involved through participation.

Know Your Book

If you have chosen your book on the basis of the Book Selection Checklist, then you are already well acquainted with it. If not, skim through it, noting features such as:

1. Sound words for which you can make the sound rather than reading the word.
2. Places where you might substitute the listener's name for the name used in the book.
3. Picture details you might ask a listener to look for if you are reading to one or two children.

4. Places in the story where you might want to pause and ask your listeners to guess what comes next.
5. Repetitious phrases where children can join in.
6. Items or objects the children will need to have concrete experiences with.

Attention-Getting Devices

Your story reading will only be successful if you have your listeners' attention. It will be a poor experience for both you and the children if you have to stop to reprimand disruptive children. It is better if they are all ready and eager for you to begin. You can be assured they will if you begin, not with the story itself, but with an attention-getting device to help the children settle down and focus their attention on the book you are about to read.

One of the simplest and most effective devices is to use the cover of the book in some way. You might, for instance, ask the children something about the cover illustration. Here are some examples:

1. Today our story is *Things I Like*. Do you see the little monkey climbing the tree? What do you suppose that monkey is going to like to do in this story?
2. This story is about some children who have found hats and shoes and clothes in the closet. It is called *The Dressed-Up Book*. What do you think those children are going to dress up to look like?
3. The name of this book is *I Wish I Could Fly*. Do you think a turtle like this can really fly? What might happen to him if he tried?
4. Here is *Moon Jump*, our story book for today. This is about a boy and his toy bear who like to jump. Where do you think they might try to jump?
5. *Cloudy* is a gray cat who likes to come and go secretly. How do you think Cloudy might do that?

An Interesting Voice

Do you enjoy reading aloud to your children? Your voice often reflects your feelings. If you are enthusiastic about story reading, the children will know it by the tone of your voice. They love to have the teacher dramatize the story by making her voice scary or whispery or way down deep. Can you do that? Most of us don't know until we try. Even then, we're not sure how we come across. Turn on the tape recorder during story reading time, and play the tape for yourself later when you're alone. Do you like the way you read the story? Practice alone with a tape recorder until you have got it the way you want it.

Child Involvement Through Participation

The egocentric nature of young children means that they will enjoy a story more if they are somehow a part of it. As the story reader, you can get children directly involved in a number of ways. You might, for instance, ask children to find a certain item in the book illustrations as you read. In *The Wheels on the Bus* (Kovalski, 1987), can the children find five babies crying? In *Old MacDonald Had a Farm* (1989), can the children find what happened to Old MacDonald when the skunk appeared? What tails can your children find in *The Dressed-Up Book* (Stinson & Collins, 1990) when all the children in the story are sitting at the table eating?

In a large group, direct child participation often disrupts the group because everyone wants a turn. Avoiding that problem is another reason for reading to small groups and individuals. But even with a small group, you can keep control of what happens by calling a particular child by name to respond, instead of opening it to everyone.

Your children may want to respond by singing the song or repeating the words as you turn the pages of *The Wheels on the Bus* (Kovalski, 1987) or *Old MacDonald Had a Farm* (1989).

For groups that are not used to sitting still and listening to a story, you may not want to interrupt the flow of the story with individual involvement for a while. You need to decide whether your priority for the children is to complete a story without interruptions or to get the children involved by offering them opportunities to participate.

Extending the Book Experience

For books to be meaningful to children, you as teacher or aide need to be prepared to extend their book experience into the total life of the classroom. Books should not be relegated to a reading corner alone. They can play a vital role in the entire curriculum if you are book-conscious enough to make them do so. When you notice children pretending to be fire fighters after a visit to the local firehouse, place an appropriate book in the dramatic play area. A fish book should be stationed next to your aquarium, and a gerbil book next to the gerbil cage. When you go outside looking for leaves in the fall, take a tree identification guide with you.

The storybooks reviewed earlier in this chapter can be extended into the life of the classroom as well. *Cloudy* (King, 1989) can be read on a cloudy day. *The Wheels on the Bus* (Kovalski, 1987) can be read before or after the class goes on a field trip by bus. *I Wish I Could Fly* (Maris, 1986) can be read after the children have visited the seashore or a pond, or when you set up a terrarium with a turtle or a frog. *The Dressed-Up Book* (Stinson & Collins, 1990) can give you and the children ideas for dressing up and pretending in your dramatic play area. Bring in a box of clothes, hats, shoes, ties, jewelry, and paraphernalia for the children to try on after reading this book.

Many teachers like to use book recordings, filmstrips, or videotapes with their children. This is not nearly as appropriate or meaningful as an adult's actual reading of a story. It is a passive experience for the children, with no chance for personal interaction. As with television, book videos tend to provide an entertainment experience rather than a learning one. Young children learn far less when they sit and listen or watch than when they become actively involved.

Children will eventually want to compose their own stories. The teacher can take dictation from individuals or small groups who want to tell a story about a pet, a personal experience, a field trip, or a photo. These stories can be made into books for inclusion in the book corner. Children gain an even greater appreciation for language and books when they create their own.

SUMMARY

Some of the activities discussed in this chapter to help children develop communication skills include:

Stress-Free Environment
Name games
Naming Follow-the-Leader
Praise, not correction

Necessity for Speaking
Greeting period
Hand puppet
Oral messages
Verbal directions

Verbalizing Feelings
Books about feelings
Pictures showing emotions
Photocopying books

Child-Adult Communication
Teacher station
Private conversation

Bilingual Children
Spanish hour
Book reading
Community volunteer
Tape recording
Wordless books
Bilingual puppet
Dramatic play

Child-Child Communication
Mixed age groups

Articulation
No correcting
Model language

Language Understanding
Talking Cards

Language Production
Puppetry

Vocabulary
Word lotto
Secret Whisper
Toy telephones

Confidence
Acceptance
No pressure

Book Selection
Identify with character
Situation familiar
Setting familiar
Attractive illustrations
Distinctive words
Exciting action
Satisfying ending
Story short

Word Play
Finger plays
Books

Listening Skills
Hearing check
Storytelling
Teacher model
Environment sounds
Self-talk
Parallel talk

Book Reading
Know book
Attention-getting
Interesting voice
Child participation

LEARNING ACTIVITIES

1. Read Chapter 6, "Advancing Communication Skills" and answer Question Sheet 6–A.
2. View Videopak E, "Speaking and Listening Skills" and answer Question Sheet 6–B.
3. Read one or more of the books listed under Suggested Readings. Add 10 cards to your file with specific ideas for helping children develop communication skills. Include the reference source on each card.
4. Observe and record the language skills of all of your children using the Language Assessment Checklist.
5. Choose a child who may be having language problems as indicated on the Language Assessment Checklist; make a Learning Prescription for him based on the results; carry out one of the activities you suggest.
6. Review ten children's books, making a card file for each, filling out the Book Selection Checklist and mounting it on the front of the card; on the reverse side, record a book extension activity you can use with children.
7. Read one of the above books with the children, using attention-getting devices and child involvement activities discussed in the chapter. (Trainer can observe.)
8. Read a second book with the children, using attention-getting and child-involvement activities, followed later with a book extension activity. (Trainer can observe.)
9. Complete the Chapter 6 Evaluation Sheet and return it to your trainer or college supervisor.

QUESTION SHEET 6–A

(Based on Chapter 6, "Advancing Communication Skills")

1. How does the drive to communicate assist a child in his language development?
2. What factors other than physical ones can interfere with a child's normal development of language?
3. What factors seem to be important in order for communication to occur in the preschool classroom? Why?
4. Why should you not correct a child's language mistakes? How, then, can you help the child improve?
5. Using one of the reasons for communication in your classroom, tell what kind of activity you could set up to promote that communication?
6. What kind of activity could you set up to help children learn to verbalize their feelings?
7. What does confidence have to do with children's speaking in a preschool classroom? How can you strengthen confidence?
8. What can you expect in articulation from the speech of a three- or four-year-old child?
9. In what different ways can the use of puppets promote language skills?
10. How can you help children who speak a language other than English?

QUESTION SHEET 6–B

(Based on Videopak E, "Speaking and Listening Skills")

1. Why is it necessary for a caring adult to be present during the early stages of a child's language development?
2. Why should you make an assessment of children's speaking and listening skills early in the program year?
3. What should you do with the assessment once it is complete?
4. How can you best help a nonverbal child improve language production?
5. How can dramatic play be used in promoting speaking and listening skills?
6. What kinds of activities during mealtime can promote language skills?
7. What should a teacher do specifically to serve as a good language model?
8. How can room arrangement promote language development?
9. How does multi-age grouping promote speaking skills?
10. What kinds of language accomplishments should you comment on favorably? Give examples.

SUGGESTED READINGS

Barton, B. (1986). *Tell me another: Storytelling and reading aloud at home, at school, and in the community.* Markham, Ontario: Pembroke Publishers. (Heinemann Educational Books, Inc., NH)

Beaty, J. J. (1990). *Observing development of the young child* (2nd ed.). Columbus, OH: Merrill.

Burke, E. M. (1990). *Literature for the young child.* Boston: Allyn and Bacon.

Cascardi, A. E. (1985). *Good books to grow on.* New York: Warner Books.

Cech, M. (1990). *Globalchild: Multi-cultural resources for young children.* Ottawa, Ontario: Child Care Initiatives.

Dowell, R. I. (1987). *Move over Mother Goose: Finger plays, action verses and funny rhymes.* Mt. Rainier, MD: Gryphon House.

Dumtschin, J. U. (1988). Recognize language development and delay in early childhood. *Young Children, 43*(3), 16–24.

Genishi, C. (1988). Children's language: Learning words from experience. *Young Children,* Vol. 44(1), 16–23.

Glazer, J. I. (1991). *Literature for young children* (3rd ed.). Columbus, OH: Merrill.

Holzman, M. (1983). *The language of children.* Englewood Cliffs, NJ: Prentice-Hall.

Jalongo, M. R. (1988). *Young children and picture books: Literature from infancy to six.* Washington, DC: National Association for the Education of Young Children.

Jenkins, P. D. (1980). *The magic of puppetry: A guide for those working with young children.* Englewood Cliffs, NJ: Prentice-Hall.

Lindfors, J. W. (1987). *Children's language and learning.* Englewood Cliffs, NJ: Prentice-Hall.

Oppenheim, J., Brenner, B., & Boegehold, B. D. (1986). *Choosing books for kids.* New York: Ballantine Books.

Pflaum, S. W. (1986). *The development of language and literacy in young children* (3rd ed.). Columbus, OH: Merrill.

Schmidt, V. E., & McNeill, E. (1978). *Cultural awareness: A resource bibliography.* Washington, DC: National Association for the Education of Young Children.

Teale, W. H., & Martinez, M. G. (1988). Getting on the right road to reading: Bringing books and young children together in the classroom. *Young Children, 44*(1), 10–15.

Trelease, J. (1982). *The read-aloud handbook.* New York: Penguin Books.

CHILDREN'S BOOKS (MULTI-CULTURAL)

African

Aardema, V. (1975). *Why mosquitoes buzz in people's ears.* New York: The Dial Press.

Daly, N. (1985). *Not so fast, Songololo.* New York: Viking Penguin.

Grifalconi, A. (1987). *Darkness and the butterfly.* Boston: Little, Brown.

Grifalconi, A. (1990). *Osa's pride.* Boston: Little, Brown.

Grifalconi, A. (1986). *The village of round and square houses.* Boston: Little, Brown.

Feelings, M. (1974). *Jambo means Hello: Swahili alphabet book.* New York: The Dial Press.

Lewin, H., Illustrated by Lisa Kopper. (1983). *Jafta.* Minneapolis, MN: Carolrhoda Books.

Steptoe, J. (1987). *Mufaro's beautiful daughters.* New York: Lothrop, Lee, and Shephard.

African American

Bogart, J. E. (1990). *Daniel's dog.* New York: Scholastic.

Caines, J., Illustrated by Ronald Himler. (1977). *Daddy.* New York: Harper and Row.

Dragonwagon, C., Illustrated by Jerry Pinkney. (1986). *Half a moon and one whole star.* New York: Macmillan.

Greenfield, E. Illustrated by Moneta Barnett. (1976). *The first pink light.* New York: Thomas Y. Crowell.

Greenfield, E. (1988). *Grandpa's face.* New York: Philomel Books.

Greenfield, E. (1975). *Me and Nessie.* New York: Thomas Y. Crowell.

Grimes, N., Illustrated by Tom Feelings. (1986). *Something on my mind.* New York: Dial Books.

Havill, J., Illustrated by Anne Sibley O'Brien. (1989). *Jamaica tag-along.* Boston: Houghton Mifflin.

Johnson, D. (1990). *What will Mommy do when I'm at school?* New York: Macmillan.

Keats, E. J. (1968). *A letter to Amy.* New York: Harper and Row.

Keats, E. (1975). *Louie.* New York: Greenwillow Books.

Keats, E. (1978). *The trip.* New York: Greenwillow Books.

Petrie, C. (1982). *Joshua James likes trucks.* Chicago: Children's Press.

Stolz, M. Illustrated by Pat Cummings. (1988). *Storm in the night.* New York: Harper and Row.

Amish

Steffy, J., Illustrated by Denny Bond. (1987). *The school picnic.* Intercourse, PA: Good Books.

Appalachian

Rylant, C., Illustrated by Diane Goode. (1982). *When I was young in the mountains.* New York: E. P. Dutton.

Caribbean

George, J. C. (1978). *The wentletrap trap.* New York: E. P. Dutton. (Bahamas)

Greenfield, E., Illustrated by Amos Ferguson. (1988). *Under the Sunday tree.* (Bahamas) New York: Harper.

Lessac, F. (1987). *My little island.* New York: Harper.

Lloyd, E. (1978). *Nini at carnival.* New York: Thomas Y. Crowell. (Jamaica)

Pomerantz, C., Illustrated by Frane Lessac. (1989). *The chalk doll.* (Jamaica) New York: Harper.

Wolkstein, D. (1981). *The banza.* New York: The Dial Press. (Haiti)

French

Bemelmans, L. (1977). *Madeline.* New York: Penguin.

Hispanic

Atkinson, M. (1979). *Maria Teresa.* Chapel Hill, NC: Lollipop Power.

Ets, M. H. (1978). *Gilberto and the wind.* New York: Penguin.

Garcia, R. (1978). *My Aunt Otilia's spirits.* San Francisco: Children's Book Press.

Sonneborn, R., Illustrated by Emily A. McCully. (1987). *Friday night is Papa night.* New York: Penguin.

Japanese

Battles, E. (1978). *What does the rooster say, Yoshio?* Chicago: Albert Whitman.

McDermott, G. (1978). *The stonecutter.* New York: Penguin.

Takeshita, F., & Suzuki, M. (1989). *The park bench.* Brooklyn, NY: Kane/Miller Book Publishers. (English & Japanese)

Native American

Ata, T. (1989). *Baby rattlesnake.* San Francisco: Children's Book Press.

Baylor, B., Illustrated by Peter Parnall. (1974). *Everybody needs a rock.* New York: Charles Scribner's Sons.

Cohen, C. L., Illustrated by Shanto Begay. (1989). *The mud pony.* New York: Scholastic.

DePaolo, T. (1983). *The legend of the bluebonnet.* New York: G. P. Putnam's Sons.

Scott, A. H. (1972). *On Mother's lap.* New York: McGraw-Hill.

Russian

Asch, F., & Vagin, V., Illustrated by Vladimir Vagin. (1989). *Here comes the cat!* (English & Russian) New York: Scholastic.

Tolstoy, L., Illustrated by Erika Klein. (1988). *Varya and her greenfinch.* Mt. Rainier, MD: Gryphon House.

Vietnamese

Surat, M. M., Illustrated by Vo-Dinh Mai. (1983). *Angel child, dragon child.* Milwaukee, WI: Raintree.

Tran-Khanh-Tuyet. (1977). *The little weaver of Thai-Yen Village.* San Francisco: Children's Book Press.

Xiong, B. (1989). *Nine-in-one, grr! grr!* San Francisco: Children's Book Press.

CHILDREN'S BOOKS (OTHER)

Brown, M. (1947). *Goodnight moon.* New York: Harper & Row.

Carlson, N. (1990). *Arnie and the new kid.* New York: Viking Penguin.

Hazen, N. (1973). *Grownups cry too.* Chapel Hill, NC: Lollipop Power.

Hutchins, P. (1969). *The surprise party.* New York: Macmillan.

Hutchins, P. (1976). *Don't forget the bacon!* New York: Penguin.

Kraus, R. (1980). *Mert the blurt.* New York: Simon and Schuster.

McCloskey, R. (1948). *Blueberries for Sal.* New York: Viking.

Rey, H. (1973). *Curious George.* Boston: Houghton Mifflin.

Stanton, E., & Stanton, H. (1978). *Sometimes I like to cry.* Chicago: Albert Whitman.

Udry, J. (1961). *Let's be enemies.* New York: Harper & Row.

Viorst, J. (1971). *The tenth good thing about Barney.* New York: Atheneum.

Westcott, N. B., (illus.). (1988). *The lady with the alligator purse.* Boston: Little, Brown.

Yashima, T. (1958). *Umbrella.* New York: Viking.

Zion, G. (1957). *Dear garbage man.* New York: Harper.

Zion, G. (1959). *The plant sitter.* New York: Scholastic.

Zolotow, C. (1969). *The hating book.* New York: Scholastic.

Handicaps

Greenfield, E. (1980). *Darlene.* New York: John Day.

Litchfield, A. B. (1976). *A button in her ear.* Chicago: Albert Whitman.

Mack, N. (1976). *Tracy.* Milwaukee, WI: Raintree Editions.

Rabe, B. (1981). *The balancing girl.* New York: E. P. Dutton.

Wordless

Crews, D. (1980). *Truck.* New York: Greenwillow Books.

DePaolo, T. (1978). *Pancakes for breakfast.* New York: Harcourt, Brace, & Jovanovich.

Ormerod, J. (1982). *Moonlight.* New York: Viking Penguin.

Ormerod, J. (1981). *Sunshine.* New York: Lothrop, Lee, & Shepard Books.

Prater, J. (1985). *The gift.* New York: Viking Penguin.

VIDEOTAPES

Beaty, J. J. (Producer). (1979). Preschool book experience (Videopak F), and Speaking and listening skills (Videopak E), *Skills for preschool teachers* [videotapes]. Elmira, NY: Mc-Graw Bookstore, Elmira College.

Educational Productions, Inc. (Producer). *Oh say what they see; Let's talk; Now you're talking;* and *Between you and me* [videotape]. Portland, OR: Educational Productions, Inc.

Oglan, J. (Producer). *Whole language learning* [videotape]. Washington, DC: National Association for the Education of Young Children.

CHAPTER 6 EVALUATION SHEET
ADVANCING COMMUNICATION SKILLS

1. Student _____

2. Trainer _____

3. Center where training occurred _____

4. Beginning date _____ Ending date _____

5. Describe what student did to accomplish General Objective

   _____

   _____

6. Describe what student did to accomplish Specific Objectives

   Objective 1 _____

   _____

   Objective 2 _____

   _____

   Objective 3 _____

   _____

7. Evaluation of student's Learning Activities
   (Trainer Check One)   (Student Check One)

   _____ Highly superior performance   _____

   _____ Superior performance   _____

   _____ Good performance   _____

   _____ Less than adequate performance   _____

Signature of Trainer: Signature of Student:

_____   _____

Comments:

7 Advancing Creative Skills

General Objective

To promote children's creativity through playful expression and freedom of activity.

Specific Objectives

- ☐ Arranges a variety of art materials for children to explore on their own.
- ☐ Accepts children's creative products without placing a value judgment on them.
- ☐ Gives children the opportunity to have fun with music.

W hen we speak of a creative person, we generally mean someone who has original ideas, who does things in new and different ways, who uses imagination and inventiveness to bring about novel forms. Can young children be creative like this?

Not only can they be, they are. Creativity seems to be intuitive in young children, something they are born with. From the very beginning they have the capacity to look at things, to hear, smell, taste, and touch things from an entirely original perspective—their own. After all, preschool children are new and unique beings in a strange and complex world. The only way children can make sense of things in their world is to explore with their senses: try things out, see what makes them the way they are, see if they can be any different.

Young children bring to every activity a spirit of wonder, great curiosity, and a spontaneous drive to explore, experiment, and manipulate in a playful and original fashion. This is creativity. It is the same impulse that artists, writers, musicians, and scientists have.

You may respond that not all children behave like this. Some show little creativity, or little interest in creative-type activities. As we noted in the chapter on cognitive skills, some children show little interest in anything new. They will not engage in any activities unless directed by the teacher. These are the children who need our special assistance in recapturing the creativity they were born with.

Acceptance and Encouragement

Creativity flourishes only where it is accepted and encouraged. Infants, toddlers, and preschoolers who have been dominated by the adults around them and not allowed to do anything their own way will not show much creativity. They have already learned the sad lesson that experimenting only gets them into trouble. Children who have been the victims of neglect, lack of love, harsh discipline, or overprotection seem to lack the spark of creativity, as well.

It is extremely important that, as a teacher or aide in a preschool program, you help to rekindle that spark. It is imperative that young children be able to use the creative skills of pretending, imaginative thinking, fantasizing, and inventiveness in learning to deal with the complex world around them. Strange as it may seem, these are the skills that will help them most in problem solving, getting along with others, understanding their world, and eventually, doing abstract thinking. Promoting creativity is, in fact, a most effective way to promote intellectual development.

Freedom

The key to setting up an environment that promotes creativity is freedom. Children need to be free to explore, experiment, manipulate, invent, and pretend spontaneously. Having an adult show them how or tell them what to do defeats this purpose. Adults do not see things or use things as children do. Young children need the opportunity to work out many ideas on their own and in their own way, without adult direction or interference.

ARRANGES A VARIETY OF ART MATERIALS FOR CHILDREN TO EXPLORE ON THEIR OWN

When most teachers think of creativity, the art area comes to mind first. Unfortunately for young children, this is often the least creative area in the entire classroom, because it is entirely adult-directed and nothing happens spontaneously. Adults get out the art supplies, set up activities on tables, instruct the children on how to use them, and stay at the tables to make sure they follow directions. This is not creative art. It is really a manipulative activity when done like this, or an exercise in following directions. Structured activities like these should not be banished from the classroom, since they are entirely appropriate for promoting manipulative and direction-following skills. It is just that teachers and children should not confuse them with creative art.

As mentioned previously, the key to creativity is freedom. Children need to be free to explore, experiment, invent, and pretend with art materials just as they do with blocks or dress-up clothes. Adults rarely consider it necessary to remain in the housekeeping corner to make sure the children dress up "properly" or play roles "correctly," yet this all too frequently happens with art.

Process vs. Product

We need to step back and think, what is our primary purpose for having art in the classroom? Is it to have children paint a nice picture or make a lovely collage to take home to mother? If this is true in your classroom, then you have confused the product of art with the process. Most preschool children do not yet have the skills or the development level to turn out an accomplished art product. Our goal should instead be to assist children in becoming involved in the process of creativity. It is the process of creating that is most important in young children's development.

We should not be faulted for making the mistake of focusing on the product. It is much easier to see a painting than a process. Moreover, no one ever told us this was not the proper way to "teach" art. After all, isn't everyone more concerned with the picture than with the process of painting it?

Not everyone. Take a look at the children in your classroom who are involved in painting. The only thing that seems to matter to them is the experience, that is, the process. They focus on their product only after adults have made a fuss about it, after they have learned that this is the way to please adults. Before that, they seem more interested in things like smearing the paint around, slapping one color on another, moving the brush back and forth, covering everything they have painted with a new color. This is the process of art—and it is how creativity is born.

Art Activities

Now that you know the true state of affairs, how can you set up your art activities to promote children's freedom to create? First of all, you need to have at least one easel, and keep it out and ready for use every day. Then you should have certain art materials permanently within children's reach. Have paper, paints, brushes, crayons, felt-tip markers, paste, and construction paper available for daily use when the children arrive. For instance, children can choose to easel paint during the free choice period. No teacher direction or assistance is needed. Children learn to handle the brush and control the paint by themselves.

Observe a beginner and you'll see how she manages. The new painter spends a great deal of time trying out which hand to use, the best way to hold the brush, how to get paint from jar to paper, how to move paint around on the paper, and how to control the drips. In other words, she is "manipulating the medium" rather than painting a picture.

To help your children manage this new medium, you might consider cutting a few inches off the long paint brush handle. Most easel brushes are the right thickness for pudgy fingers, but too long for preschoolers to manipulate easily. You might want to put out only one or two colors of paint until children are ready to handle more. You might also want to mix the tempera paint powder a little thicker to make it easier for beginners to control. Use liquid starch to thicken it.

Art Supplies

Art supplies should be kept on low shelves next to the children's tables or work space to make it easier for children to see and select from what is available and later return items to their shelf space when they are finished. You will want several kinds of paper, and plenty of it, as well as paste, glue, scissors, crayons, felt-tip pens, colored chalk, finger paints, yarn pieces, popsicle sticks, pipe cleaners, and collage scraps. Let children know they are free to select from the materials at the art table to use as they wish.

Have at least one easel in the classroom and keep it out and ready for use every day.

At other times, you may want to set up the art activity before the children arrive, and let them "play" with it creatively during free choice periods. Take dough, for example. In the beginning, you may want to mix the dough and have it ready for the children to explore and experiment with when they come in. Perhaps you'll put out rolling pins and cookie cutters for the children to use by themselves. You can do this for a number of days or weeks with different implements, once the children's interest in rolling pins and cookie cutters has waned. After they have exhausted the possibilities for manipulating the medium, you can involve them in the fun of measuring and mixing the dough themselves before they play with it. Another time, you can have them add food coloring of varying colors for an entirely different effect.

Still another time, put out colored chalk, dishes of water, and brown paper grocery sacks. Children can experiment by drawing on the sacks with or without water for different effects. The chalk can be dipped in water each time the child draws. Another time, bring in chalkboards or pieces of slate for the children's drawing experiments.

No matter what art materials you use, arrange them so the children can be creative with them on their own. Collage scraps, paste, and backing paper can be waiting for children on one of their tables. What they do with these items is up to them. Another day, have food coloring, medicine droppers, and jars of water waiting.

Finger painting can be done on smooth paper, on tabletops, or on large sheets of butcher paper on the floor. The point is to set up the activity so that children can create with it on their own. Occasionally you may have to get involved to get the children started, but then you can withdraw and let them go to it by themselves.

The same principles apply to mixing paint. Let children experiment on their own with two colors at first. Yellow and blue make green; yellow and red make orange; blue and red make violet. After experimenting with one pair of colors, put out two pairs of different colors at the same time, and later three pairs.

ACCEPTS CHILDREN'S CREATIVE PRODUCTS WITHOUT PLACING A VALUE JUDGMENT ON THEM

If freedom is the most important aspect of creativity, then acceptance is the second most important. You must accept unconditionally whatever the child produces, just as you accept the child himself unconditionally. Not all children may live up to the standards you expect, but that does not mean you don't accept them and value them as human beings. As a professional in a preschool program, you are obligated to accept every child equally, whether they are clean or dirty, rich or poor, black or white, smiling or withdrawn—it matters not. They are all children. They have come to your center. They are yours to guide regardless of their qualities.

The same is true of their creative products. A smudge of brown covering an easel paper may mean a breakthrough to a child struggling to conquer the medium of drippy paint and awkward brushes. You must accept it for what it is: not a painting but a process, the results of a difficult struggle with the medium. In addition, you must accept it honestly. What should you say? Not: "That's a beautiful painting, Charles," because it may not look so to you. How about: "You surely used a lot of paint in your work today, Charles!" That is an honest appraisal of what happened, and the child can accept that.

On the other hand, a child may have done a representational drawing and want your reaction to it. If you are not sure what to say because you don't know what the drawing represents, you can respond by commenting on the artistic elements of the drawing. Its color, its patterns, its shape, the lines used, the texture of the painting, and the placement of the painting on the paper are all good possibilities. To ask a child, "What is it?" may be a real put-down when the child knows it is a fire engine. Instead, you might say, "I like the way you used the red color. What do you think?" or "I really can see that picture. The colors are bright and beautiful."

Some teachers ask children, "Do you want to tell me about your picture?" This is certainly a nonjudgmental comment, and may even elicit information about the picture that you can follow up on. However, what the child is showing you may not be a picture at all, but the results of the artistic process she was following. She will probably not be able to articulate that. Furthermore, children don't always want to talk about their paintings and drawings. Showing them to you may be only an indication that they are finished and want you to see what they did.

To other children, their art is private. They may not want to talk about it nor even show it to you. That should be their choice. You should, however, give them the opportunity to hang their work on the wall where art is displayed if they want to. If they do, let them place it where they want, as well. You may give them the choice of mounting their work first on backing paper to show it off better.

Stages of Art Development

You will become more appreciative of children's art if you understand the various developmental stages children go through in drawing when they are allowed to express themselves spontaneously. From 2 to 3 years old, children mainly scribble. This is an important stage and should not be discouraged if we want children to develop drawing skills. Scribbling is to drawing what babbling is to speaking. Children everywhere tend to make these same markings in the same way at approximately the same age (Kellogg, 1969).

Sometime between 2 and 4 years of age, the scribbles take on outline shapes such as circles, ovals, squares, triangles, and crosses. Between the ages of 3 and 5 children begin to make designs from the shapes they have been drawing. Although there are an unlimited number of possibilities, children usually draw only a few favorites over and over, such as "radials" and "suns." Between the ages of 4 and 5 their designs often take the form of a person. These so-called "tadpole people" grow out of "suns," with the rays of the sun becoming the arms, legs, and hair of the person, and the circle becoming the face and the body. All children seem to make their first people this way.

By the age of 5, many children are at a pictorial stage, creating representational drawings. Whether they continue developing talent in art during their elementary school years depends as much on the freedom and acceptance they have received during the preschool years as it does on inborn skill.

It is important for both you and the children's parents to know about the stages of art development in young children, so that when a 3-year-old shows you a page of scribbles, you will not be tempted to dismiss it as "only scribbles." Instead, you will recognize it as the child's first exciting step in the developmental process of learning to draw.

To demonstrate that you really accept children's art work, whether scribbles or pictures, you can make a collection of each child's paintings over a number of weeks or months. You can display children's paintings attractively in your room. For instance, you can put them on backing paper or in frames. You can also take instant photos of children working at easels as well as photos of their completed works. You might include these photos in a scrapbook about each child.

Attitudes Toward Children's Art

Can you also accept artwork that is radically different from the norm? Some adults are uncomfortable with children's originality. They believe children should be taught to conform—that there is only one way to play with toys or to paint pictures. They have great difficulty accepting red grass or purple sky.

This kind of attitude will quickly kill creativity in an early childhood classroom. Creativity demands a spontaneity that many adults do not exhibit because they have not allowed it to develop. Artists, on the other hand, have somehow escaped the inhibitions imposed on most of us. Preschoolers have the same great artistic potential because they have not yet experienced these inhibitions.

Give your children the opportunity to develop this most satisfying aspect of their nature while there is yet time. Do not insist that their paintings and drawings must represent something. Many will not have reached this stage in their artistic develop-ment. Instead, give them your support regardless of the outcome of their efforts.

If they are in the process of creating a finger painting, for instance, let them complete the experience. Do not stop them when the painting looks good to you. The final result may be a smudge of colors, but it is their expression, not yours. Your support, in this case, has been your restraint from stopping them when the painting suited your taste.

If you allow children the freedom to experiment and create with color, you may be amazed at the results. Their abstract art compares well with that of professionals. Researchers who have studied this phenomenon believe it reflects the natural creative urge of all human beings. Most preschool children are able to express this drive in wholly original ways—as artists do—because they do not know any different. Everything they do and experience is new and fresh to them. They have not yet learned to conform to an adult standard. Let us strive in our programs to keep creativity alive in young children as long as possible.

Some of your children may be ready to represent things in art. They, too, need the freedom to explore. Don't insist that they make the sky blue and the grass green. Let them play with painting a picture just as they do with building a block construction. One teacher tried without success to make a child paste cutout red "chimneys" on the roof of his house where the teacher thought they belonged instead of on the lawn beside the house where the child had placed them. Finally, the exasperated child looked up at the teacher and declared, "They're firecrackers!"

GIVES CHILDREN THE OPPORTUNITY
TO HAVE FUN WITH MUSIC

Children need adult role models to dramatize how we want them to behave. This is as true in the creative arts as it is in eating food at the lunch table. The cliché is true that children will do as we do, not as we say. If you want your children to be creative, then it is up to you to lead the way.

Your creative actions should be as natural and spontaneous as you want the children's to be. In other words, don't direct the children to watch what you're doing and copy you. What you hope children will do is not an imitation but an original action spurred by your leadership.

Are you afraid to sing in front of others? Many of us are. Could it have something to do with our own improper introduction to music? We owe it to our children to avoid the same mistake with them.

Let's find a way to sing in the classroom. You don't need to be able to carry a tune; many of the children can't either. All that really matters is that you have fun with sound. If you are having fun, the children are bound to. Start with a monotone chant. Make up your own if you don't know any.

Hap-py day,
Hap-py day,
Let's have a
Happy, happy day!

Clap while you are chanting. Some of the children may follow your lead and clap along with you. Repeat the chant a few times, and perhaps some of the children will join in. This isn't done during a formal "music period." Let's not make music formal. It can be done any time you feel like it. Maybe something makes you feel happy. Maybe everyone is busily working and it makes you feel good. You are doing your song or chant because it is the way you feel like expressing an emotion. Whether or not the children respond doesn't matter, but your acting in this spontaneous and creative way sets the stage for children to make up songs or chants when they feel good too.

What other situations during the day can you convert to songs or chants? How about pick-up time?

We're picking up the blocks,
We're picking up the blocks,
Clunk, clunk, clunk, clunk,
We're picking up the blocks.

We're picking up the trucks,
We're picking up the trucks,
Clack, clack, clack, clack,
We're picking up the trucks.

This can be chanted or sung to the tune of "The Farmer in the Dell." If the children join in, let them help you invent words for the other items to be picked up.

Singing or chanting directions can apply to any number of situations: putting on outside garments, setting the table, washing hands, or getting out cots for the afternoon nap—when you can whisper the chant.

You can sing or chant a welcome to the children in the morning or when using their names throughout the day. Here are some beginning lines just to get you started:

Where is Bobby? ("Where is Thumbkin?")
Where, oh where, is nice little Lisa? ("Paw Paw Patch")
Joel, Joel, come to lunch. ("Skip to my Lou")
Here comes Joyce through the door. ("This Old Man")

You or the children may want to make up finger plays to go along with your songs. Sing a song at least once a day, and you'll soon be doing it more often. You'll know it was worth the effort when the children begin singing them back to you.

Manipulating the Music Medium

What other kinds of musical experiences do the children have in your classroom? Do they consist mainly of records, with singers who tell the children how to move their bodies? This, of course, is not creative music. It compares closely to the manipulation of art materials we discussed earlier. There is nothing wrong with recorded music per se. It just isn't creative music.

Children need to play with music as they do with blocks, trying out different combinations, breaking them up, and starting all over. And again, as with art, it is the process that is important, not the product. Songs—the end result—may be highly satisfying, but if they are not arrived at freely and in fun, they may never be sung outside the classroom.

Initially, children will do with music just what they do with art: learn to manipulate the medium. This sounds strange when we talk about music, but it is the natural way young children learn any new skill if we give them the opportunity. In other words, they need the chance to play with sounds and rhythm.

You can set up a sound-making table in a noisy area of the classroom. Sound makers can be a series of small containers, such as empty tuna cans, juice cans, margarine cups, and covers, with a collection of seeds, beans, rice, and pebbles the children can place inside the containers to shake. Have a record or cassette player on the table that the children can use by themselves, along with several records or tapes of rhythmic music. Let them try shaking the containers to music. They may want to record and play back the results.

Another time, use containers as drums. Add a collection of Tinkertoy or homemade drumsticks with tape wrapped around the ends to cut down on noise, and let the children practice drumming to music.

You can also use metal containers as drums, using large spoons as drumsticks. Let the children fill a set of jars or glasses with varying amounts of water, and tap them with a spoon. Put out a large collection of "junk" items and encourage the children to invent their own music makers. You may call this noise rather than music, but don't tell the children that, if you want them to continue creatively. This stage of music-making compares to the scribble stage in art and the babble stage in speaking. After the children have learned to manipulate the medium with ease, they may want to make their own rhythm instruments. Books such as *Your Children Need Music* (Greenberg, 1979) tell how.

Instruments

Don't make the mistake of using rhythm instruments only as a group activity. Individuals need chances to make their own music by themselves as well as with others. That is why it is important to maintain a music corner with a record or tape player. Rhythm instruments can be hung on a pegboard for use during the free choice periods. You can limit the volume on the record player by taping down the knob, if this seems a problem.

Children do not need instruments to make music. They can sing, hum, clap, and tap their feet or fingers. You may want to introduce them to clapping during circle time. Let them clap out name chants: "Here-comes-Bren-da," with a clap for each syllable. Or children may want to play follow-the-leader with clapping patterns: one child claps out a rhythm, then the other children try to imitate it. These games can be recorded and played back.

If you bring in an instrument to play, make it one that the children can also try out. Remember, it is the music maker who gets the most out of the experience. Children can strum on an autoharp if you press down the chord buttons. Have a child sit next to you and strum as you press the chord buttons and sing a song with the rest of the group. They can take turns until everyone gets a chance. Another adult instrument that children enjoy is the electric keyboard. Small keyboards bring the piano down to size for preschool children. Harmonicas are also fun for children to use on their own. Buy enough small harmonicas for a group to learn to use by blowing out and drawing in. Kazoos can be fun, too. Have children march as they play. When the children are finished, clean the instruments carefully with disinfectant wipes and put them away to prevent the spread of germs by mouth.

Once you realize that many opportunities for individual play and experimentation with instruments are essential at the preschool level, your music program will take on an entirely different character.

Other Creative Activities

Each activity area in the classroom can promote creativity in children if you set it up for children to use on their own. Sand and water tables are sources for imaginative play when interesting accessories are located within the children's reach. Manipulative materials and table toys promote creativity when children are free to choose what they want and to use them in imaginative ways. Even the book area can be creative when teachers model the creative use of stories by making up their own and encouraging children to do the same.

Creative movement activities have been discussed earlier in Chapter 4, "Advancing Physical Skills." Dramatic play and block building, two other creative areas, will be discussed in Chapter 9, "Promoting Social Skills."

SUMMARY

This chapter has focused on the goal of promoting children's creativity through playful expression and freedom of activity in the areas of art and music. By allowing children to experiment with materials and colors, and then by accepting their artistic efforts and products as the beginning stages of a developmental process, we support children's continued creative development. Although teacher-directed art has a place in the curriculum in promoting children's direction-following and manipulative skills, it should not be confused with creative art in which the child is in control of manipulating the medium her own way to discover what will happen.

Music can also promote creativity in children when teachers use it themselves in a relaxed and enjoyable manner. To encourage music production in the preschool classroom, teachers must lead the way by chanting, singing, and providing musical toys and instruments. Children need to become actively involved in creating their own music, and not merely passive listeners to records and tapes. Clapping, tapping, and other rhythm activities can help lead children into song. Rhythm instruments can be made by the children and kept out for their use. Child-size adult instruments such as the harmonica speak to this instinctive need within most children to express themselves in music.

LEARNING ACTIVITIES

1. Read Chapter 7, "Advancing Creative Skills" and answer Question Sheet 7–A.
2. View Videopak A, "Setting Up the Classroom" and answer Question Sheet 7–B.
3. Read one or more of the Suggested Readings, and add 10 cards to your file with specific ideas for helping children develop creative skills. Include the reference source on each card.
4. Set up an art area the children can use independently different from the way it is now. Observe and record what happens on three days. Discuss results with trainer.
5. Allow children to paint (finger, easel, or table painting) on their own and observe the process. Discuss the results with the children in ways that show acceptance. Discuss this activity with trainer.
6. Make a collection of children's paintings or drawings that illustrate the stages of art children go through. Discuss with trainer how your collection illustrates the stages.
7. Do a singing/chanting activity with children using ideas from this chapter. (Trainer can observe.)

8. Set up a sound or rhythm instrument activity for individuals or small groups to use. (Trainer can observe.)

9. Complete the Chapter 7 Evaluation Sheet and return it to your trainer or college supervisor.

QUESTION SHEET 7–A

(Based on Chapter 7, "Advancing Creative Skills")

1. What is a creative person like?
2. What seems to kill creativity in children?
3. What can preschool teachers do to keep creativity alive in children? Why should they?
4. What is meant by the expression, "confusing the product with the process?" How can this affect children's art?
5. Why should children be allowed to "play" with art materials?
6. Why is it important to accept children's creative products even if they do not seem well done or attractive?
7. Why is it important to understand the developmental stages children go through in learning to draw?
8. How can you get the children in your classroom to sing?
9. What other ways can children become involved with making music?
10. How can adult instruments be used in preschool music?

QUESTION SHEET 7–B

(Based on Videopak A, " Setting Up the Classroom")

1. How can a child feel good about his creativity in the preschool classroom?
2. How does the arrangement of the block area allow children to be creative in it?
3. How can children be creative in the dramatic play area?
4. What kinds of art equipment might you have available for children's use every day?
5. Why should art materials be kept on low shelves near the art tables?
6. Why should you hang children's art products on the wall at a child's eye level?
7. Can children be creative with manipulative materials? How does room arrangement encourage this?
8. What is one creative table game you could make for your children?
9. How can water play be arranged for children to use it creatively?
10. Why should children learn to use record or tape players by themselves?

SUGGESTED READINGS

Attuck, S. M. (1982). *Art activities for the handicapped.* Englewood Cliffs, NJ: Prentice-Hall.

Bayless, K. M., & Ramsey, M. E. (1991). *Music: A way of life for the young child* (4th ed.). Columbus, OH: Merrill.

Beaty, J. J. (1990). *Observing development of the young child* (2nd ed.). Columbus OH: Merrill.

Beaty, J. J., & Tucker, W. H. (1987). *The computer as a paintbrush: Creative uses for the personal-computer in the preschool classroom.* Columbus, OH: Merrill.

Brashears, D. (1985). *Dribble drabble: Art experiences for young children.* Mt. Rainier, MD: Gryphon House.

Bos, B. (1978). *Don't move the muffin tins: A hands-off guide to art for the young child.* Roseville, CA: Turn the Page Press.

Burton, L., & Kuroda, K. (1981). *Artsplay: Creative activities in art, music, dance, and drama for young children.* Menlo Park, CA: Addison-Wesley Publishing Company.

Christoplos, F., & Valletutti, P. J. (1990). *Developing children's creative thinking through the arts.* Bloomington, IN: Phi Delta Kappa.

Greenberg, M. (1979). *Your children need music.* Englewood Cliffs, NJ: Prentice-Hall.

Hitz, R. (1987). Creative problem-solving through music activities. *Young Children, 42*(2), 12–17.

Jalongo, M. R., & Collins, M. (1985). Singing with young children! Folk singing for non-musicians. *Young Children, 40*(2), 17–22.

Jenkins, P. D. (1980). *Art for the fun of it.* Englewood Cliffs, NJ: Prentice-Hall.

Kellogg, R. (1969). *Analyzing children's art.* Palo Alto, CA: National Press.

Moomaw, S. (1984). *Discovering music in early childhood.* Boston: Allyn and Bacon.

Schirrmacher, R. (1986). Talking with young children about their art. *Young Children, 41*(5), 3–7.

Uhlin, D. (1984): *Art for the exceptional child.* Dubuque, IA: William C. Brown.

Warner, S. (1989). *Encouraging the artist in your child (even if you can't draw).* New York: St. Martin's Press.

CHILDREN'S BOOKS

Carle, E. (1984). *The mixed-up chameleon.* New York: Harper and Row.

Hutchins, H. (1987). *Ben's snow song.* Toronto, Canada: Annick Press.

Jonas, A. (1989). *Color dance.* New York: Greenwillow Books.

Jones, C. (1990). *This old man.* Boston: Houghton Mifflin.

Kherdian, D., & Hogrogian, N. (1990). *The cat's midsummer jamboree.* New York: Philomel Books.

Komaiko, L. (1987). *I like the music.* New York: Harper and Row.

Lionni, L. (1982). *Let's make rabbits.* New York: Pantheon Books.

Martin, B. (1983). *Brown Bear, Brown Bear, what do you see?* New York: Holt, Rinehart, & Winston.

Rounds, G. (1989). *Old MacDonald had a farm.* New York: Holiday House.

Williams, V. B. (1984). *Music, music for everyone.* New York: Mulberry Books.

VIDEOTAPES

Beaty, J. J. (Producer). (1979). Setting Up the Classroom (Videopak A), *Skills for preschool teachers* [videotape]. Elmira, NY: McGraw Bookstore, Elmira College.

National Association for the Education of Young Children (Producer). (1990). *Music across the curriculum* [videotape]. Washington, DC: NAEYC.

South Carolina Educational TV (Producer). *Art and young children,* and *Music movement with young children* [videotape]. Columbia, SC: SCETV

CHAPTER 7 EVALUATION SHEET
ADVANCING CREATIVE SKILLS

1. Student _____

2. Trainer _____

3. Center where training occurred _____

4. Beginning date _____ Ending date _____

5. Describe what student did to accomplish General Objective

   _____

   _____

6. Describe what student did to accomplish Specific Objectives

   Objective 1 _____

   _____

   Objective 2 _____

   _____

   Objective 3 _____

   _____

7. Evaluation of student's Learning Activities
   (Trainer Check One)   (Student Check One)

   _____ Highly superior performance   _____

   _____ Superior performance   _____

   _____ Good performance   _____

   _____ Less than adequate performance   _____

Signature of Trainer: Signature of Student:

_____   _____

Comments:

8 Building a Positive Self-Concept

General Objective

To help children improve their self-concept through your attitude and behavior toward them.

Specific Objectives

- ☐ Accepts every child as a worthy human being and lets him or her know with non-verbal cues.
- ☐ Helps children accept and appreciate themselves and each other.
- ☐ Provides many activities and opportunities for individual children to experience success.

T he formation of a self-concept begins at birth and is still very much in the development stage during a child's preschool years. How a child eventually comes to feel about himself is the result of an accumulation of contacts and experiences with other people and with the environment. If most of these contacts have been positive, the child should feel good about himself. If an infant has been loved and cared for, picked up and cuddled, fed and changed properly, provided with a stimulating environment, then he begins to develop a perception of himself as a likable human being. If he is not neglected or left alone too much, not scolded too harshly or restricted too severely, not nagged at constantly, in turn, he will tend to like the other human beings around him and behave as they want him to.

If, on the other hand, the child has accumulated an unending series of negative responses from other people and the environment, he will come to believe there is something wrong with him. Infants and young children are highly egocentric; they view everything as if they are the source of all that is happening around them. If everything they do receives a negative response, they quite naturally assume it is their fault and that they are somehow not good. This egocentricity sometimes carries children's guilt to extremes of which parents are totally unaware. In cases of parental separation or divorce, the child frequently feels that he is to blame.

It is up to you and your classroom staff to help your children experience as many positive interactions with people and things as possible. You need to be aware, however, that it is from an accumulation of responses, and not just from one or two instances, that the self-image grows. You will therefore want to be consistent in your behavior toward a child so that he receives a clear, ungarbled message of your positive feelings toward him.

ACCEPTS EVERY CHILD AS A WORTHY HUMAN BEING AND LETS HIM OR HER KNOW WITH NON-VERBAL CUES

Your first step in helping a child accept and feel good about herself is to accept the child yourself, totally and unconditionally. This sounds so obvious that you may wonder about its inclusion. Of course you accept the unhappy child—just as you accept all of the children in your classroom. But do you accept her totally and unconditionally? If you are human like the rest of us, you may have children you favor above others, and children you do not like as well. What about the loud and aggressive child? What about a child who is never clean? What about the overweight child? The one who whines? The one who tattles? You need to sort out any negative feelings about such children and make a change in them before you can hope to bring about changes in the children's feelings about themselves.

A simple way to start is to make a list of all the children in your class. After each name, write down frankly and honestly what you like about each child and why, as well as what bothers you about each and why. Then write down your reaction to the child in the classroom. For example:

Marie

Like: her quiet way of playing
Why: I like quiet children.
Dislike: her uncleanliness
Why: I dislike dirtiness.
My reaction in class: I leave her alone.

Joshua

Like: when he gives me a hug
Why: I like children to be affectionate.
Dislike: His temper tantrums
Why: I don't like the way he disrupts the whole class when he doesn't get his way.
My reaction in class: I often pat his head; hold him in my lap.

When you have finished, go back through the list and ask yourself for each child: Do I really accept this child totally and unconditionally? Do my day-to-day reactions convey to the child that I accept him as he is?

This does not mean that you must accept disruptive and destructive behavior from the child. Instead, you should accept the child as an individual to be valued no matter how she looks or how she behaves. It means you will help each child overcome negative behavior through your respect for children as individuals. If you find from your list that you do not do this with certain children, then you need to begin changing your attitude.

You can start by listing as many positive things as you can about each child whom you have not accepted totally. Keep a pencil and pad handy during the day and make a special effort to observe and record only positive things about the child. These notes, like your original set, are for your eyes only. They should be kept in a private place, to be disposed of when you finish with them.

Non-verbal Cues

You demonstrate your acceptance of children through non-verbal cues. Children understand how you feel about them by the way you act toward them rather than by what you say. Your tone of voice, for instance, conveys as much or more meaning than your words. How do you sound to the child you seem to have trouble accepting totally? Switch on your cassette tape recorder when you are in an activity area with the child. After class, play back the tape and listen to yourself. Ignore everything on the tape but the tone of your voice. Play it low enough so you cannot even make out the words. Are you satisfied with what you hear? If not, you may want to make a note to yourself about changing the tone of your voice, perhaps making it softer, or keeping the scolding tone out of it. You should remember, of course, that the accumulation of such contacts with a child helps form the self-image, not just this one incident.

What about your face? How does it look to a child? Do you scowl or frown very much? Do you smile a lot? Try smiling at the unhappy child. Children reflect the people around them. If nobody ever smiles at them, why should they feel like smiling themselves? Be persistent in your smiling. Eventually you will get a smile in return.

Nearness and touch are important cues of acceptance to preschool children. Affection is usually expressed through a hug, a hand on the shoulder, an arm around the waist, or sitting or standing close to someone. Most children crave this affection. Those who seem not to, who instead withdraw from touch or contact, may indeed have self-concept problems, or may merely be shy. Your non-verbal cues of acceptance with these children may have to be smiles and a friendly voice until they feel better about themselves and become more at ease in the classroom. Do not allow the current exaggerated concern about "good touches and bad touches" to alter your display of affection toward your children. Your "good touches" are necessary for the growth of a positive self-concept in your children.

It is important for all the adults in the preschool classroom to behave consistently toward all the children. If you are the head teacher or team leader, it is your responsibility to make sure this happens. If you notice that a classroom worker seems to favor one child or ignore another, you may want to have a team meeting at which all of you do the exercise of listing each child's name, along with your likes, dislikes, and reactions. The harm created by an adult showing favoritism toward a child in a preschool classroom lies in the non-verbal cues this action conveys to each of the other children. It says very clearly: this favored child is somehow more likable than I am; or, I am not as good as this other child.

Your acceptance of and your positive reactions toward all of the children in your class are thus extremely important aids to the growth of a healthy self-concept for each child. Just as you make periodic assessments of children's feelings about themselves, you must constantly check on your own feelings about the children as well.

HELPS CHILDREN ACCEPT AND APPRECIATE THEMSELVES AND EACH OTHER

How do children feel about themselves in your classroom? A child's self-concept is an elusive thing to pin down. One way to begin assessing self-concept is through observing the child and recording his behavior according to a checklist. The Self-Concept Checklist in Table 8.1 can help you and your colleagues determine a child's perception of himself. To be checked, these behaviors should occur consistently, or they may not represent an accurate picture of the child.

It is important at the outset that you try to determine how children feel about themselves. Since they have difficulty expressing this verbally, you must determine it through observing and recording a child's particular responses or behaviors as he or she interacts with other children and activities. Add this information to each child's records and use it as you make individual plans for him or her.

For children who have few checkmarks, you and your co-workers will need to provide special opportunities for strengthening their self-concepts. Perhaps the most critical indicator of a child's self-image is the entry, "Smiles, seems happy much of the time." The child who does not smile or act happy demonstrates obvious evidence of troubled feelings within. What can you do to help?

Mirrors, Photos, Tapes

Besides accepting the child yourself, the most important role you can play is to help children accept themselves and each other. Children need to know what they look like to accept themselves. A full-length mirror is a necessity in the classroom. Children will

TABLE 8.1 Self-Concept Checklist

_____	Looks at you without covering face when you speak to child
_____	Can identify himself/herself by first and last name
_____	Seeks other children to play with or will join when asked
_____	Seldom shows fear of new or different things
_____	Is seldom destructive of materials or disruptive of activities
_____	Smiles, seems happy much of the time
_____	Shows pride in his/her accomplishments
_____	Stands up for his/her rights
_____	Moves confidently, with good motor control

Permission is granted by the publisher to reproduce this checklist for record keeping.

use it not only in the dress-up corner, but at odd moments during the day. They are curious about themselves. Is this what they really look like? You will find they use mirrors quite differently from adults who, after all, already know what they look like.

Young children are trying to sort themselves out and find out who they are. Hand mirrors serve the same purpose, giving a close-up view of the face for a child sitting at a table. Keep more than one in the classroom.

An instant-print camera is another good way to promote self-concept. Take many photos of each child during the program year. Instant prints are more meaningful to a child when she has just participated in an activity. Now she can see how she looks as the builder of a block house or dressed as a fire fighter.

Take photos of children and their parents when you make home visits, to demonstrate your acceptance of the parents as well as the child. Display the photos at the center or in personal scrapbooks the children may want to make.

Photograph each child doing an art project, feeding a classroom pet, on a field trip, making a puzzle, going down a slide, or talking with a friend. Have pictures of individuals laminated for the children to use on an attendance chart or job chart, with hooks for the photos of the children in attendance or those appointed to a certain job for the day. Enlarge another photo of each child, glue it to wood or cardboard, and cut it into puzzle pieces to be kept in separate containers in the manipulative area.

A tape recorder may serve the same purpose. Spend time with individuals or small groups, recording each of their voices, playing it back, and discussing it. Children may want to tell something about themselves, their pets, their families, or their homes. They may want to tell a story, sing a song, or pretend to be someone else. When they learn to use the tape recorder on their own, they can tape each other's voices.

Self-Concept Name Games

Children enjoy the same feeling seeing their names as they do seeing their image in a mirror or in a photo. Some children may already know how to print their names. Many will know at least the first letter of their name. Use children's printed names in every way you can think of, not only to help them learn to recognize their names, but also to make them feel good about themselves. "J-O-S-H-U-A—those are my letters. That's me!"

Play Find Your Name Card with a small group of children and their name cards in a pile on a table. Play Match Your Name Card with duplicate name cards and the cards on the attendance chart. Read books that feature names, such as *Andy (That's My Name)* (DePaola, 1973), about a boy with the letters of his name on blocks which the big kids take. Bring in sets of alphabet blocks with duplicate blocks of each letter, and let individuals try to make their own name out of blocks.

If you have a classroom computer, be sure to have at least one name program. *Early Games* (Springboard, 1984) contains a game called Names, in which a child types in his name one letter at a time, presses RETURN, and then watches the monitor as his name flashes on the screen in exciting patterns and colors accompanied by sound effects.

Children's Books

Children can learn to accept themselves and others through stories about children who have the same concerns as they do. *Will I Have a Friend?* (Cohen, 1971) shows Jim's familiar worry about finding a friend on the first day of nursery school. *The Shy Little Girl* (Krasilovsky, 1970) is older, but she has the same friendship problem. *The Very Little Boy* (Krasilovsky, 1962) is not big enough to do anything interesting until he suddenly begins to grow. *Much Bigger Than Martin* (Kellogg, 1976) is a humorous treatment of sibling rivalry on the part of the little brother who finally finds a way to become much bigger than Martin. But Jason, the perfect little bear in *I'm Terrific* (Sharmat, 1977), has to become "the new me" in order to keep his friends. In *I Like Me!* (Carlson, 1988), a little girl pig likes herself in everything she does, even when she makes mistakes.

Accepting Diversity in Children

The children in your classroom may well reflect the multi-ethnic, multi-cultural, rich, poor, gifted, and handicapped tossed salad of humans that makes America an exciting place to live these days. If you as an early childhood professional cherish each youngster as a worthy and special person, your children will follow your lead in accepting each of their classmates themselves. To assist you in this acceptance, keep in mind the following guidelines:

1. Stress similarities, but honor differences.
2. Build on the child's strengths.
3. Have high expectations for everyone.

First of all, as previously mentioned, you yourself must accept the child as he or she is: his looks, his language, his culture, her clothing, her handicap, her voice. You show your acceptance by your tone of voice, your smile, your words, your actions. Greet each child cheerfully every day. Help each youngster to feel at home in your classroom.

Although you may note that certain children have a different skin color, hair style, language, or handicapping condition, each is a child like the others with similar needs for your attention, affection, and support. There is no need for you to treat any child as different, or to vary your behavior from one another.

You are the behavior model the children watch for cues as to how they should behave toward a child they perceive as "different." If the children see that you behave toward that child just as you do toward them, they will feel safe in doing the same. For instance, if the children discover that Alberto doesn't speak the same way they do, you can agree with them, pointing out matter-of-factly: "Many people in the world speak different languages. Would you like to learn some words from Alberto's language?"

In other words, you should deal with each child just as you deal with every other child. The child who is overly aggressive and the child who is overweight also need your acceptance. The child with leg braces and the child with a hearing aid are children first of all, not handicapped children. They need to feel they are not different from the others, because feeling different usually means feeling inferior, and often invites teasing and ridicule on the part of other children.

You should begin to help children who do not seem to feel good about themselves by identifying their strengths and helping them to build on those strengths. A child who speaks Spanish can help the others learn to count in Spanish. A hearing-impaired child may be able to show the others how to sign "hello." The aggressive child may be a wonderful climber who can help others master the jungle gym. The shy child may turn out to be the class computer expert who can share her skills with the rest.

Finally, you should have high expectations for everyone in the class. With your support and guidance, each of your children should be able to participate in most of the activities. A wheelchair-bound child who cannot climb the monkey bars can pull himself around them with a rope for physical exercise. A shy child can whisper through

Everyone can do something well. Help each child discover his particular skill.

a puppet if speaking aloud is too painful. A non-English-speaking child can tape-record a wordless picture book in her own language for another child to hear.

Whatever the activity, you should expect and encourage—but not force—everyone to join in. If the children are singing, a hearing-impaired child could join in by playing a rhythm instrument or beating a drum. A child who doesn't speak the language could hum the song on a kazoo. The shy or withdrawn child could have a puppet whisper the words. An excellent book that promotes such an approach is *Alike and Different: Exploring Our Humanity with Young Children* (Neugebauer, 1987). It presents an anti-bias curriculum for young children, which deals with gender and racial stereotypes, gifted and handicapped children, and diversities such as multi-cultural and interracial children.

PROVIDES MANY ACTIVITIES AND OPPORTUNITIES FOR INDIVIDUAL CHILDREN TO EXPERIENCE SUCCESS

One of the most important factors influencing the development of a healthy self-concept is success. Children of this age need to experience success to feel good about themselves. If children can successfully perform the activities and use the materials you provide, the experience can boost their self-concepts. Achieving success outside their home environment is very important for young children. They need this experience over and over again to build a good feeling about themselves, that they are able to accomplish meaningful things.

You should make sure that activities and materials are appropriate for your children's developmental levels. In other words, don't put out the most complicated puzzles, books, and art projects at the beginning of the year. Nor should you stress competition in your classroom at any time. Your children will meet that soon enough in the outside world. Their experience in your classroom should give them breathing space—time to develop positive feelings about themselves as worthy persons who can accomplish the interesting and challenging activities in your program. Winning or losing can come later, when their positive self-concept has grown stronger.

Although children should be able to choose from any of the games and materials you provide, you can steer those who have difficulties toward the simpler materials and activities. All children need to experience success. For those who seldom sit still long enough to complete an activity, you might consider sitting with them and encouraging them to complete it.

Some children are so fearful of failure that they just won't try. You may need to help them step by step to succeed. Hand the frustrated puzzle-maker a piece and let him try to find where it goes. Encourage him to try again. "You can find it, Jeremy, look again." Hand him another piece if he doesn't take one on his own. When the puzzle is completed, ask him if he wants an instant print photo of the puzzle for his personal scrapbook that each child is making. This may be the first time Jeremy has completed a puzzle. He will be proud of his accomplishment if you show him that you are, too.

Building on the Child's Strengths

Everyone can do something well. Help each child discover her particular skill, then build on it. Perhaps the child with poor motor coordination can grasp a spoon and stir well. It is up to you, then, to provide activities in which that child can experience similar success: mixing gelatin, powdered drinks, powdered paint, or dough. Add similar activities to extend the successful experience. Let that child be in charge of the melon baller when the children put together a fruit salad. Think of other implements that the child might use successfully: a paper punch to count the number of children in class each day; a pencil sharpener; or a food mill to grind up cooked apples or pumpkins. Maybe that child can be a drummer in your music-making activities.

You may want to list such skills on individual cards for each child with space for the dates when they accomplish something new. Parents need to know about your goals for their children, and you need to know about their goals as well. Discuss with them what children are able to do by themselves in your classroom, so that parents can encourage them to accomplish similar things at home.

Strengthening a Child's Independence

Children's concepts of themselves receive an exceptional amount of strengthening as they learn how to do things on their own. Some preschool teachers do not realize this, and think they are helping children by tying their shoes, zipping their jackets, serving their food, and pouring their milk. Children do not protest. After all, they have been little and helpless all those years before coming to the center.

But now is the time for children and the adults around them to change. As children grow and change, the adults around them should, too. This is one reason for your child development center: to help young children grow and develop independence.

You might first list all the tasks children in your center could accomplish successfully on their own, for example:

Take off, put on outer garments
Button, zip clothes
Hang garments in cubby
Get out paints, puzzles, etc.
Put on own paint apron
Mix paints
Make play dough
Help with clean-up, pick-up
Go to bathroom
Wash hands
Brush teeth
Set table
Fold napkins
Serve food

Pour drink
Feed animal pet
Help clean animal cage
Play musical instrument
Operate tape recorder, record player
Operate computer
Answer telephone
Hammer nails, saw wood
Cut with scissors
Cut with knife
Use vegetable scraper
Get out ingredients for cooking activity
Follow recipe chart
Print own name
Get out and put away cot
Fold blanket
Climb up and down climber
Ride tricycle

This is a partial list. Can your children do these things? More important, are they allowed to? One teacher might say, "I would never allow a 3-year-old to use a sharp knife. He might cut himself." But another teacher may reply, "All my children learn to handle dangerous implements such as knives and saws so they won't get hurt. If they should ever slip and cut themselves, that too is a learning experience, and we have bandages and sympathy always at hand."

Some classroom staffs worry about children using tape recorders and record players because they are expensive and easily broken. Others report that they try to purchase the most durable recorders, those that will best survive children's handling. They believe it is extremely important for children to be able to use these recording tools by themselves. Consequently, they are willing to spend as much time as necessary to instruct young children in the value and proper use of the equipment and monitoring the children until they are able to use it independently.

Parent's Expectations

Find out what children can do on their own at home from both the parents and the children themselves. You may be pleasantly surprised. However, if your goals and those of the parents diverge sharply, you may want to find out why. Parents need to know what children of this age should be able to accomplish so they do not limit their children. You need to know what parents expect of their children at home to help guide your own expectations in the center. Both you and the parents need to realize the importance of independent accomplishments in the development of a child's positive self-concept.

Society's Expectations

Children's accomplishments are as much a function of societal expectations as anything else. Certain societies, for instance, expect preschool boys to handle a two-foot machete or bush knife safely and responsibly.

The point is that your children can and will try to accomplish whatever you and their parents decide is appropriate. Hopefully, you will set your sights high.

Children's Books About Independence

Fictional characters who solve problems by themselves help strengthen preschoolers' feelings about their own abilities. *Sara and the Door* (Jensen, 1977) tells about a little girl who shuts the door on her coat and must handle the situation on her own. In *I Can Do It By Myself* (Little & Greenfield, 1978), Donny overcomes his problems and fears to buy his mother a birthday present all by himself. *I'm in Charge!* (Drescher, 1981) relates a little boy's humorous handling of household tasks while his mother is at work and his father can't be disturbed. In *I'll Do It Myself* (Marton, 1989) Michelle all of a sudden takes charge of brushing her own hair. Although her first attempts are not all that successful, she is eventually rewarded.

Teacher's Role

You may agree with the theory of helping every child succeed at something, but still you may wonder how you can implement such a concept when you have 15 or 20 children in your classroom. No matter how many children you have, the concept is feasible, if you have set up the physical environment along the lines discussed in Chapter 3, so that children can become independent and self-directed in their activities. The physical arrangement and kinds of materials should allow children to become involved with activities on their own, without your direction.

Your role in the classroom is to set up activities that the group can enjoy, but that particular individuals will especially benefit from, and then to help involve those individuals in the appropriate activities.

Your role also includes stepping back and observing individuals and how they become involved, so that you can decide what else you need to do and how else you should try to meet their needs. You are not in this alone. Whether you are a teacher, a teacher's assistant, or a volunteer, you are a part of a team. When one of the team is leading a group project, someone else should be free to operate on a one-to-one basis with the child who needs special help in improving his self-concept.

SUMMARY

This chapter has discussed methods for improving the self-concept of your children through your attitude and behavior toward them. First of all, you must accept each of the children and show them that you do, through non-verbal and verbal cues. Smile at them. Encourage them with words. Let them know how you feel about them. Then you must find ways for them to accept themselves and one another. They begin to accept themselves in the classroom environment when they find that they can succeed in the activities and tasks they encounter. They begin to accept one another when they see your modeling behavior of acceptance toward all of the other children. Then, when they find that you give them opportunities to become independent in classroom activities, they develop pride in their accomplishments and a real boost in their positive feelings about themselves.

LEARNING ACTIVITIES

1. Read Chapter 8, "Building a Positive Self-Concept" and answer Question Sheet 8–A.
2. View Videopak C, "Self-Image and Self-Control" and answer Question Sheet 8–B.
3. Read one or more of the Suggested Readings. Add 10 cards to your file with specific ideas for helping children develop a positive self-concept. Include the reference source on each card.
4. Assess the self-concept of every child in your classroom using the Self-Concept Checklist.
5. Make a list of all the children in your class, and after each name write down frankly and honestly what you like about the child and why, what you dislike about the child and why, and your reaction to the child in class.
6. Choose a child you have perhaps not accepted unconditionally, and try to change your attitude by listing for three days all the positive things you see that child do. Show your approval with non-verbal cues, and record the results.
7. Plan and carry out several activities with a child who seems to have a low self-concept based on ideas in this chapter. (Trainer can observe.)
8. Work with children with diversities in looks, behavior, abilities, language, or background, and help them to accept one another through your modeling behavior and an activity you set up. (Trainer can observe.)
9. Complete the Chapter 8 Evaluation Sheet and return it to your trainer or college supervisor.

QUESTION SHEET 8–A

(Based on Chapter 8, "Building a Positive Self-Concept")

1. How is a child's self-concept formed?
2. What is the first step you should take to help a child accept himself?
3. Why are nonverbal cues important to a young child?
4. What nonverbal cues can you give a child to show you like him?
5. What art activities can help improve a child's self-concept? How?
6. Why is it important for children to experience success? How can they do so in your classroom?

7. Why should you not stress competition in your classroom?

8. How does developing independence help improve a child's self-concept?

9. What do expectations—yours, a parent's and society's—have to do with a child's self-concept?

10. What is your role in helping children with low self-esteem?

QUESTION SHEET 8–B

(Based on Videopak C, "Self-Image and Self-Control")

1. What things make a child feel good about himself?

2. How does setting the table help strengthen a child's self-concept?

3. What kinds of things help a child develop a negative self-image?

4. How many positive incidents does it take to establish a good self-concept?

5. How does classroom arrangement affect self-image?

6. Why is it important for the child to have a private cubby?

7. What are some classroom activities that help a child develop a positive self-image?

8. How can children's own ideas be used in the classroom to strengthen their self-concepts?

9. How can the use of a camera help strengthen the self-image?

10. How does the way the teacher handles children's negative behavior affect their self-concept?

SUGGESTED READINGS

Balaban, N. (1985). *Starting school: From separation to independence, a guide for early childhood teachers.* New York: Teachers College Press.

Beaty, J. J. (1990). *Observing development of the young child* (2nd ed.). Columbus, OH: Merrill.

Berne, P. (1988). Nurturing Success. *Pre-K Today,* 33–37.

Bos, B. (1982). *Before the basics.* Roseville, CA: Turn the Page Press.

Briggs, D. C. (1970). *Your child's self-esteem.* Garden City, NY: Doubleday.

Clemens, S. G. (1983). *The sun's not broken, a cloud's just in the way: On child-centered teaching.* Mt. Rainier, MD: Gryphon House.

Hitz, R., & Driscoll, A. (1988). Praise or encouragement? New insights into praise: Implications for early childhood teachers. *Young Children, 43*(5), 6–13.

Hopkins, S., & Winters, J. (Eds.). (1990). *Discover the world. Empowering children to value themselves, others, and the earth.* Philadelphia: New Society Publishers.

Kostelnik, M. J., Stein, L. C., & Whiren, A. P. (1988). Children's self-esteem: The verbal environment. *Childhood Education, 65*(1), 29–32.

Neugebauer, B. (Ed.). (1987). *Alike and different: Exploring our humanity with young children*. Redmond, WA: Exchange Press.

Purkey, W. W., & Novak, J. M. (1984). *Inviting school success: A self-concept approach to teaching and learning*. Belmont, CA: Wadsworth.

Samuels, S. C. (1977). *Enhancing self-concept in early childhood*. New York: Human Sciences Press.

Thompson, J. J. (1973). *Beyond words: Nonverbal communication in the classroom*. New York: Citation Press.

Yawkey, T. D. (Ed.). (1980). *The self-concept of the young child*. Provo, UT: Brigham Young University Press.

CHILDREN'S BOOKS

Cohen, M. (1971). *Will I have a friend?* New York: Collier.

Carlson, N. (1988). *I like me!* New York: Viking Penguin.

DePaola, T. (1973). *Andy (that's my name)*. Englewood Cliffs, NJ: Prentice-Hall.

Drescher, J. (1981). *I'm in charge!* Boston: Little, Brown.

Hutchins, P. (1978). *Happy birthday, Sam*. New York: Viking Penguin.

Hutchins, P. (1971). *Titch*. New York: Viking Penguin.

Jensen, V. A. (1977). *Sara and the door*. Reading, MA: Addison-Wesley.

Kellogg, S. (1976). *Much bigger than Martin*. New York: Dial Press.

Krasilovsky, P. (1970). *The shy little girl*. Boston: Houghton Mifflin.

Krasilovsky, P. (1962). *The very little boy*. Garden City, NY: Doubleday.

Little, L. J., & Greenfield, E. (1978). *I can do it by myself*. New York: Thomas Y. Crowell.

Maris, R. (1983). *My book*. New York: Viking Penguin.

Marton, J. (1989). *I'll do it myself*. Toronto, Canada: Annick Press.

Ross, D. (1980). *A book of hugs*. New York: Thomas Y. Crowell.

Sharmat, M. W. (1977). *I'm terrific*. New York: Scholastic.

COMPUTER SOFTWARE

Early games. (1984). Minneapolis, MN: Springboard.

VIDEOTAPES

Beaty, J. J. (Producer). (1979). Self-image and self-control (Videopak C), *Skills for preschool teachers* [videotape]. Elmira, NY: McGraw Bookstore, Elmira College.

CHAPTER 8 EVALUATION SHEET
BUILDING A POSITIVE SELF-CONCEPT

1. Student _____

2. Trainer _____

3. Center where training occurred _____

4. Beginning date _____ Ending date _____

5. Describe what student did to accomplish General Objective

   _____

   _____

6. Describe what student did to accomplish Specific Objectives

   Objective 1 _____

   _____

   Objective 2 _____

   _____

   Objective 3 _____

   _____

7. Evaluation of student's Learning Activities
   (Trainer Check One)   (Student Check One)

   _____ Highly superior performance   _____

   _____ Superior performance   _____

   _____ Good performance   _____

   _____ Less than adequate performance   _____

Signature of Trainer: Signature of Student:

_____   _____

Comments:

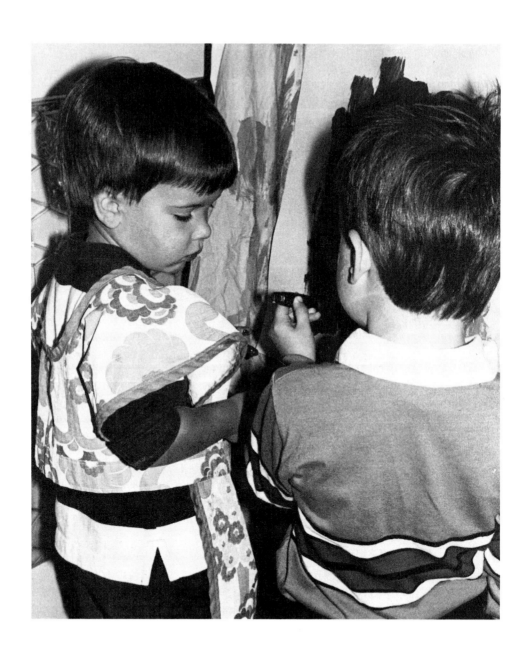

9 Promoting Social Skills

General Objective

To promote children's social development by helping them learn to get along with others.

Specific Objectives

☐ Provides opportunities for children to work and play cooperatively.
☐ Helps, but does not pressure, the shy child to interact with others.
☐ Provides experiences that help children respect the rights and understand the feelings of others.

Many of us understand that young children are highly self-centered beings, and that this is a necessary step in the human growth pattern for the individual to survive infancy. We are also aware that as children grow older, they need to develop into social beings as well to get along in society.

Children in your center must learn to work and play cooperatively, not only because you expect it of them, but because they are in a group situation that demands it. They need to be able to get along with the other children in their peer group. It may not be easy for some.

PROVIDES OPPORTUNITIES FOR CHILDREN TO WORK AND PLAY COOPERATIVELY

Three-year-olds, for instance, may be more attuned to adults than to other children. After all, they are not far removed from the toddler stage, when they were almost completely dependent upon an adult caregiver. Suddenly they are thrust into a group situation, where adults do not have time for them exclusively, nor do adults expect them to act as dependent, self-centered beings. Young children do not expect this to happen when they first come into a group situation. It is quite an adjustment for some children.

It is up to you and the other staff members to recognize this problem and help ease children into becoming social beings who can work and play happily with other children. This is no chore for some children; they have learned these skills elsewhere. For others, you must work carefully to set up opportunities to help them become part of the group.

To recognize quickly which children already display social skills and which ones may need help in developing these skills, you may want to observe each of your children using the *Social Skills Checklist* in Table 9.1. Be as unobtrusive as possible as you observe each child during pretend group play. This information will give you insight into the development of individual children so far as social play is concerned. You will learn which children are able to gain access to group play, take on pretend roles, adjust their actions to the group, take turns, and resolve conflicts on their own.

Children learn these skills by their involvement in spontaneous play with other children, not by being taught by a teacher. The teacher's role is to set up situations where children can pretend and then observe each child using a checklist to determine where the child stands in social skills development. The teacher can then encourage—but not pressure—children who need special help to become involved with others. For children who need special help learning to take turns or avoid conflicts, for instance, the teacher can set up situations outside of group play where children can practice the skills they will be learning spontaneously during play.

For example, bring in a pair of hand puppets, one for you and one for a child who frequently gets involved in sharing conflicts with another child. Ask the child if she would like to play puppets with you. Introduce the puppets. You might name her puppet "Sadie-Share-the-Toy," and yours can be "Donna-Don't-Give-Up." Have your puppet get involved with hers over a sharing conflict. You could have your puppet say:

"Look what I've got. I found this neat Ninja Turtle over on the toy shelf." (Refer to a real toy like this to get the child's attention.)

Her puppet might respond: "Can I see it? I want to play with it, too."

Yours can reply: "No, it's mine. I found it first. You can't have it."

At this point, you can intervene to speak as yourself. Ask the child what Sadie-Share-the-Toy could say to persuade Donna-Don't-Give-Up to share the Ninja Turtle. Also, discuss strategies that probably won't work. Then continue the role-playing until Sadie finally gets the toy. The result of getting the real toy to play with when she exhibits the proper behavior will reinforce the behavior and help the child understand what works and what doesn't work in sharing.

TABLE 9.1 Social Skills Checklist (Pretend Play Groups)

_____	Plays in solitary manner away from group
_____	Plays parallel to other children but alone
_____	Seeks other children to play with or joins group
_____	Pretends or takes role that satisfies own needs
_____	Adjusts actions to satisfy group needs
_____	Takes turns with roles or toys
_____	Carries on appropriate dialog with other players
_____	Solves interpersonal conflicts without teacher's help

This example illustrates the way young children learn sharing through play. When children are involved in conflicts, direct commands or speeches about sharing by adults are not nearly so effective.

Dramatic Play

One of the most effective opportunities for children to learn and practice social skills is during the spontaneous pretend play that takes place in the dramatic play area. Most classrooms have an activity area where children are encouraged to pretend and take on roles. Sometimes this area is called the "housekeeping" or "doll" or "family" corner, and contains equipment such as a play stove, refrigerator, sink, table, and dress-up clothes. These props encourage children to take on the family roles they see at home: mother, father, baby, sister, brother.

What is the point, you may ask? Why should we encourage children to fantasize? Isn't it bad for them? Not at all, according to child development specialists. Young children spend a great deal of time pretending, whether or not we encourage it. It seems to be their way of making sense of the people and the world around them.

In a preschool classroom, this kind of activity gives children an opportunity to be part of a group. If they are shy about interacting, they can become acquainted with others through the roles they take on. They can "hide" behind their roles, so to speak, in the way a shy child hides behind a puppet. Dramatic play is a unique opportunity you can provide for learning social skills. To get along with the other players, children must learn to share, take turns, adjust their actions to the group, and resolve conflicts without an adult's help.

We know about the importance of peer pressure among older children. Child development research has only recently come to recognize how important peers are to younger children as well. They exchange information about the world around them; they offer suggestions to one another on appropriate ways to behave; and some even try to impose their will on others in the group. Children learn what is expected of them, whether or not they decide to conform to this pressure.

In addition, children observe how others are treated by their peers, what works and what doesn't work in interpersonal conflicts, and how far their peers can go to try to get their own way. Aggressive children learn that the others will not accept their overbearing ways. The others may demonstrate their feelings by stopping the play altogether when things get out of hand, or by refusing to let their aggressive peers join in play the next time. Not only does the aggressive child learn a lesson when such negative peer responses happen again and again, but the other child players also learn that they might experience similar reactions from the group if they behave in an aggressive manner.

Besides teaching children social skills, dramatic play also gives them the opportunity to try out the real-life roles they see enacted around them. It helps them understand what it is like to be a mother or a brother. They begin to see things from another perspective, often trying on for size the roles they will eventually play as adults. While they play these roles in the classroom, they are becoming socialized in a much more effective way than any adult could teach them. They learn to follow peer directions, take leader or follower roles, compromise their own desires, and resolve inter-peer conflict—all through spontaneous play.

Another benefit of dramatic play is to help children master uncomfortable feelings. Adults are sometimes unaware of the frustrations children feel at being small and helpless in a grown-up world. Pretending to be an adult helps children gain some control over their world and work out fears and frustrations. They can pretend about going to the doctor and getting a shot, going to a strange school next year, or staying overnight with a babysitter and thus lessen the trauma of the real event.

Furthermore, dramatic play helps children clarify new ideas and concepts about society and the world around them. As they gain information about unfamiliar people and situations, children are able to make it understandable by incorporating it into their imaginative play. After a plumber comes to his house, a child might play out the situation in the housekeeping corner and begin to understand it better. Dramatic play, in other words, gives concrete meaning to abstract ideas.

Finally, dramatic play helps young children develop creative skills by forcing them to use their imaginations. They make up the roles, situations, rules, and solutions. The drama can be as elaborate or simple as the players make it. And strangely enough, it is through imaginative play that children come to understand the difference between fantasy and reality. The real world becomes more real to children who have opportunities to pretend.

Dramatic Play Areas

You will want to have a permanent area in your classroom for this kind of dress-up play. It can be a household area such as a kitchen or bedroom, because those are the areas most familiar to children, thus encouraging them to play familiar family roles. Other dramatic play areas may also be appropriate from time to time. For example, you may want to set up a grocery store, shoe store, or post office after the children have visited one of these sites on a field trip. Children can bring empty cartons, cans, and boxes to fill the shelves of a store.

Dramatic play can take place with smaller toys in other areas of the classroom, serving the same socialization purpose. You can encourage dramatic play in the block corner by mounting pictures at child's eye level of activities involving the field trip sites the children have visited: a store, farm, zoo, pet store, or post office. Then you must provide appropriate toys and props to accompany the play: figures of people and animals, little cars and trucks, string, tubing, or small boxes. Let the children use these props on their own in any way they want. To be effective, pretend play must be spontaneous.

Do the same near the sand or water table and in the manipulative area. A supply of miniature people, animals, cars, trucks, boats, and doll furniture is essential if you are committed to promoting imaginative play. Many early childhood educators favor unpainted wooden miniatures because these props put greater demands on the children's imaginations than do realistic figures. Children, on the other hand, often prefer the more realistic figures.

It is not necessary to spend a great deal of money equipping your classroom. Large and small cardboard milk cartons can be cut down and covered with vinyl adhesive paper as buildings in dramatic play. Cutouts of figures and vehicles from magazines can be pasted to cardboard backings. Parents can donate old hats, shoes, purses, necklaces, and wallets for dress-up accessories.

The book *Be What You Want to Be* (Fiarotta, 1977) is full of illustrated suggestions for using cartons, containers, tubes, cups, yarn, cord, bottle caps, and wallpaper paste to make props for play stores, offices, florists, or pizza parlors. The book gives directions for making everything from cardboard telephones and cash registers to typewriters and top hats. Be aware, though, that these are items for teachers to make, not preschool children.

Motivation

To stimulate children in their pretend play, you may want to take them on brief field trips around the corner or down the street. The most mundane places are exciting to young children, who see the world with fresh vision because it is new to them. A barbershop, laundromat, gas station, or even a parking lot can be the focus of fascinating imaginative play for these adventurers. It is up to you to provide the props for them to carry out their drama when they return to the classroom.

Another stimulus to pretending is reading a book such as *Owliver* (Kraus, 1974) about a boy who loves to act out various roles, with the enthusiastic support of his mother, or *Jim Meets the Thing* (Cohen, 1981) in which a scary television program prompts the characters to pretend scary roles. In the simply written book *Let's Pretend* (Greydanus, 1981), the three children characters pretend to be spies, spying first on their dog and then their cat. In *The Trek* (Jonas, 1985), a girl on her way to school pretends she is on a trek through an African jungle with creatures spying on her. In *Regards to the Man in the Moon* (Keats, 1981), Louie invites the inner-city neighborhood kids to blast off with him in his old washing-machine space ship on an imaginary trip to the moon.

Another book to motivate pretending is *In the Attic* (Oram, 1984), in which a little boy climbs into an imaginary attic and finds all kinds of wonderful creatures to play with. *The Train* (McPhail, 1977) takes place at night in the bedroom of a little boy who loves trains and finds that his own model train has turned into a real train with passengers and an engineer. In *Mashed Potato Mountain* (Gugler, 1988), Jamie turns his plate of potatoes, gravy, and broccoli into a strange world of white mountains, brown rivers, and green forests.

Teacher's Role

Your initial role in dramatic play may be that of an observer. You will want to determine which children take part in dramatic play and which never do. Can they take turns? Can they resolve conflicts? Who are the leaders? The followers? What roles do they play? How long do they sustain their roles? What do they know about the situations they are dramatizing?

Suppose a child named Vicki, for instance, constantly refers to the "superman" in her apartment building whenever she plays house. Once you are aware of her confusion between the comic book hero, Superman, and the "super" or superintendent of a building, you can help her understand the difference by discussing these terms later during a group activity.

Children's fear of doctors may also surface in dramatic play. If you observe that children have mistaken ideas about what doctors do, do not interrupt the play to "set them straight." Instead, take note of their misconceptions for future clarification. You may later want to read a story about a child who visits the doctor, or a humorous animal adventure such as *Curious George Goes to the Hospital* (Rey, 1966). Or you may feel that the children have been able to work out their fears satisfactorily on their own in their dramatic play.

What happens in the dramatic play area is determined somewhat by the way you set it up, what equipment and furniture are available, and what paraphernalia you put out. If the children have expressed fear of police officers, for example, you may want to put out appropriate props—say, a police cap—especially after a classroom visit from an officer.

If you observe that a certain child is not participating in dramatic play, or is not staying with a role or interacting with others in their roles, you may want to help him get involved by playing a role yourself. "C'mon, Rob, let's visit Joyce's store. You carry the pretend money. What shall we buy?" When the child seems involved and comfortable, you can ease out of your role the same way you entered.

For new groups of children who seem to have no idea how to get started in dramatic play, you may even have to assign roles and start the play by taking a role yourself. When things are going smoothly, you can withdraw. "Let's go to the beach," you might say. "Does anybody want to go to the beach with me? Okay, let's pack our swimming suits. The bags are on the shelf. Rachel, you bring the picnic basket. Rob, you bring the beach ball. I'll bring the towels. Sharon, would you like to drive the bus to the beach?" Of course, all of this is pretending. If you happen to have bags or baskets for props, all the better. If not, the children can pretend they have them.

When dramatic play begins to get wild or seems to disintegrate, you may need to step in and change its direction. When a race with tiny cars in the block building area has disintegrated into squabbles and shouting, you might ask, "What do race car drivers do when the race is finished?" If you have the props on hand, you may be able to redirect the children into "washing and polishing their race cars." For miniature cars, children can use milk cartons open at both ends as car wash buildings to drive through. They can use old cut-off toothbrushes to clean the cars and paper tissues to polish them. You can help the children improvise.

Block Building

The dramatic play area is one place where children's imaginative play can help them develop socially, emotionally, and intellectually. The block area is another. Children carry on their role-playing in this area in a similar but scaled-down manner. Unit blocks are used realistically to construct roads, bridges, and buildings, or more abstractly as cars, planes, spaceships, or anything else a child's imagination can conceive. Children play with the constructions they create both realistically and imaginatively, depending upon their experience with life, with blocks, and with pretending.

Before children role-play in the block corner, they need to spend a great deal of time in exploratory play with the blocks. They need to handle and manipulate the blocks, carry them around, push them and roll them, fill containers with them, and dump them out.

Very young children nearly always begin their initial experiences with blocks this way. They are exploring the medium. Even older children who have had no experience with unit blocks begin this way.

No matter how old they are, children seem to go through certain consecutive stages as they learn to use blocks by themselves. First attempts at building usually take the form of lining up blocks in rows on the floor, or stacking them vertically in towers. Children eventually learn through experimentation how to "bridge," that is, connect the space between two blocks with another block. This breakthrough in construction techniques allows them to make more elaborate structures. Enclosing a space, a doll, a toy, or a car with blocks seems to be the next step in their natural block building development. After they have discovered and practiced these basic building techniques, children often go on to build complicated structures or stack up blocks in intricate patterns. The key to their development here, as in other curriculum areas, is the freedom to explore the materials on their own, unhindered and undirected by adults.

Occasionally, a child does not seem to know how to get started in block building. This might be an instance where you want to intervene. How would you go about it? Sometimes your presence in the block corner will entice a shy or insecure child into the area. You might then ask the child to get you a long block from the shelf if she doesn't seem to know what to do. Put the block down and ask her to get another block. Ask the child where to place it. Get her involved in selecting and placing other blocks one by one. Once she is involved, you can withdraw, as in dramatic play. Tell the child you'll be back in a few minutes to see how many other blocks she has placed on the structure and what it will look like. Your role should be one of support for the shy or unsure child, and that of observer for the rest.

You will soon become aware of which children build by themselves and which ones build parallel to the others but on their own. You will also learn which children are able to build cooperatively with other children, the final step in the socialization process. Keep records of the children's progress on individual file cards along with their Social Skills Checklist results.

It is important not to use pressure. It is not up to you to make Paul play with Mike. You need to provide the opportunity for both, but they must make the contact on their own. This will often happen automatically after both feel secure in the block area. That means they need to experiment with blocks on their own. They need to do a great deal of solitary and parallel building before they gain the confidence to cooperate with other children.

Frequently, the first social contacts involve conflict. "He took my block!" or "She won't let me play!" Often, as teacher or assistant, you will be drawn into the situation because the children want you to settle it. A situation of uncontrolled anger, destruction of materials, or harm to other children demands that you step in. Firmly but calmly, you must enforce previously established limits of not letting children hurt one another or harm materials.

On the other hand, you can let the children handle many of their own problems with each other once they feel they have your support. Give them masking tape to mark off boundaries for building. Help them make a sign that asks others not to knock down the building. Help them set the kitchen timer to 5 minutes per child so they can take turns with a favorite truck in the block area. Let children give out tickets to other builders who would like to join in. Ask the children what they want to do to solve the problem. You and your children can come up with dozens of effective ideas to help them resolve conflicts. You can anticipate such problems if you take a few minutes to observe the children in the block area.

You must remember, of course, that adult direction stifles the children's imagination. You may need to encourage children at the outset to help them get started, but then you should tactfully withdraw. You may need to help redirect their play when it gets out of hand, but then step aside. For dramatic play to be truly effective in developing social skills, children need to manage their social roles by themselves.

HELPS, BUT DOES NOT PRESSURE, THE SHY CHILD TO INTERACT WITH OTHERS

For children who have difficulty interacting with others, you may need to help them get started, but do so with great care and without pressure. If a child doesn't seem to participate in group enterprises, you will first want to assess the situation by observing.

Stages of Play

Does the child play happily by herself? Solitary play is often the first step in socialization with peers. As the child gains confidence, she may become more involved with group activities, even though still playing her own game alongside the others—this is called *parallel play*. Eventually she will interact with others in true cooperative play. You do not need to intervene to help the child work through these stages. They should occur naturally over a period of time if you and the child's peers accept and support her.

The Shy Child

On the other hand, the shy or unsure child may need your help to get involved. One way to help the child get started, as mentioned previously, is to take a role yourself for a brief period, then remove yourself when the child seems comfortable playing with others. You could say, "Come on, Jeanie, let's visit Rob's grocery store and buy some food for lunch. You carry the purse, and I'll bring the baby. What shall we buy?" or "Shall we visit Rosa's house today, Jeanie? You knock on the door and see if she is home." Sometimes the shy child lacks the social skills to gain entry to play groups. Your modeling of the appropriate behavior and dialog in this way can help.

Sometimes the seemingly shy child has other reasons for not interacting with others. One teacher learned that a boy who usually played by himself in a vacant corner was not shy at all. He came from a family of 10 and had no toys or space of his own at home. He simply needed to get away and be by himself. In another program, an extremely bright child was already reading at age 4 and was simply not challenged by activities the others engaged in, so he preferred to do his own thing.

Children are individuals, as well we know. If children seem happy in self-contained play, invite but don't push them into a group activity. They may in fact do better on their own. We need to respect these differences in children as we do in adults. Don't give up entirely on the so-called loners, however. Some children are simply overwhelmed by large groups. You might begin by inviting them to do something with one other friend: look at a book together, help pick up toys, set the table together, get out the cots for nap, or go to the office to get the mail. The two friends may eventually participate in group activities on their own.

Friendship

Friendship among young children is not necessarily the same as it is among older children or adults. A preschooler values friends for their abilities to meet her needs, rather than for their personalities. The young child needs a friend to help build a block

Preschoolers value friends for their abilities to meet their own needs.

building, or play fire fighter, or push a wagon around. Because young children are so self-centered, early friendships are often one-sided and fluid. A friend is valued for satisfying certain needs of the other child. Someone who shares a toy or plays with a child is considered a friend, for the moment at least.

For the child who has difficulty finding a friend in the classroom, the teacher can sometimes help the child by modeling the appropriate behavior. Put on a hand puppet and have the child put on one. Have your puppet ask the child's puppet to do something. Could they build a tower together? Perhaps this child could also show another child how to do something he is familiar with. Could they saw wood together, make a puppet talk, read a book, build a block building together?

Reading books about friendship sometimes helps children deal with their own feelings. In *Will I Have a Friend?* (Cohen, 1967), Jim worries about whether he will find a friend on the first day of nursery school. In *Best Friends* (Cohen, 1971), Jim and his friend have a falling out, but make up when an emergency situation brings them back together. In *We Are Best Friends* (Brandenberg, 1982), Robert has to deal with the loss of his best friend Peter, who moves away. In *The Hating Book* (Zolotow, 1969), two girls have a falling out over a misunderstanding.

Classroom Materials

Classroom materials can sometimes help shy children become involved with others. Materials through which they can project yet not reveal themselves totally are best. A toy telephone, for instance, allows them to talk to other children indirectly until they feel comfortable enough for a more direct encounter. A teacher can initiate such a pretend phone call. Puppets, dolls, or toy animals allow shy children the same protection. A stuffed animal can act as a security blanket as well as a way for an unsure child to approach someone else. In *Will I Have a Friend?* (Cohen, 1967), Paul makes his initial contact with Jim through a tiny truck he shows to Jim.

Making friends with the classroom guinea pig or rabbit can be the first step toward making friends with another child. The teacher can help the child become involved with a classroom animal to get this process started. Find out what the shy youngster is interested in, and use that as a prop to help her become involved with others.

PROVIDES EXPERIENCES THAT HELP CHILDREN RESPECT THE RIGHTS AND UNDERSTAND THE FEELINGS OF OTHERS

Self-centered people, whether children or adults, have great difficulty seeing things from a point of view other than their own. Because of this, egocentric young children disregard the rights of those around them. If a child wants a toy another child is playing with, he may take it forcefully. He does not do this to be mean; rather, the social skills of sharing, taking turns, and waiting turns are simply not yet part of the young child's behavior. These skills must be learned.

Modeling

Children can learn from your example as well as from the other adults in the classroom. Make it obvious that you respect their rights and will stand up for them if necessary. Make it a point to thank children who wait for a turn or share. Do this again and again, and some of the children will begin to imitate this behavior. Because children also imitate peer behavior, your modeling will spread throughout the classroom as children see others behaving this way.

Bring in a special toy or activity for sharing and taking turns. For example, to demonstrate taking turns, read a storybook such as *Everybody Takes Turn* (Corey, 1980). Then you can show a small group of children a new toy or stuffed animal that they might all want to play with. How can they decide who will get the first turn, and the next? How long should a child be allowed to play with the toy? You can talk about these problems and decide on solutions together. Perhaps the children would like a sign-up list where everyone who wants a turn can sign his own name—even in scribble writing. Or they might want to regulate turns by drawing tickets with numbers that indicate the order of each child's turn. Maybe they would like to regulate the time with a 3-minute egg hour-glass. Then it is up to the children to put these skills to use in the spontaneous group play situations that you promote during free-choice time.

Standing Up for Rights

You may need to help a shy or bilingual child stand up for her rights. First of all, children need to know you will respect each child's rights; then you can help individuals stand up for their own rights.

When conflicts arise, it is often impossible for the teacher to determine who was right and who was wrong. Try not to deal with children's conflicts on this basis. Instead, listen to each child in a noncommittal way. Let each have a say. Then ask each of them what they think should be done about the problem. For example, Michelle says Anthony took the toy cash register that she was playing with. Anthony says that he had had it first and left it only a few minutes to find some toy money. When he came back, Michelle had taken it. You can best help the children recognize each other's rights if you first listen to each child and then ask what each one thinks should be done to solve the problem. Finally, if the two still disagree, tell them you will take the cash register until they have agreed on a solution to resolve the conflict. When they have agreed, they can come tell you and get the cash register.

No matter how you handle conflict, it is important to be consistent. If you handle interpersonal problems in the same objective manner every time, the children will come to trust you and understand that you will treat each of them fairly in their dealings with one another. This gives them a good basis for handling problems on their own eventually. They can try out different strategies to see which ones work best. Sometimes the only solution is for the teacher to keep the disputed toy until another day.

Children's Books

Discussing problems of rights and feelings with individuals and small groups is another way to help children see things from a different point of view. You can sometimes motivate these discussions by reading an appropriate story. *Everybody Takes Turn* (Corey, 1980) explains the concept of taking turns in simple, understandable terms. The book *Sharing* (Gomi, 1981) shows two little girls sharing candy, an apple, colored paper, and even the love for their cat. *Frederick* (Lionni, 1967), about the little mouse who is different from others and gathers memories of sunshine and flowers instead of grain for the long winter months, might stimulate a discussion about a child who wants to be different. Other books dealing with this topic are *Oliver Button Is a Sissy* (De Paola, 1979), about a little boy who likes to dance, and *The Story of Ferdinand* (Leaf, 1977), also published in Spanish, about a bull who was too gentle to fight.

Reading *Nobody Listens to Andrew* (Guilfoile, 1957) can lead to a discussion about how someone feels when no one will listen to him. *Even That Moose Won't Listen to Me* (Alexander, 1988) treats the same theme from Rebecca's point of view. *Sam* (Scott, 1967) is still another book about the same dilemma—no one in Sam's family allows him to do anything with them until he finally cries in frustration. *Ira Sleeps Over* (Waber, 1972) might initiate a discussion about how it feels to be teased.

Marty McGee's Space Lab, No Girls Allowed (Alexander, 1981) is a wonderful story of a little girl and a baby sister who are finally allowed in their brother's off-limits space lab when it turns out that only they can make Marty's space helmet work. Children's treatment of one another is also the theme of *If He's My Brother* (De Paola, 1979), a simple cartoon-like story in which a boy asks questions about how to treat his various possessions, and finally, about how to treat his brother. Your children can have an interesting time deciding on the answers.

As children begin to internalize these ideas through their experiences in the classroom, their social behavior should also change from self-centeredness to cooperation and respect for the rights of their peers.

SUMMARY

This chapter has discussed ways to promote children's social development by helping them learn to get along with others. It is often difficult for children of this age, who are egocentric by nature, to work and play well in a group setting. Their experiences in the dramatic play area can provide opportunities for them to work out relationship problems with their peers. Through dramatic play, children learn to see things from another's point of view. They exchange information with one another, often about appropriate ways to behave. They learn to share, take turns, and wait for a turn. To facilitate such play, the teacher needs to observe and record information about individuals and their social skills development, such as who is playing in a solitary manner, parallel to others, or in a group; and who can pretend, adjust actions to satisfy group needs, take turns, or carry on appropriate dialog. The teacher's role will be to stimulate such play in the first place by taking children on field trips, setting up pretend situations to extend their field trip learning to the classroom, and supporting them in their efforts. When play disintegrates, the teacher may need to find ways to extend the play further by posing a question or suggesting a new direction. The teacher also helps children to stand up for their own rights and respect the rights of others by modeling such behavior, listening to each side when conflict ensues, and helping children resolve their own problems.

LEARNING ACTIVITIES

1. Read Chapter 9, "Promoting Social Skills," and answer Question Sheet 9–A.
2. View Videopak D, "Dramatic Play," and answer Question Sheet 9–B.
3. Read one or more of the Suggested Readings. Add 10 cards to your file with specific ideas for helping children develop social skills. Include the reference source on the back of each card.
4. Observe each child as he or she engages in dramatic play using the Social Skills Checklist; record and interpret the results, noting children who may need help.
5. Choose one or more of the children who may need help developing social skills and use ideas from this chapter to help him or her improve.
6. Bring in props and set up a dramatic play area around a new theme based on a new or different activity or field trip you and the children are involved with. Observe and record your children's reactions. (Trainer can visit.)
7. Bring in new pictures and accessories for the block building area to encourage non-participants to engage in block building. You may need to get involved directly. (Trainer can observe.)
8. Read to a small group of children a storybook about one of the following themes: being different; being treated unfairly; not being listened to; standing up for rights; understanding people's feelings. Discuss with the children how they would feel in similar situations. Use hand puppets if you want. (Trainer can observe.)
9. Complete the Chapter 9 Evaluation Sheet and return it to your trainer or college supervisor.

QUESTION SHEET 9–A

(Based on Chapter 9, "Promoting Social Skills")

1. Why should children have to change their egocentric natures when they come to your center?
2. How can you help bring about this change?
3. What social skills can children learn through dramatic play?
4. What stages do children seem to go through as they learn to play with unit blocks?

5. How can you help get a child involved who does not seem to know how to play with blocks?

6. How can you help a shy child get involved in playing with others?

7. How do friendships between preschoolers differ from those between older children?

8. How can the use of classroom materials help a shy child overcome shyness?

9. How can preschool children learn to take turns?

10. In cases of conflict, how can you help a child stand up for his rights if you do not know who was right or wrong?

QUESTION SHEET 9–B

(Based on Videopak D, "Dramatic Play")

1. What kinds of imagining or pretend play do young children do?

2. Why do children do this kind of pretending?

3. How does dramatic play help a child handle fears and frustrations?

4. How does dramatic play help a child clarify unfamiliar situations?

5. How does dramatic play help children improve their communication skills?

6. How does dramatic play encourage socialization?

7. How should you set up the dramatic play area if you want these things to happen?

8. What should be the teacher's role in dramatic play?

9. How can the teacher extend children's learning in a play situation?

10. What can the teacher do when play disintegrates?

SUGGESTED READINGS

Beaty, J. J. (1990). *Observing development of the young child* (2nd ed.). Columbus, OH: Merrill.

Buzelli, C. A., & File, N. (1989). Building trust in friends. *Young Children, 44*(3) 70–75.

Edwards, C. P. (1986). *Promoting social and moral development in young children.* New York: Teachers College Press.

Fiarotta, P., & Fiarotta, N. (1977). *Be what you want to be!* New York: Workman Press.

Honig, A. S. (1987). The shy child. *Young Children, 42*(4) 54–64.

Koste, V. G. (1978). *Dramatic play in childhood: Rehearsal for life.* New Orleans, LA: Anchorage Press.

Provenzo, E. F., Jr., & Brett, A. (1983). *The complete block book.* Syracuse, NY: Syracuse University Press.

Rogers, D. L., & Ross, D. D. (1986). Encouraging Positive Social Interaction Among Young Children. *Young Children, 41*(3) 12–17.

Rubin, Z. (1980). *Children's friendships.* Cambridge, MA: Harvard University Press.

Smilansky, S. (1968). *The effects of sociodramatic play on disadvantaged preschool children.* New York: John Wiley & Sons.

Smilansky, S. (1990). *Facilitating play: A medium for promoting cognitive, socioemotional and academic development in young children.* Gaithersburg, MD: Psychosocial and Educational Publications.

Smith, C. A. (1982). *Promoting social development of young children: Strategies and activities.* Palo Alto, CA: Mayfield.

Webb, R. A. (1977). *Social development in childhood.* Baltimore, MD: Johns Hopkins University Press.

Zimbardo, P. G., & Radl, S. L. (1981). *The shy child.* New York: Doubleday.

CHILDREN'S BOOKS

Alexander, M. (1988). *Even that moose won't listen to me.* New York: Dial Books for Young Readers.

Alexander, M. (1981). *Marty McGee's space lab, no girls allowed.* New York: Dial Press.

Brandenberg, A. (1982). *We are best friends.* New York: Greenwillow Books.

Cohen, M. (1971). *Best friends.* New York: Macmillan.

Cohen, M. (1981). *Jim meets the thing.* New York: Greenwillow.

Cohen, M. (1967). *Will I have a friend?* New York: Macmillan.

Corey, D. (1980). *Everybody takes turn.* Chicago: Albert Whitman.

De Paola, T. (1976). *If he's my brother.* Englewood Cliffs, NJ: Prentice-Hall.

De Paola, T. (1979). *Oliver Button is a sissy.* New York: Harcourt Brace Jovanovich.

Gomi, T. (1981). *Sharing.* South San Francisco: Heian International.

Greydanus, R. (1981). *Let's pretend.* Mahwah, NJ: Troll Associates.

Gugler, L. D. (1988). *Mashed potato mountain.* Windsor, Ontario: Black Moss Press.

Guilfoile, E. (1957). *Nobody listens to Andrew.* New York: Scholastic.

Jonas, A. (1985). *The trek.* New York: Mulberry Books.

Keats, E. J. (1981). *Regards to the man in the moon.* New York: Collier Books.

Kraus, R. (1974). *Owliver.* New York: Windmill and Dutton.

Leaf, M. (1977). *The story of Ferdinand.* New York: Penguin.

Lionni, L. (1967). *Frederick.* New York: Pantheon Books.

McPhail, D. (1977). *The train.* New York: Penguin.

Oram, H. (1984). *In the attic.* New York: Henry Holt and Company.

Rey, H. A. (1966). *Curious George goes to the hospital.* New York: Scholastic.

Scott, A. H. (1967). *Sam.* New York: McGraw-Hill.

Waber, B. (1972). *Ira sleeps over.* Boston: Houghton Mifflin.

Zolotow, C. (1969). *The hating book.* New York: Harper.

VIDEOTAPES

Beaty, J. J. (Producer). (1979). Dramatic play (Videopak D), *Skills for preschool teachers* [videotape]. Elmira, NY: McGraw Bookstore, Elmira College.

Educational Productions, Inc. (Producer). *Time together: Learning to play with young children* [videotape]. Portland, OR: Educational Productions, Inc.

CHAPTER 9 EVALUATION SHEET
PROMOTING SOCIAL SKILLS

1. Student _____

2. Trainer _____

3. Center where training occurred _____

4. Beginning date _____ Ending date _____

5. Describe what student did to accomplish General Objective

   _____

   _____

6. Describe what student did to accomplish Specific Objectives

   Objective 1 _____

   _____

   Objective 2 _____

   _____

   Objective 3 _____

   _____

7. Evaluation of student's Learning Activities
   (Trainer Check One)   (Student Check One)

   _____ Highly superior performance   _____

   _____ Superior performance   _____

   _____ Good performance   _____

   _____ Less than adequate performance   _____

Signature of Trainer: Signature of Student:

_____   _____

Comments:

10 Providing Guidance

General Objective

To promote the development of self-control in young children through positive guidance.

Specific Objectives

☐ Uses positive prevention measures to help eliminate negative behavior in the classroom.

☐ Uses positive reinforcement techniques to help children learn appropriate behavior.

☐ Uses positive intervention methods to help children control their negative behavior.

C hildren who feel good about themselves are less prone to exhibit disruptive, negative behavior. Nevertheless, you and your classroom are not the only influences in the children's lives. Their interactions with others—parents, siblings, peers, neighbors, strangers—as well as their own personalities have a distinct bearing on how they will behave around you. Some children enter your classroom smiling, with good feelings about their self-worth, and with cooperative behavior that reflects these feelings. Other children come with as many as 3 or 4 years of accumulated negative experiences that are reflected in the disruptive or negative way they behave. How can you help such children learn appropriate positive behavior?

If you are aware that much of young children's negative behavior stems from insecurity and a negative self-image, you will eventually conclude that punishment, harsh treatment, loud commands, and scolding on your part do not provide solutions. These responses are themselves negative behaviors, and only reinforce a child's poor self-image. While punishment may stop negative behavior temporarily, it does not help the child build the inner, long-lasting control he needs to get along in the world.

Preschool children have been sent to your classroom to develop manipulative skills, improve large motor coordination, learn social skills, develop language, develop creativity, learn certain cognitive concepts, and improve their self-image. You should also include "learning appropriate behavior" as a learning goal. You should put this goal at the top of your list for certain children, and go about teaching it as you would any skill. Young children need objective, not emotional, guidance in the area of learning appropriate behavior.

USES POSITIVE PREVENTION MEASURES TO HELP ELIMINATE NEGATIVE BEHAVIOR IN THE CLASSROOM

Learning Environment

First of all, you need to anticipate problem behavior and set up your learning environment to prevent it. Young children may run around wildly if your classroom arrangement gives them the space to do so. Children may squabble over toys and materials if there are not enough for everyone, or if these items are not appropriate for the developmental level of the children. Likewise, children may become bored with books and toys if the "same old ones" are always on the shelves, with nothing new ever added or none of the old ones put away.

You can eliminate some of the causes for disruptive behavior in a preschool classroom by rearranging the room and providing more materials. Situations that cause such behavior include:

1. Too few activities and materials
2. Activities and materials not appropriate for developmental levels of children
3. Too much room to run around
4. Activity areas not clearly defined
5. Classroom geared for total group activities rather than individual and small group activities
6. No duplicates of favorite toys or materials
7. No change in old materials, books, toys

By setting up your classroom as described in Chapter 3, "Establishing a Learning Environment," you will go a long way towards reducing friction between children, in addition to giving yourself more free time to work with small groups and individuals who need special help.

Orderly Sequence of Events

Another positive measure you can take to prevent disruptive behavior among children is to maintain a stable and orderly sequence of events on a daily basis. You should maintain the daily schedule in the same order so that children feel secure in knowing what will occur and what comes next. Although the home life of some of your children may be chaotic, their classroom life should be stable enough to have a calming influence on their behavior. Have an illustrated daily schedule chart mounted at the children's eye level. Refer to it daily, so that children begin to understand the sequence of events.

The sequence should be a balanced one. Active play should be followed by quiet activities. Have a quiet or rest period after vigorous outdoor play. But there is no need to force children to rest if they have not been active enough to need it. (See Chapter 12, ''Providing Program Management''.)

A Minimum of Waiting

Don't keep children waiting. You can anticipate that some youngsters will act in a disruptive manner if you make them stand in line for long periods while waiting to go out or have them sit at tables with nothing to do while waiting for lunch. If such negative behavior occurs, it is your fault, not the children's. Plan your schedule so that long waits are unnecessary. However, if unanticipated waiting should occur, then be prepared with a transition activity to keep the children's interest and attention. Read or tell them a story, do a finger play, sing a song, or play a guessing game or a name game.

A Maximum of Time

Giving children plenty of time is another ''trick of the trade'' that experienced preschool teachers have found valuable in preventing negative behavior. Give children time to choose activities, time to get involved, time to talk with friends, time to complete what they are doing, time to pick up. Your program should be relaxed and unhurried. It takes young children longer to do things than we often anticipate. They need this time to accomplish things on their own. If they feel pressured because you impose your own time limits on them, they may behave disruptively. We owe it to young children to provide plenty of time.

  Pickup time is often an occasion for disruptive behavior on the part of some children. If this is the case in your classroom, you can anticipate the behavior and be ready to diffuse it. Some teachers announce to the entire class: ''It's 5 minutes to pickup time.'' This may not be the most effective thing to do. Most preschool children have a poor concept of 5 minutes, or any length of time, for that matter. For some, the announcement may be the signal to leave their activity area quickly so they won't have to pick up.

  It may be more effective on your part to go to certain areas and quietly tell the children, ''You can finish playing now. I'll be around in a few minutes to help you get started picking up.'' It is important for adults to contribute to pickup. Some children are too overwhelmed with all of the blocks or toys scattered across the floor to know how to get started. Involve them in a pickup game, such as: ''Let's use a big block as a bulldozer to push all the little blocks over to the shelf.'' Once they get started, you can leave and go to another area.

Child Involvement in Rules

Another positive measure for preventing negative behavior is to involve the children in making the rules for the classroom. If children know what is expected of them, they often behave better and more cooperatively in complying with the rules. At circle time, talk to the children about rules: ''What kind of rule shall we have about the toys and materials?" Rules such as "Children Who Got Materials Out Should Help Pick Up" and "Use Materials Carefully" may evolve from this discussion. Have the children help you make a few simple rules about materials and equipment. You will want to post these rules illustrated with stick figures in the appropriate area:

Block Area: "Build Only as High as You Can Reach"
Computer Area: "Wash Hands Before Using Keyboard"
                 "Two Children at a Time on Computer"
                 "Sign Up on Clipboard for Turn"

Children can then help regulate themselves if someone tries to disrupt the activity. In addition, pre-literate children will learn to interpret these signs if you and the other children read them aloud and refer to them.

Setting Limits

You and your co-workers need to set your own limits for children's behavior, for example, that they will not be allowed to hurt themselves or each other or to damage materials. These limits can then be enforced consistently, firmly, and without shame or blame by the staff. Without limits, children may frequently test you to see how far you will let them go. They need to be satisfied that you will not allow destructive things to happen. They need to feel secure in the classroom environment to expend their energies on constructive activities. Your staff needs to keep these limits clearly in mind as well, since they too will be responsible for enforcing them.

Other rules regarding the number of children allowed in activity areas, taking turns, and sharing materials can be regulated partly by the children themselves through the physical arrangement of the classroom.

Force Unacceptable

Finally, we should not force young children to participate in group activities. Some are just not ready to be involved with large groups that seem overwhelming to them. Others may not feel secure enough in the classroom environment to join a group. You should invite but not pressure such children. If you anticipate that certain children will not join in and will instead be disruptive, then have an activity or task ready for them. Give them a choice: "If you don't want to join us, Jeffrey, here is a storybook for you to read. When you're finished, you may want to join us. If not, you can read another book."

USES POSITIVE REINFORCEMENT TECHNIQUES TO HELP CHILDREN LEARN APPROPRIATE BEHAVIOR

Positive Reinforcement

Positive reinforcement helps the teacher focus attention on a child's desirable behavior and ignore the negative behavior. Teachers frequently focus on negative behavior because it is so effective at attention-getting. Frequently, the disruptive child is simply crying out for adult attention, even if it means punishment. When we respond to such misbehavior, even with punishment, we do not change it—even though we may stop it temporarily—but only reinforce it. A response of any kind leads the child to believe: "If I do this, they will pay attention to me."

Therefore, we must shift our attention from the negative to the positive. This is no simple task—it will take a concerted effort on your part and that of the other staff members to shift attention to the positive and ignore the negative behaviors of the children. This kind of shift requires the changing of a mind-set. You must take definite steps to bring about such a change in yourself before you can expect a child to change.

You can begin to accomplish this change by making a list of the positive behaviors that a disruptive child displays during the day. Share the list with other staff members. Each time the child displays a positive behavior, reinforce her with a smile, a touch, or a word of encouragement. Each time she displays a disruptive behavior, try to ignore it. If you must stop the behavior because it involves harm to another child or to a piece of equipment, simply remove the other child or the equipment from the setting. Do not make eye or verbal contact with the disruptive child at this time. But as soon as the child exhibits desirable behavior, go to her and express your pleasure. Do this as soon as possible, so the child receives the message that you will respond to her positive behavior but not to her negative actions.

Be sure the other adults in the classroom respond to the disruptive child the same way. There is no need to get angry or upset, speak loudly, or punish the child. You and your co-workers need to keep in mind that "discipline" for young children means "learning appropriate behavior" or "learning self-control." For young children to learn self-control, you and your staff must provide them with many such learning opportunities.

You may have to practice this new way of responding a number of times before you can expect results from the children. Have another staff member watch you do it; then talk about it. Let that person try it, too, with the same child. Work on this method until you make it work for you. This technique takes more time to get results than forcing a child to stop his misbehavior. In the end, however, it is more worthwhile, because the behavior control comes from within the child rather than from the outside. It is a step for the child toward developing self-control, and a step away from depending on the adults around him to control his behavior.

Focus on Victim, Not Aggressor

When things get out of hand and one child hurts another, your first concern should be for the victim rather than the aggressor. You must, of course, stop the unacceptable behavior, but do so by focusing on the victim. This is contrary to the way most adults naturally react in cases of child conflict. Ordinarily, the teacher rushes to stop the aggressor and even punishes that child. However, this tends to reinforce the misbehavior by giving the first attention to the aggressor. If you go first to the victim, the surprised aggressor will get the message that she cannot gain your attention with such misbehavior. Do not forget, however, to respond to the aggressor as soon as she displays positive behavior. This is the time to discuss with the child, in a matter-of-fact way, her inappropriate behavior, that you cannot let her or anyone else hurt another child, and that you appreciate the way she is behaving now. This is also the time to discuss with her what else she could do when she gets angry, rather than hurt the child she is upset with.

Model Appropriate Behavior

How can the disruptive child learn acceptable, appropriate behavior? You and your co-workers need first to explain and then to model this behavior. Children learn a great deal by example. Say to a child: "When you are angry at another child, you need to tell that child how you feel. What could you say to her? Try it." If the child does not know how to express anger in words, you can demonstrate. Tell him: "I would say to Sharon: 'Sharon, you spilled paint on my paper. That makes me very angry!'"

You as a teacher need to model this behavior. You need to express your own feelings to the child: "Rob, I am really upset that you hit Sharon instead of talking to her about what happened. You need to tell her in words how you feel, and not hit her." If you follow up with this advice again and again, children will pick up on it. Eventually, you will hear your children saying to one another: "Tell him in words. Don't hit him."

You need to maintain your own self-control. When you become angry with children, you need to calm down before talking to them. Yelling at children puts you in the same position as the child who is out of control. It is not helpful to either of you. Children are in your program to learn how to handle their own strong emotions. They want someone to prevent them from getting out of control. They look to you to model this controlled behavior.

You also need to model courteous behavior. Treat the children with the same respect as you would treat a friend. Don't yell across the room at a child who is demonstrating inappropriate behavior. Walk over to the child and talk to her quietly, in a courteous but firm manner: "Brenda, you took the paint brush away from Rachel before she was finished. She is really upset about it. You will need to give it back to her now. If you want to paint, you can sign up for a turn." You may also need to let a child practice or role-play her actions or words. "Rachel, let's go over to Brenda, and you tell her how you feel. What are you going to say to her?"

USES POSITIVE INTERVENTION METHODS TO HELP CHILDREN CONTROL THEIR NEGATIVE BEHAVIOR

No "Time-Out" Chair

Most teachers heave a sigh of relief when they hear about the demise of the "time-out chair," one of the intervention methods that has been popular in early childhood classrooms for children who are out of control. The "time-out chair" is "out" in many

The teacher needs to model courteous behavior when a child is having difficulties. Treat the child with the same respect as you would a friend.

classrooms today, since it is no longer considered a positive intervention method. It was always a struggle for teachers to get really out-of-control children to sit in the chair in the first place, and their noisy protests and crying tended to disrupt the entire classroom. The more submissive children allowed themselves to be placed in the chair, but at what cost to their self-concepts? The "time-out chair" was not supposed to isolate children since it was placed within the classroom, but the other children kept away, anyway. It was not supposed to be a punishment, just a time for disruptive children to calm down. Nevertheless, their peers still viewed them as being punished and shunned them—a particularly insidious and unpleasant sort of punishment. The chair was not supposed to be a threat, yet there it sat, a very definite threatening presence in an otherwise pleasant environment—like a dunce chair from an old-time schoolroom—waiting to be occupied.

We are glad to see it go, along with other negative intervention techniques that tend to put down a child instead of teaching appropriate behavior.

Accepting Negative Feelings

What will you do, then, when children become angry or upset and begin to act out their feelings? First of all, don't wait for this to happen and then be forced to react negatively. You need to anticipate your children's behavior and be prepared for them to be out of sorts, as you yourself are from time to time.

Once you acknowledge that negative feelings are a natural part of a young child's growth and development, you will be able to take the next step more readily, that of accepting these feelings. It's all right for children to feel angry or frustrated or upset. Acceptance does not mean approval; it means only that you recognize this negative part of children as well as their positive aspects, and will help them change. Acceptance is the first step in helping children control the negative aspects of their behavior.

In addition, accepting a child's negative feelings helps to defuse them. You need to display your acceptance by not becoming angry or upset yourself. You need to stay calm and respond to the child in a matter-of-fact tone of voice. Your unruffled behavior is the first step in calming the child. Your actions say to him: "If the teacher doesn't get upset, then it can't be so bad."

Verbalizing Negative Feelings

Next, you need to help children express their negative feelings in an acceptable manner. Helping them find a harmless means of expression will defuse these feelings. Otherwise, the children may burst out again as soon as you turn your back.

Verbalizing feelings, that is, expressing them in words, is one of the most effective ways to get them out. Expressing anger, jealousy, or frustration in words helps to relieve the emotion. Your calm voice may be all it takes to soothe the child: "How do you feel, Jennifer? Tell me how you feel." If the child will not talk directly to you, she may talk to a hand puppet you hold, or through a hand puppet she holds. Be patient. A child caught up in an emotional outburst often needs time to calm down enough to talk.

Redirecting Negative Behavior

On the other hand, a hostile, crying child may not be able to respond verbally. Instead, a classroom activity may help him calm down and regain control of himself. Water play is an especially soothing activity. If you don't have a water table, you can fill the toy sink in the housekeeping corner or a plastic basin on a table for an upset child to play with.

Clay and dough are also excellent for children to use to work out frustrations. Encourage them to knead the material or pound it with their fists or a wooden mallet. Beanbags serve the same purpose. Let children expend their negative energy constructively by throwing a beanbag or a foam ball at a target.

Finger painting also helps children release negative energy. Consider keeping a quiet corner with a comfortable rocking chair and space for water play, dough, or finger painting. If children know you will help and support them in releasing negative feelings nondestructively, they will begin to assume more control themselves.

Books can sometimes be helpful in a stressful situation. For example, children often become upset when a new baby enters the family and will act out their feelings in the classroom. Thus it is a good idea to have several books that discuss this event. You will want to read and discuss the books with all the children, but they will give special comfort to the child who is directly affected. Popular books of this nature are *Peter's Chair* (Keats, 1967), *A Baby Sister for Frances* (Hoban, 1964), *Nobody Asked Me If I Wanted a Baby Sister* (Alexander, 1971), *When the New Baby Comes I'm Moving Out* (Alexander, 1979), *She Come Bringing Me That Little Baby Girl* (Greenfield, 1974), and *I Love My Baby Sister (Most of the Time)* (Edelman, 1984).

Other books to help children get over feeling upset are *Alexander and the Terrible, Horrible, No Good, Very Bad Day* (Viorst, 1972); *I Was So Mad!* (Simon, 1964), also published in Spanish; *The Grouchy Ladybug* (Carle, 1977); *How Do I Feel?* (Simon, 1970); *Sometimes I Like to Cry* (Stanton & Stanton, 1978); and *The Temper Tantrum Book* (Preston, 1969).

The children's behavior will often give you clues as to how to deal with them to strengthen their self-control. Here are some behaviors that have occurred in preschool classrooms as described by the teachers involved, along with suggestions for ways the teacher might deal with the behavior.

Destructiveness; Hitting

> Daryl is a real problem in the center. He is extremely de-
> structive to the toys and equipment; and he endangers the
> other children when he hits or pushes them. When he hits
> them with the toys, it can really hurt.

Compulsive hitting and damaging things may well be a tensional outlet for this boy. His teacher, Lynn, needs to be firm and consistent in not allowing Daryl to hurt other people or things. She needs to convey this idea to Daryl firmly but not harshly each time she stops him. Lynn needs to accentuate any positive behavior Daryl displays toward people or things with positive remarks. "Daryl, you and Bobby played so well together today," or "Daryl, I really appreciate how carefully you put the toys away." Finally, Lynn needs to redirect Daryl's negative behavior. Perhaps he can take out his feelings on a homemade "punching pillow." On the other hand, Lynn may decide that Daryl needs most of all to calm down to control his inner frustrations.

Playing at a water table may be a soothing activity for him. Lynn will undoubtedly have to try several approaches to see which works best for Daryl.

Whining; Tattling

> Nancy would be a likable child if only she'd stop her constant whining. She is always coming to the teacher with tales about other children doing things to her, and she always tells them in a whining voice.

David, the teacher, has already formed a judgment against Nancy by saying she "would be a likable child if only . . ." David needs to start by changing his own attitude and then showing Nancy that he accepts her as she is. The whining and tattling should be ignored as much as possible. Instead, David should concentrate on Nancy's positive behavior and praise her for ordinary things, saying, for example, "Nancy, you and Sue played so well this morning." David may want to tape-record Nancy's voice when she plays with others in the dramatic play area or converses at the lunch table. Later, they can listen to the tape together, with the teacher making comments such as: "It really sounds nice when you talk so cheerfully, Nancy. Don't you like the way you sound?"

Biting

> Ronnie is a biter. Every time someone does something he doesn't like, he'll give them a hard bite before they even know what's happening.

Here again, it sounds as though the teacher, Donna, first needs to change her attitude. Already Ronnie has been labeled "a biter." He is undoubtedly a boy with great frustrations that need an acceptable outlet. As with Daryl, the teacher needs to stop Ronnie from hurting others and direct him into an acceptable channel for releasing his tensions. Since he seems to release energy through his mouth, perhaps he could chew on something when he gets upset. Calming activities such as water play might also be effective. In addition, Donna needs to show Ronnie throughout the day that she cares about him and accepts him as a good person.

Thumb-Sucking

> Julie is a shy child who always has her thumb in her mouth no matter how many times you remind her about it.

An outside reminder is not going to help Julie stop her thumb-sucking when it gives her such comfort. For a teacher to constantly call attention to this behavior not only reinforces it, but probably makes Julie feel bad that she is always doing something that offends the teacher. Thumb-sucking is a satisfying and tension-relaxing behavior for her. The teacher first needs to accept Julie as she is and then will be able to help her find an appropriate substitute behavior. The adult in the classroom to whom Julie most readily responds should talk with her about thumb-sucking and why people dislike it. Julie herself must want to stop before any efforts will be effective. Because she uses her thumb and mouth to release pent-up tension, Julie might substitute more suitable tension-releasing activities using thumb and/or mouth. Could she chew gum? If this is not acceptable, perhaps she could hold some small object in her hand—a tiny doll or miniature car or some clicking device. Or she may agree to bandage her thumb as a reminder not to suck it. Julie needs extra support and affection in the classroom to make her feel good about herself. In this instance, it may not be helpful to praise her for not sucking. There may be too many relapses and therefore too much built-up guilt. The sensitive teacher may instead know when to ask Julie, "Is it working?" If the answer is no, the teacher may ask, "Do you want to try something else?" Children are people, too; if treated with respect, they can make such decisions to help themselves.

Temper Tantrum

> When Ricky can't have the toy he wants right away, he throws himself down on the floor and kicks and screams

Some adults regard this kind of behavior as that of a "spoiled child." It is instead a release of great tension. Not much can be done for a child during the duration of the tantrum. It is best to move other children away and go about the business of the classroom. Afterwards, the teacher needs to comfort the child and suggest other outlets. Perhaps Ricky could pound on a pillow or kick a ball. Lynn, his teacher, might do well to purchase a tetherball for just such occasions. She can fasten it on a short rope to a low place in the corner for children to kick when they are out of sorts like this. Lynn will need Ricky's cooperation, though, to achieve any kind of success. Perhaps he will be willing to cooperate when he realizes that he is warmly accepted and loved in the classroom despite his moments of rage. Patience will be necessary on everyone's part. There will undoubtedly be many lapses before Ricky learns to substitute ball-kicking for tantrum-throwing.

Overaggressiveness

> Lyle seems to take pleasure in hurting others. He looks around the room to see which boys are doing something interesting, then goes over to them and breaks up their building, throws something at them, takes away their toys, or pushes them down. He is a new boy at the center and hasn't made any friends.

In fact, Lyle has probably been trying hard to make friends. Some children use this aggressive technique to do so. They are making contact as best they know how, even though it produces negative results. The teacher, David, has passed judgment on the behavior by saying that "Lyle seems to take pleasure in hurting others" without understanding the reason for it. David will need to change his attitude to succeed in helping Lyle control his behavior. Since Lyle seems desperate to make a contact with another boy, perhaps David can ask Lyle and one other boy to do some chores for him, or he can put Lyle in charge of a group activity such as woodworking. With time and patience, this problem should work itself out as Lyle becomes accepted by the group. David should set an example, though, by demonstrating his own acceptance of Lyle.

Things to Avoid

There are certain adult behaviors that you and your staff should avoid. Although some of the following actions may make children behave, at least temporarily, they may be extremely destructive to their self-concepts and their ability to develop control over their behavior.

1. Do not talk about a child in a place where the child can hear you.
2. Do not use judgment words such as *good, bad, stupid,* or *slow* when referring to a child.
3. Do not constantly nag or scold.
4. Do not correct a child's speech.
5. Do not embarrass or humiliate a child.
6. Do not compare a child with siblings.
7. Do not accentuate negative things about a child.
8. Do not stress competition between children where someone wins and someone loses.
9. Do not withhold food (such as dessert) as a punishment.
10. Do not use physical punishment against a child.

Your efforts to improve the children's self-control will be rewarded as the children learn to control their behavior in the center. In addition, parents may notice their children's growth in this regard and help support your efforts at home. The child with special behavior problems may require concerted and cooperative effort on the part of both home and center to effect a change. It is surely worth the effort.

SUMMARY

The goal of guidance is to promote the development of self-control in young children. You can accomplish this goal through positive prevention measures: arrange the learning environment to prevent disruptive behavior; offer an orderly sequence of daily activities to promote feelings of security; keep "waiting" time for children at a minimum but "time" to accomplish things at a maximum; and involve children in making classroom rules and setting their own limits. In addition, children learn self-control through positive reinforcement of their appropriate behavior. For example, each time a disruptive child displays a positive behavior, you can give the child a smile, a touch, or a word of praise. You should ignore negative behavior as much as possible or respond matter-of-factly without making eye contact. Positive intervention techniques that help children control negative behavior no longer include the use of the "time-out chair" because of its detrimental effects on children. Instead, teachers intervene by first accepting children's negative feelings themselves, then helping children verbalize their feelings, and finally redirecting children's negative behavior into constructive activities such as finger painting, play dough, water play, and beanbags. Your own modeling of calm yet firm behavior should also help children feel less upset and more in control in times of stress.

LEARNING ACTIVITIES

1. Read Chapter 10, "Providing Guidance," and answer Question Sheet 10–A.
2. View Videopak C, "Self-image and Self-control," and answer Question Sheet 10–B.
3. Read one or more of the Suggested Readings. Add 10 cards to your file with specific ideas for helping children develop self-control. Include a reference source on the back of each card.
4. Make an assessment of the classroom based on the items mentioned on page 206. Make changes where necessary. Record the effects of the changes on the children.
5. Observe and record children standing in line. The next day, use a transition activity with children standing in line. Discuss the difference. (Trainer can observe.)
6. Observe a disruptive child for a day, and write down all of the positive behavior he or she displays. Show that you approve by smiling or giving a word of praise. Record the results.
7. Bring in a new activity or material through which children under stress can express or work out negative feelings, and use it with a child. (Trainer can observe.)
8. Read an appropriate book to a child who displays negative feelings. Record the results.
9. Complete the Chapter 10 Evaluation Sheet and return it to your trainer or college supervisor.

QUESTION SHEET 10–A

(Based on Chapter 10, "Providing Guidance")

1. Why is punishment an inappropriate method for correcting a child's disruptive behavior?
2. How can your arrangement of the learning environment prevent negative behavior?
3. Why is an orderly sequence of daily events important in helping to eliminate negative behavior?
4. Why is it your fault if children's negative behavior occurs while they stand in line or wait for lunch?

5. Why should children be involved in making rules and establishing limits? What should these limits be?

6. What is "positive reinforcement" and how does it work to bring about self-control in children with behavior problems?

7. Why should you focus on the victim rather than the aggressor in cases of one child hitting another?

8. How do children learn appropriate behavior in the classroom?

9. Why is the "time-out chair" no longer considered an effective method for controlling children's negative behavior?

10. How does the redirecting of negative behavior work?

QUESTION SHEET 10-B

(Based on Videopak C, "Self-Image and Self-Control")

1. What does self-image have to do with the way a child behaves in the classroom?

2. Why is it important in the development of self-control for a child's peers to show they accept him?

3. How does coping with the environment affect a child's self-control?

4. How does classroom arrangement affect a child's self-control?

5. What does a child's participation in classroom chores have to do with self-control?

6. What has to happen for children to assume control over their behavior?

7. What is the best way for a teacher to enforce limits in a classroom area when children get out of hand?

8. How should the teacher deal with negative behavior on the playground?

9. What rule should you follow for children to gain the teacher's attention?

10. Do you agree with the statement, "Self-control and self-image go hand in hand"? Explain.

SUGGESTED READINGS

Beaty, J. J. (1990). *Observing development of the young child* (2nd ed.). Columbus, OH: Merrill.

Briggs, D. C. (1970). *Your child's self-esteem.* Garden City, NY: Doubleday.

Cherry, C. (1983). *Please don't sit on the kids.* Belmont, CA: Pitman Learning.

Cherry, C. (1981). *Think of something quiet.* Belmont, CA: Pitman Learning.

Clewett, A. S. (1988). Guidance and discipline: Teaching young children appropriate behavior. *Young Children, 43*(4) 26–31.

Cary, E. (1979). *Without spanking or spoiling: A practical approach to toddler and preschool guidance.* Seattle, WA: Parenting Press.

Essa, E. (1983). *Practical guide to solving preschool behavior problems.* Albany, NY: Delmar.

Honig, A. S. (1985). Compliance, control, and discipline. *Young Children, 40*(2) 50–58.

Kersey, K. (1986). *Helping your child handle stress.* Washington, DC: Acropolis Books.

Marion, M. (1991). *Guidance of young children* (3rd ed.). Columbus, OH: Merrill.

Mitchell, G. (1982). *A very practical guide to discipline with young children.* Marshfield, MA: Telshare Publishing.

National Association for the Education of Young Children. (1988). Ideas that work with young children: Avoiding 'Me against you' discipline. *Young Children, 44*(1) 24–29.

Williamson, P. A. (1990). *Good kids, bad behavior: Helping children learn self-discipline.* New York: Simon and Schuster.

CHILDREN'S BOOKS

Alexander, M. (1971). *Nobody asked me if I wanted a baby sister.* New York: Dial Press.

Alexander, M. (1979). *When the new baby comes I'm moving out.* New York: Dial Press.

Carle, E. (1977). *The grouchy ladybug.* New York: Thomas Y. Crowell.

Edelman, E. (1984). *I love my baby sister (most of the time).* New York: Viking Penguin.

Greenfield, E. (1974). *She come bringing me that little baby girl.* Philadelphia: J. B. Lippincott.

Hoban, R. (1964). *A baby sister for Frances.* New York: Harper and Row.

Keats, E. J. (1967). *Peter's chair.* New York: Harper and Row.

Marzollo, J. (1980). *Uproar on Hollercat Hill.* New York: The Dial Press.

Preston, E. M. (1969). *The temper tantrum book.* New York: Viking Penguin.

Simon, N. (1970). *How do I feel?* Chicago: Albert Whitman.

Simon, N. (1974). *I was so mad!* (Also in Spanish) Chicago: Albert Whitman.

Stanton, E., & Stanton, H. (1978). *Sometimes I like to cry.* Chicago: Albert Whitman.

Viorst, J. (1972). *Alexander and the terrible, horrible, no good, very bad day.* New York: Atheneum.

VIDEOTAPES

Beaty, J. J. (Producer). (1979). Self-image and self-control (Videopak C), *Skills for preschool teachers.* Elmira, NY: McGraw Bookstore, Elmira College.

National Association for the Education of Young Children (Producer). *Discipline: Appropriate guidance of young children.* Washington, DC: NAEYC.

South Carolina Educational TV (Producer). Guiding behavior of young children. *Calico pie.* Columbia, SC: SCETV.

CHAPTER 10 EVALUATION SHEET
PROVIDING GUIDANCE

1. Student _____

2. Trainer _____

3. Center where training occurred _____

4. Beginning date _____ Ending date _____

5. Describe what student did to accomplish General Objective

   _____

   _____

6. Describe what student did to accomplish Specific Objectives

   Objective 1 _____

   _____

   Objective 2 _____

   _____

   Objective 3 _____

   _____

7. Evaluation of student's Learning Activities
       (Trainer Check One)   (Student Check One)

   _____ Highly superior performance   _____

   _____ Superior performance   _____

   _____ Good performance   _____

   _____ Less than adequate performance   _____

Signature of Trainer: Signature of Student:

_____   _____

Comments:

11 Promoting Family Involvement

General Objective

To encourage family involvement in center activities to promote their children's positive development.

Specific Objectives

☐ Involves parents in participating in children's program.
☐ Recognizes and supports families of different make-ups.
☐ Supports families and children under stress.

P arent involvement has long been a part of most preschool programs, but only in recent years have we come to realize just how important this involvement can be. Research shows us that programs with a strong parent component have the longest-lasting positive effects on children. Not only do children change and improve their skills as a result of their preschool experience, but their parents change as well. Parents who are directly involved in their children's preschool programs are much more likely to encourage their children's development at home and to support their learning during the later school years. Even parents who are not directly involved but show enthusiasm for their children's preschool programs promote their children's self-esteem and reduce discipline problems both at home and at school.

INVOLVES PARENTS IN PARTICIPATING IN CHILDREN'S PROGRAM

Parents can be involved in many ways and at many different levels in their children's early childhood programs. These are only several of the possibilities:

1. Visiting the program
2. Attending the classroom team meeting to help plan for their child
3. Volunteering as a teacher's assistant
4. Receiving training and working as a paid classroom assistant
5. Helping the classroom staff on a field trip
6. Visiting the program to read a story or sing a song with the children
7. Making equipment or materials for the program

223

8. Bringing something of their culture or language to the program (stories, songs, dances, foods, words)
9. Putting on a money-raising project for the center
10. Visiting the classroom as a community helper or to demonstrate their occupation
11. Becoming a member of the board or Policy Action Council or other decision-making body
12. Carrying out at home with their child an activity they learned at the center
13. Joining the program's parent club and participating in activities
14. Taking instruction in nutrition, cooking, parenting, or another topic in a workshop sponsored by the program

Most parents will not become involved automatically. You must take the initiative, letting them know they are welcome and helping them find a comfortable way to contribute to their child's welfare while in your program.

If parents' only experience has been with public school programs, they may not realize how important their role is for their child's success in your classroom. Parents of preschool children are their child's most important role model. If they ignore or downplay their child's school experience, the child may not take it seriously herself. If they do not know what learning is going on in the preschool, they can hardly support or extend that learning at home.

Thus, it is vital for teachers to find a way to involve the parents of each child in some aspect of your program. It may not be easy, especially with parents who work during the day or with parents whose own school experience has left them with negative feelings about classrooms and teachers.

Focus on the Child

The most effective approach to parent involvement is to focus on the child, not the program. What does the child like? What are the child's favorite kinds of activities? Does he like to sing or color? Have books been read to the child? Which ones? What do the parents want their child to learn in the early childhood classroom? Should the teacher know anything special about the child and his needs? Parents are concerned about their children's welfare; if you focus on this from the beginning, you will quickly capture their attention.

During the intake interview or enrollment process at the beginning of the school year, you or another program member can invite parents to become involved and offer them specific choices. For example, a parent could eat lunch with his child once a month; read a story to a small group at "story time" on any Friday; walk to the park with the group any time they go; be the librarian in charge of child care magazines and pamphlets for the parents; be a "telephone parent" who calls other parents when it is time for the monthly parent meeting; be the "transportation parent" who brings parents who have no car to the meeting; or gather news from parents for the parent newsletter.

On the other hand, the parent may have an idea for the monthly parent workshop: for example, something she would like to learn about low-cal cooking, shopping on a tight budget, learning games to make from throw-away items, or positive discipline techniques for a hard-to-control child.

You may not meet your children's parents until school begins. Some teachers, however, visit their children's houses at the beginning of the year and take pictures of the children and their families by their front door to be included in the personal scrapbooks children will be making in school. Children not only need to make a transition from home to school, but also to be assured that the teacher and the program accept and respect their home and parents.

Beginning School

Many programs begin with a staggered entrance process so that all the parents and children do not come on the same day at the same time. Half the children, for instance, may come on the first day, and half on the next; or half in the morning, and half in the afternoon. On those first days, each half of the class stays only part of the time. Invite parents or other family caregivers to bring their children and stay themselves for the brief class session. You and your staff can divide your time between the parents and their children. The children and parents should be invited to explore the room. You can set up puzzles or a water table for them, as well as the permanent activity areas.

In the meantime, one of you can talk with the parents, asking about what their child likes to do at home and what the parents hope to see the child accomplish in the program. Jot down this information on a file card for each child. The parents may have already discussed this with the program's parent worker, but it is still a good way for the classroom staff to reinforce the notion that the program cares about the parents and their child and will go out of its way to express this care.

Invite parents to stay until the child feels comfortable without them. This may take several days for some children. If parents work, they may be able to manage to come to work late on the first days of the program. If not, they may be able to send another family member. Some parents may have difficulty knowing when to leave after several days, but the staff can assist them. From the beginning, let parents know that they should plan to stay a shorter time every day as their child becomes more involved in the classroom activities. In the meantime, a staff member should make sure the child becomes busily engaged and then signal the parent when it is a good time to leave.

Home Visits

The beginning of the school year may be the time to arrange home visits. You can tell parents that you want to drop by in a few weeks to let them know how their child has adjusted to the center, and that you intend to visit all the parents for the same purpose. Plan the visit for a mutually agreeable time.

It is important to state your intention at the beginning of the program; otherwise, parents may feel threatened by a home visit, fearing that their child has done something wrong. You must of course follow up with the visit.

Some parents may be uneasy about a teacher visiting their home, thinking their home might not measure up to the teacher's expectations. At the same time, some teachers may be uncomfortable with home visits because they find themselves removed from the familiar "territory" of the classroom. Both teachers and parents will feel more at ease with one another if they focus on the child. This is the purpose of the home visit: to see the child in the home setting and talk with the parents about how the child is getting along in preschool.

Take along a photo of the child pursuing a favorite activity: building a block structure, painting a picture, dressing up to play a role, or making a puzzle. You may also want to take some of the child's art work to share or a book she especially likes. Leave the book behind for a family member to read to the child. Talk about the scribbles on the child's paper as being the first step in the development of drawing skills. Before leaving, invite the parents to visit the school at a particular time to watch or participate in some activity.

A home visit like this is important not only for the teacher to gain insight into the child's home and family background, but also for the family to learn that you care enough about their child to take time to visit the home.

Parents' Classroom Visits

What should parents do when they visit the classroom? Sit and watch? Join in their child's activity? Greet the parents at the door and let them know what they can do. At first, they will probably want to sit and watch; later, they can participate in some way if they want. Raymond's mother was invited to stir the instant gelatin the children were making for snack. Michelle's grandmother read the children a story when she came to visit. Mike's mother went on a nature walk with the class when they gathered colored leaves.

Some children will act up when their parents are in the classroom. Parents need to be aware that this is neither unusual nor wrong. To distract such children, you might give them a special role to play, an errand to do, or something to be in charge of. On the other hand, you might give their parents a teacher's role: reading a book to a small group, overseeing the woodworking area, or being in charge of playing a record or tape. For some children, the best thing to calm them down is for them to do an activity with their parents. Perhaps they can make a puzzle with their parents, do an easel painting, or build with blocks. Or invite the child and parent to look at the classroom book collection together and select a book to sign out and take home.

Materials as Connectors

For some programs, materials make the best connector between home and school. Parents can understand the purpose of bringing a book home or sending empty containers to school. Again, the focus is on the child. Keep a duplicate collection of children's books in paperback that can be borrowed and taken home on a daily basis.

Children can sign out for one book at a time at the end of the session and return it in the morning. If they forget, they will need to return it before taking out another book. In the same manner, you can have a toy lending library with a duplicate set of the toys you use in the classroom, such as cars, trucks, figures of people, animals, and doll furniture. Children can sign out their favorite toy and keep it overnight.

Ask parents to collect empty containers and send them to school for the children's pretend supermarket. Ask them to send dress-up clothes, hats, shoes, belts, wallets, and purses. Scraps of cloth, scraps of wood, Styrofoam containers, margarine cups, and paper towel tubes are other useful items they can save for the classroom.

Family members can collect milk cartons of various sizes and meet at the center for a "block-making bee" to cover their milk cartons with contact paper for use as blocks. You may not have time for all the materials you would like to make for individuals; parents can help. Invite parents to a puzzle-making session and provide them with two enlarged photos of their children, along with clear contact paper and cardboard backing. They can make two picture puzzles of each child by gluing the photo to the cardboard, laminating it with clear contact paper, and cutting it into simple puzzle sections to be kept in a manila envelope. They can leave one puzzle on the manipulative materials shelf and take the other one home.

Parents as Classroom Volunteers

Encourage parents to volunteer in the classroom on a regular basis if they feel comfortable in this role. Parents who are successful interacting with children when they visit may want to return as volunteers. You will need to talk with such parents about program goals, your goals for individual children, and what the parents themselves would be comfortable doing during their time in the classroom. Stress the importance of teamwork and how they will become a part of the classroom team. Also discuss the roles of the other team members, so that parents understand their own role and how to carry it out. Remember that a successful volunteer effort takes time and effort on the part of the classroom staff.

You can post signs in each activity area to tell volunteers and visitors what the children are doing and what the volunteer's role can be. For example, in the book area, the sign might say: "Children are free to choose any book to read during free-choice period. Volunteers and visitors may want to read a book to a child if the child is interested." In the art area, the sign might say: "Children are encouraged to try out art materials on their own. Volunteers and visitors may want to observe the children and encourage them, but let them do art activities without adult help."

In the beginning, you may want the parent volunteers to observe both children and teachers, focusing on certain areas of the Teacher Skills Checklist, so that they have a better understanding of how staff members carry out program goals. The area of guidance is one that often needs explanation. Let each parent spend time observing how staff members "Use positive reinforcement techniques to help children learn appropriate behavior" or "Use positive intervention methods to help children control their negative behavior." At the end of the observation time, you will want to sit down and discuss what the parent observed. You should discuss not only the

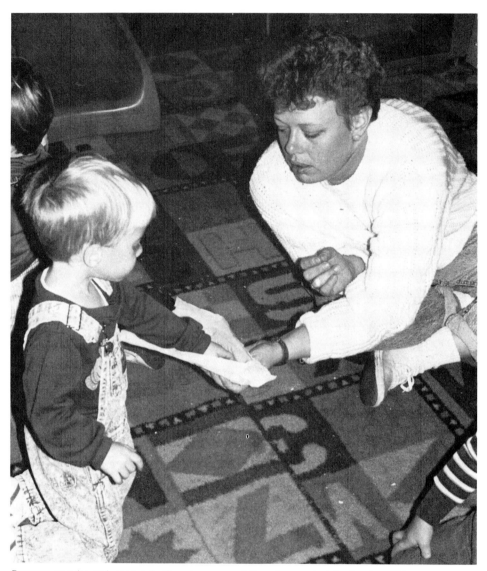

Parents can be volunteers in the classroom if they learn what their role will be and how they can carry it out.

methods for guiding children, but also why certain methods are used. Ask how the parent handles the same behavior at home.

At first, you may want volunteers to work in only one or two curriculum areas of the classroom until they become used to the children and the program. You or one of your team members need to give help and support to volunteers, as well as intervening with sensitivity when things do not go well. Have how-to booklets available to lend to volunteers or suggest that they view videotapes about the curriculum area or guidance method they are working with. Invite volunteers to planning sessions and in-service training programs. When they have acquired enough contact hours in your program, some volunteers may want to prepare for CDA (Child Development Associate) assessment.

You will soon recognize which volunteers are most helpful. Make rules to prevent your program from being overwhelmed with classroom volunteers. Select one day a week for one volunteer at a time, or you may want to regulate the number of times each parent can volunteer. Remember, volunteers should be a help in the program, not a hindrance.

RECOGNIZES AND SUPPORTS FAMILIES OF DIFFERENT MAKE-UPS

Life and family styles of the 1990s are far different from those of the traditional American family, which typically consisted of mother as homemaker, father as breadwinner, and children whose first group experience occurred in public school kindergarten. Today's families may be blended, extended, single-parent, bilingual, culturally diverse, or dependent on child care—often from infancy on.

Single-Parent Families

A tremendous increase in the number of single-parent families occurred in the 1970s and '80s. Increases in the divorce rate and the incidence of out-of-wedlock births among teenage girls and young women are principally responsible. Adoption of children by single parents is also on the rise. Although women head most single-parent families, some men have joined their ranks.

Early childhood programs need to recognize and accept such families. Single parents can maintain strong, functioning families with the proper support. Teachers must be aware, though, that children also need special support during the turmoil of family breakup, and that parents need special treatment to find time to meet with preschool teachers. Some early mornings, evenings, or weekends may need to be set aside for parent-teacher meetings. It is your professional responsibility to make the initial contact and arrange your schedule to meet that of a family member.

Blended Families

Many, if not most, divorced parents eventually re-marry. When both parents bring children from a previous marriage, the newly formed family is referred to as *blended*. Blended families can offer their children the same kind of support as their primary families did. Often, however, it takes time for families and children to build secure relationships with one another, especially if the original family breakup was difficult. Children, especially young children, seem to suffer most immediately from this stress, taking on feelings of guilt, shame, and rejection.

Preschool teachers need to be aware of the stress factors possible in blended families, and show both children and their parents that they are accepted and cherished in the program. Again, it is up to the program to make the initial contact and set up parent-teacher meetings at the convenience of the family.

Culturally Diverse Families

Families from cultures different from that of the majority of classroom parents are referred to as *culturally diverse*. They may be recent immigrants to the United States from Haiti, Cuba, Puerto Rico, Mexico, Viet Nam, India, or Japan. They may be ethnic minorities such as Native American or African American families. They may speak only their native language or be bilingual in English as well. Their economic backgrounds will be as diverse as their nationalities. Immigrants come for economic opportunities as well as political refuge. This has always been the case in the United States. These families expect that a program like yours will help their children to become adjusted to the new country, its language, and its customs. They also expect that their own culture and language will be respected and not put down.

You or a member of your classroom team needs to make the initial contact with these families as well. If the parents do not speak English, then take along a native-language speaker, or arrange for an older sibling who speaks English to be present. It is important that initial meetings be face-to-face at a location convenient to the parents.

Working Parents

No matter what the make-up of the family, you should expect that many parents will be working and not at home during the day. This means that parents depend on their child's preschool more than ever for quality care, concern, and support for their children. Help assure your children's parents that this is the case. Take the initiative to contact the parents and arrange for meetings at their convenience. This should be an important part of the job description of *every* early childhood caregiver.

As a child caregiver, you need to recognize and support *every* family make-up that your children represent. Parents are their children's most important role models. Families set the stage for their children's successes or failures in life. Thus, early childhood programs must be deeply involved in supporting the families of their children.

Family Support of Programs

It is just as important that the children's families support your program. In fact, this seems to be the key to child gains in preschool: if parents show enthusiasm for their children's preschool programs, then children profit greatly from the programs. In cases where parents are unenthusiastic or even negative about the program, children do not gain in self-esteem or behavior improvement. Thus, it is up to you to get your program's message across to parents and families: that your program can help their children to grow and develop emotionally, socially, physically, intellectually, in language skills, and creatively, if they—parents and families—support what you are doing. You, in turn, must recognize and support the families in their role in raising their children.

How do you do this? Your turn comes first: you must first recognize the families of your children by accepting them, just as you do their children. You may not understand or even agree with their life styles; that is their business, not yours. Your particular role in accepting your children's families is to support them in their child-rearing. To do this, you must develop a two-way communication with parents and families. You must not only communicate to parents what is happening with their children in your program, but also elicit from them what their expectations are and how you can support what they are trying to achieve.

Two-Way Communication

We often pay mere lip service to the notion that the parents are the child's first and most important teachers, yet it is true. To recognize this fact, we must turn our parent-involvement effort into an interactive process in which we are not the only ones speaking and telling our story. Parents need to communicate to us their goals for their child and their efforts to achieve those goals. This does not mean we should pry into family matters. Again, the focus is on the child. It means we should try to come together on common ground: what is best for their child. We will support them in their efforts and will expect them to support us in ours.

If we find that the two sets of goals are different, we need to find ways to communicate to parents about why we are doing what we are doing, as well as eliciting the same information from them. Parents need to know that their youngster's preschool program will support their efforts to help the child grow and learn and that the program wants their support, too. The program's child-rearing techniques may indeed be different from their own, but the parents need to know that both are acceptable. Child abuse, of course, is not acceptable; but two-way communication with parents involved in child abuse is just as important to help such families correct the situation.

Sometimes the differences focus on behavioral goals. Parents may expect their children to play quietly, sit still and listen to the teacher, or keep their clothes clean. The program, on the other hand, may expect children to become involved with all the activities—both quiet and boisterous ones—to become independent of the teacher, make their own choices, and not to be concerned with keeping clean when it is more important to experience all the activities.

Teachers and parents need to talk about these goals, face-to-face if possible. Set up a time when you can meet with each family. Can one of the parents visit the class, perhaps on a lunch hour if both are working? Can you visit a child's home in the evening? Can parents come to an evening, early morning, or weekend parent group meeting? Can the group meeting be held in an informal location, such as a restaurant, where parents will feel more at ease?

If parents are unaware that young children learn best through exploratory play, you might consider showing a videotape to illustrate such activities. On the other hand, if you learn from parents that limited clothing resources at home make it important that their child keep clean, you will need to find ways to make sure that the child's clothing will not be damaged, and to inform the parents.

SUPPORTS FAMILIES AND
CHILDREN UNDER STRESS

The breakup of families is only one reason many young children are under stress today. Other reasons include hospitalization of themselves or a family member, moving, a parent losing a job, abuse of alcohol or drugs by a family member, the absence of a family member, and the death of a family member. Your contact with families should alert you to any causes of stress within the family, and you should discuss with the family how the program can help their child during such times. Your two-way communication with families can also alert them when you observe children displaying symptoms of stress such as uncharacteristic thumb-sucking, whining or moping around, unusual aggressiveness or tiredness, not eating, or not sleeping at nap time.

Reading books dealing with stress can be therapeutic for children. A fascinating approach to children's stress about moving is *Maggie Doesn't Want to Move* (O'Donnell, 1987) about a boy who uses the excuse that his baby sister doesn't want to move to express his own concerns. Parents are absent from home for many reasons these days. In *My Mom Travels a Lot* (Bauer, 1981), a little girl expresses the good things and the bad things about her mother being away from home. In *Dear Daddy* . . . (Dupasquier, 1985), a little girl writes a letter to her father away from home on a ship. The illustrations on every page show both the child at home and the father on the ship. *First Pink Light* (Greenfield, 1976) is a sensitive story about Tyree who tries to stay awake all night to greet his father who is returning at the "first pink light."

Overcoming grief and anguish caused by the death of a loved one cannot really be accomplished by reading a book to a child. The sensitive books now written about children experiencing death of animal pets and beloved family members are better used long after the experience, when time has begun to heal the child's loss.

Your most helpful response to any kind of stress in children may be your acceptance of them in bad times as well as good, your display of that acceptance with smiles, hugs, concerned inquiries, and your re-directing them into activities to take their minds away from the stressful situation for a while.

SUMMARY

Families can become involved in program activities in a variety of ways. They can visit the classroom to assist the staff in daily activities, field trips, or making materials. They can share with the children a song, a story, or a cultural practice. They can serve on committees or policy councils. It is up to the classroom staff to make the initial contact with families and arrange for them to visit or participate. The focus should be on the child, and it should be positive. Parents can be encouraged to volunteer their services, but then the staff needs to assist and support the volunteer parents through discussion and the assignment of specific tasks.

The program and staff need to recognize and support families of non-traditional make-up such as single-parent families, blended families, and culturally diverse families. When both parents work, teachers need to arrange meetings at times convenient for the family. Two-way, face-to-face communication is important for both the program and the family to understand the goals each has for the child involved. It is just as important for the child's development to have the family support the program with enthusiasm as it is for the program to support the child. When children are under stress because of hospitalization, absence of family members, parents' loss of job, or death in the family, the teacher can be supportive by reading therapeutic stories in some instances, having patience with the child's out-of-sorts behavior, and expressing the deepest concern and care for the child in bad times as well as good.

LEARNING ACTIVITIES

1. Read Chapter 11, "Promoting Family Involvement," and answer Question Sheet 11–A.
2. View Videopak F, "Preschool Book Experience," and answer Question Sheet 11–B.
3. Read one or more of the Suggested Readings and add 10 cards to your file with specific ideas for helping parents become involved in the preschool classroom. Include a reference source on the back of each card.
4. Communicate with a parent using an idea from this chapter that focuses on his child.
5. Get a parent involved in the program as a classroom volunteer and work with the parent in a classroom area she feels comfortable with. (Trainer can observe.)
6. Talk face-to-face with a family member about a child from a culturally diverse, single-parent, or blended family. Find out what the family's goals are for the child, and talk about the program's goals with the family member.
7. Put on a program at the center that parents can attend, with parents having input into what should be presented or being involved in working on the program in some way. (Trainer can attend.)
8. Read a book to a child or small group to help relieve stress from one of the factors discussed in this chapter. Record the results.
9. Complete the Chapter 11 Evaluation Sheet and return it to your trainer or college supervisor.

QUESTION SHEET 11–A

(Based on Chapter 11, "Promoting Family Involvement")

1. Why do preschool programs with strong parent involvement have the longest-lasting positive effects on their children?
2. What are some of the ways a parent can become involved in a preschool classroom?
3. How can the teacher help get parents involved?
4. Why should you have a staggered entrance process at the beginning of the school year?

5. How can you set up home visits without seeming threatening to parents?

6. How can you involve parents in volunteering in the classroom?

7. How can you get parent support of your program from a single-parent, blended, or culturally diverse family?

8. What does two-way communication in the parent-involvement process mean, and how can you get it started?

9. What should you do if you find that the program's goals and the parent's goals for their child are different?

10. How can children's books support children under stress?

QUESTION SHEET 11–B

(Based on Videopak F, "Preschool Book Experience")

1. How early in a child's life should a parent begin reading to the child?

2. What difference does it make whether the parents begin at this time?

3. What do parents need to know about children to choose good books for them?

4. What books might appeal to young children on the basis of their self-centeredness?

5. Name several books with fun words and phrases that children enjoy repeating.

6. Since young children like to pretend, what types of books appeal to them?

7. Why do young children respond so well to family stories?

8. Name several books that are short enough to hold the children's attention.

9. What could parents do with books besides read them to their children?

10. If parents wanted to convert favorite book characters to a flannel board activity, how could they do it?

SUGGESTED READINGS

Berger, E. H. (1991). *Parents as partners in education: The school and home working together* (3rd ed.). Columbus, OH: Merrill.

Endsley, R. C., & Bradbard, M. R. (1981). *Quality day care: A handbook of choices for parents and caregivers.* Englewood Cliffs, NJ: Prentice-Hall.

Greenberg, P. (1989). Parents as partners in young children's development and education: A new American fad? Why does it matter? *Young Children, 44*(4) 61–75.

Gestwicki, C. (1987). *Home, school, and community relations: A guide to working with parents.* Albany, NY: Delmar Publishers.

Honig, A. S. (1979). *Parent involvement in early childhood education.* Washington, DC: National Association for the Education of Young Children.

Larrick, N. (1982). *A parent's guide to children's reading.* New York: Bantam.

Maples, M. K. (1985). *Steps to CDA for home visitors.* Elmira, NY: McGraw Bookstore, Elmira College.

Murphy, A. T. (1981). *Special children, special parents.* Englewood Cliffs, NJ: Prentice-Hall.

Taylor, D., & Strickland, D. S. (1986). *Family storybook reading.* Portsmouth, NH: Heinemann.

CHILDREN'S BOOKS

Bauer, C. F. (1981). *My mom travels a lot.* New York: Frederick Warne.

Caines, J. (1977). *Daddy.* New York: Harper & Row.

Dupasquier, P. (1985). *Dear Daddy . . .* New York: Viking Penguin.

Greenfield, E. (1976). *First pink light.* New York: Thomas Y. Crowell.

Hines, A. G. (1986). *Daddy makes the best spaghetti.* New York: Clarion Books/Ticnor & Fields.

Lewin, H. (1981). *Jafta's father.* Minneapolis: Carolrhoda Books.

Lewin, H. (1981). *Jafta's mother.* Minneapolis: Carolrhoda Books.

O'Donnell, E. L. (1987). *Maggie doesn't want to move.* New York: Macmillan.

Stolz, M. (1988). *Storm in the night.* New York: Harper & Row.

Walter, M. P. (1983). *My mama needs me.* New York: Lothrop, Lee & Shepard Books.

Williams, V. B. (1982). *A chair for my mother.* New York: Greenwillow Books.

VIDEOTAPES

Beaty, J. J. (Producer). (1979). Preschool book experience (Videopak F), *Skills for preschool teachers* [videotape]. Elmira, NY: McGraw Book Store, Elmira College.

National Association for the Education of Young Children (Producer). *Partnerships with parents* [videotape]. Washington, DC: NAEYC.

South Carolina Educational TV (Producer). *Communication with parents. Promises* [videotape]. Columbia, SC: SCETV.

CHAPTER 11 EVALUATION SHEET
PROMOTING FAMILY INVOLVEMENT

1. Student _____

2. Trainer _____

3. Center where training occurred _____

4. Beginning date _____ Ending date _____

5. Describe what student did to accomplish General Objective

   _____

   _____

6. Describe what student did to accomplish Specific Objectives

   Objective 1 _____

   _____

   Objective 2 _____

   _____

   Objective 3 _____

   _____

7. Evaluation of student's Learning Activities
        (Trainer Check One)   (Student Check One)

   _____ Highly superior performance   _____

   _____ Superior performance   _____

   _____ Good performance   _____

   _____ Less than adequate performance   _____

Signature of Trainer: Signature of Student:

_____   _____

Comments:

12 Providing Program Management

General Objective

To develop an effective early childhood classroom program based on the needs of individuals.

Specific Objectives

- ☐ Uses a team approach to plan a flexible classroom schedule.
- ☐ Uses transitions and small group activities to accomplish the goals of the program.
- ☐ Plans for individual needs based on child observation and interpretation.

Daily Planning

Managing any program calls, first of all, for planning on the part of those who will carry it out. The keynote of daily planning in early childhood programs is balance. You need to make plans to accommodate a group of 15 to 20 lively youngsters, at the same time meeting their particular individual needs. Children need time to let off steam as well as periods of quiet relaxation. They need to develop large motor abilities but also the fine skill of eye-hand coordination. They should be exposed to total group doings, but not at the neglect of small group activities. While the children may be indoors for most of the day, outdoor needs must still be met. And all these activities should flow smoothly from one to the other so that children will feel the satisfying rhythm of a well-planned day.

How do you do it? If you have arranged your classroom according to the ideas in Chapter 3, you have already begun. The physical arrangement of the room indicates what activities are available and how many children can participate in each.

Is planning, then, merely a matter of scheduling time? That, of course, is part of the planning process, but there is so much more. First, planning involves knowing your children—knowing what they are like as a group and how they differ as individuals. It involves learning how they feel at different times of the day.

Take the first half hour in the morning, for instance. Do your children walk or ride to the center? Do they come bursting in from a bus as a mob or straggling in one by one with mothers in tow? Are they sleepy, cranky, hungry, or happy? What happens during the first half hour in the morning? What would you like to have happen during that time?

Goals

What goals do you have for the entire group of children for a single day? For part of the day? What special goals do you have for individuals?

Your goal for the group may be something like "helping the children learn to work and play together in harmony;" a goal for a certain part of the day may be "to improve nap time so that non-sleepers don't disturb sleepers." Your individual goals may be many and varied, for example, "helping Trish come out of her shell and respond to the other children and activities around her."

These are merely ideas. You need to organize and express your goals concretely to implement them. Others on your classroom team need to become aware of them. You need to know what others have in mind. You need to convert all goals into specific plans for the day or even for the year.

USES A TEAM APPROACH TO PLAN A FLEXIBLE CLASSROOM SCHEDULE

Team Planning

Everyone on the classroom team must be aware of how daily plans are made, when they are made, and who is involved. If you are the teacher, you realize that, for daily plans to be made and carried out, everyone on the team must participate. Participation in carrying out goals is much more effective if the participants take part in the planning. If you are an assistant or volunteer, you realize that the effectiveness of your contribution to the program depends on your input in planning the activities you are responsible for.

No single person in an early childhood classroom can or should do everything. Successful management of the program depends as much on the interpersonal relations and cooperation of the staff as on any other element. Balance is the key here, too, as the entire staff becomes involved in daily planning.

The teacher is the leader by definition, and therefore needs to take the lead in encouraging other team members to express their ideas and concerns. The lead teacher must not dominate nor allow others to dominate. The leader should ask for suggestions from the others and give them responsibility to carry out activities without interference. The assistants, on the other hand, must be willing to take on that responsibility and offer suggestions.

Assistants should be responsible along with the lead teacher for observing individual children and recording pertinent information. Teachers should involve assistants in ordering equipment and supplies, ask them to attend parent conferences and make home visits, and place them in charge of small groups. Teachers and assistants alike should participate in set-up and clean-up; the teacher should not relegate these duties to an assistant while occupying herself with more "important" activities. *Teamwork* means that the teaching team shares all the responsibilities of the classroom. When teamwork operates effectively, a visitor will not be able to tell who is the teacher and who are the assistants.

Good interpersonal communication makes teamwork possible. An effective team recognizes that the leader has overall responsibility, but is willing to work together toward a common goal. Each member trusts and respects the others, so that when things go wrong, team members are able to communicate problems and resolve them in a friendly atmosphere.

Overcoming Team Problems

Problems will occur from time to time. When two or more people work closely in the same room for long periods of time, it is only natural that they will have occasional problems. It is the responsibility of the team to take time to resolve such problems. When problems arise, the team should choose someone from the program to lead an informal dialog. This could be the program director, the educational coordinator, the family worker, or anyone else the team agrees upon. Guidelines for such a dialog include:

1. Giving attention to nonverbal communication
   a. Keeping eye contact
   b. Using a pleasant tone of voice
   c. Watching body language
2. Giving attention to verbal communication
   a. Using two-way conversation
   b. Avoiding educational jargon
   c. Speaking in non-judgmental terms
3. Using written communication
   a. Stating the problem in non-judgmental terms
   b. Asking pertinent questions
   c. Giving helpful information
4. Using listening skills
   a. Keeping an open mind
   b. Listening carefully to all sides
   c. Trying to determine what important facts have been left unstated
5. Coming to a closure
   a. Summarizing what has been covered
   b. Stating what has been agreed upon
   c. Describing what will be done and by whom
6. Having a follow-up session
   a. Describing what has been done
   b. Deciding on its effectiveness
   c. Determining further actions

Programs that schedule regular monthly team sessions are often able to resolve problems successfully. At these sessions, all team members are asked to contribute in a positive manner, following the guidelines above. Before the scheduled session, the leader asks each team member to hand in a brief written note listing three items:

1. A positive action or accomplishment of the team during the past month
2. An area of concern needing discussion and/or some kind of action
3. A question regarding the team approach

The leader reads these notes and prepares for the session, keeping in mind the need for a positive orientation. These sessions should follow up on concerns that surfaced the month before, but they can also become problem-solving and brain-storming sessions. To set the tone, the leader begins the session by sharing the positive accomplishments that team members listed in their notes. Teams who have used this approach find that the act of writing down "areas of concern" helps to diffuse emotional issues and state the case in objective terms. Having meetings like this on a monthly basis rather than when problems arise also helps to prevent interpersonal problems from developing into major communication breakdowns.

Scheduling Planning Sessions

Some staffs spend the last 15 minutes of each day to plan for the next day. It is unusual for a staff to schedule an early morning planning period, because they need to set up activities for the day and greet early arrivers. The most common time for planning sessions seems to be Friday afternoon, at which time the staff puts together daily plans for the week to follow.

In some programs, planning is more informal. A teacher may say, "We just do not have time to get together as a team, so I make up the ideas for things as I go along. I tell the others what their responsibilities are."

This teacher needs to listen to the way the director of an especially well-run day care center might respond: "My staff does not have the time either, but we feel so strongly about the importance of planning together that we take the time. We ask a mother to come in once a week and sit with the napping children while we plan, or we arrange for a senior citizen volunteer to come in and read the children a story. We feel that if we do not plan for something to happen, then nothing will happen as we want it to in our classroom. Since we started team planning, everyone is so much happier. The staff understands their responsibilities so much better. They are much more eager to carry out activities with the children, because they have contributed to the planning. Even the children are happier because of the staff's enthusiasm. We've never accomplished so much with children as we have since we started regular staff planning sessions."

Using Time Blocks

A simple but effective way many programs schedule activities is in the form of time blocks. Time blocks are periods of time of unspecified length that occur at approximately the same time every day, but with flexibility within each to allow for many things to happen. The time blocks used in many programs include:

arrival	nap time
free choice (AM)	snack time (PM)
snack time (AM)	free choice (PM)
playground	circle time
rest time (AM)	departure
lunch time	

If yours is a half-day program, your departure might occur after lunch. If your half-day schedule does not include lunch, you could substitute circle time for rest time, after which the children would depart.

The length of each time block as well as the order in which you schedule it depends on your goals, your children's needs, and daily circumstances.

The advantages for using time blocks include, first of all, flexibility. Their length can vary, although their order will remain the same. For example, arrival may take about 15 minutes every morning. But occasionally the bus will be late, so arrival time may stretch to 30 minutes or more. You may decide to omit the free-choice period entirely on such occasions and go immediately out to the playground. Since the children have been cooped up on the bus so long, they might need to get out in the open where they can release their pent-up energy. Another day, you may find the children are just too restless for circle time. What they need instead is a run around the playground.

In other words, time blocks do not tie you to specific times. Rather, they refer to activities and their sequential order. Their flexibility frees you and your staff to plan for a variety of activities within a certain block. It does not lock you into the kind of schedule that dictates: "Snack Time, 10 a.m." All you know about snack time is that it follows the playground time block, however long that should last. The two time blocks might even occur simultaneously if you decide to serve the juice outside on a hot day.

A second advantage of time blocks is their built-in balance. You can easily alternate contrasting kinds of activities simply by the order in which you schedule the particular time blocks.

Just as important is the stability your program acquires through the use of time blocks. The same periods tend to occur in about the same order every day. This promotes a sense of security among the children. Young children need this kind of structure that they can understand and that makes them feel comfortable to enjoy a variety of activities.

Finally, time blocks provide a simple system of program management for classroom workers. Their use is especially helpful to part-time volunteers, who are much more at ease with a daily schedule they can readily understand and become comfortable with.

Let us look at each of the time blocks one by one, as we would use them to plan a daily program according to our goals.

Arrival

"Helping the children learn to work and play together in harmony" was one program's daily goal. To accomplish it, the staff first looked at each time block to see:

1. What elements promote the goal
2. What elements hinder the goal
3. What changes need to be made

In reviewing their present morning arrival time block, the staff noted that their 17 children came from two separate neighborhoods. About half of them walked to the center or were driven by their parents between 8:30 a.m. and 9:00 a.m. The others came by bus in a group between 8:50 a.m. and 9:00 a.m. The teachers were on hand to greet each child individually, although they found this difficult when all the children from the bus came swarming in at one time.

As the staff reviewed the arrival period, they decided that the most helpful element was greeting children individually and having a brief conversation. The obvious negative element was the crowd of bus children arriving all at once. What began harmoniously with the walkers soon dissolved into bedlam. The staff decided to try having some individual activities on hand that would promptly separate the children after they burst into the room as a crowd.

Their most successful effort along this line turned out to be a two-part activity involving "tickets and crowns." The tickets sorted out the children, and the crowns made the center a fun place to come every morning. The staff made a cardboard name ticket for each child. Every morning the tickets were placed in some part of the room, usually on a table, for children to find when they entered. When children presented their tickets, the teachers would give them cutout paper crowns to wear, along with a cheery greeting, "Hello, it's nice to see you this morning!" The children so enjoyed this activity that it evolved into their making various headpieces for morning greeting time: Native American hats, paper soldier hats, and even headbands.

Another teacher resolved the morning mass-arrival woes by taking a photograph of each child, fastening a tab hook at the top, and hanging it on a pegboard. When a child arrived, he would find his picture and then hang it on the Job for a Day Chart next to the job he wanted. Then he would go to the teacher for his greeting and directions on his job. For instance, the job of "Zoo Keeper" might mean "feed the guinea pig."

Some teachers use books to make a connection between a child's home and the center, as discussed in Chapter 11. Morning arrival time might then become a book check-in time as well as an individualized greeting time for the child.

Once you have assessed your arrival time block on the basis of elements that promote your daily goal for children and those that hinder the goal's accomplishment, you should be able to institute changes that will make your center an exciting place to enter every day of the year.

Free Choice (A.M.)

Most programs schedule a free-choice period immediately after arrival. This is a natural follow-up because so many of the children are already involved in block building, dramatic play, and other permanent activities. This time block differs from arrival-time free play only in the expanded number of activities available. Each classroom staff member is responsible for a different planned activity, such as a table of dough, rolling pins, and cookie cutters; a table of yarn and uncooked macaroni for stringing necklaces; a portable climber and mats for jumping; a table of vegetable

To plan for individual children, it is necessary to observe and record their behavior looking for areas of strength and needs.

scrapers, carrots, celery, mayonnaise, and ketchup for making snacks and dips; a table of torn paper, buttons, paper clips, and glue for collages; story reading with puppets for a small group; or any of the many other special activities the adult staff has planned for the children.

In light of your daily goal of "helping children learn to work and play together in harmony," the staff needs to identify elements in the free-choice period that promote this goal and those that hinder its accomplishment.

You may decide that your free-choice period's most important strength is the number and quality of activities available daily, while its principal hindrance is getting the children involved in favorite activities without a fuss. Too often children insist on participating in favorite activities at the same time, and soon a squabble ensues. In such a case, you need either to make changes in the way children select an activity, or to offer more variations of favorite activities.

First, decide which are the favorite activities. You can identify these at staff planning sessions. For example, cooking and water play were identified in one classroom. Many children had trouble waiting for turns when those activities were set up. One solution was to have three tables of the favorite activity going at the same time. Set up three tables instead of one for cooking. Each table can then feature the same type of cooking activity, or each can be different, for instance, making cherry gelatin with banana slices, lemon gelatin with pineapple chunks, and orange gelatin with mandarin orange sections. Measuring out the portions can provide just enough of the gelatin fruit dessert for the whole class.

It is no more difficult for a staff to set up three of the same type of activity than three different ones. In fact, it is really an excellent way to extend learning experiences. One water activity could be to explore which things float and which sink; another could be to dissolve different food colors and pour the colored water through funnels into plastic bottles; a third activity might be to put detergent into a dishpan full of water and whip it into suds with an eggbeater.

Children can regulate their own movement from one activity to another during the free-choice period in a number of ways. When one child leaves his chair, another can take it. Or you can give out color-coded tickets for each activity which the children can trade with one another. Another possibility is to fasten four hooks, card pockets, or pegs in each area for children to hang name tags on; when a hook is empty, another child may hang his tag on it to join in. You may want to set up these same activities for several days running, until all the children have had their chance at every activity.

How long should the morning free-choice period last? It may vary from day to day, depending on the children's involvement or restlessness. If children are working and playing in harmony, it can last much of the morning. You and your staff can decide daily.

Snack Time (A.M./P.M.)

Snack time in the early childhood classroom may be a group or individual activity, depending on the preferences of the teacher, staff, and children. Most programs have snacks as a total group experience in the middle of the morning. Many teachers think that young children need the nourishment, and that it is good to come together as a group at some point after working individually or in small groups. Others believe that children themselves should determine when to snack and how much they need to eat. Instead of setting up tables for a total group snack, they make a "snack bar" available on a single table for much of the morning, encouraging children to use it whenever they want. Their rationale is a reluctance to pull children away from activities they are deeply involved in.

The same considerations apply to afternoon snack time. If the children take a long nap, you may want to have a snack ready for them when they awaken. The snack will give them a chance to re-orient themselves to their surroundings after a deep sleep. If your snack time has not been all that harmonious, ask the children themselves how they would like snack time to be organized.

Playground

Scheduling this time block depends primarily on the children and their circumstances. Are they city children who seldom get a chance to play outside? Do they come every day from long distances on a bus? If so, you may want to schedule a playground period after arrival. This gives bus children a chance to let off steam, and restless children an opportunity to expend their energy in a constructive way. Some teachers like to schedule playground first because the children already have on their outside clothing, making it easier and less time consuming for the dressing-undressing ritual. Otherwise, playground is usually scheduled toward the end of the morning.

One team found that the main hindrance to the playground period was that all three of the center's classes were outside at the same time, creating turn-taking squabbles over equipment. The simple solution was for the three teams to meet together and decide on alternating their playground time blocks.

Rest Time (A.M.)

The decision to have a rest time in the morning depends on how early the children arrive and how active they are during the morning. Some programs have a quiet time just after juice, when lights are turned off and the children put their heads down on the tables. Do your children need this? They may if they have been outside playing for half an hour or more. Without a physical workout, however, rest period can be a waste. If the teachers find themselves spending most of the rest period trying to make the children rest, it hardly seems that they need it.

Some programs choose to have "mat time" instead, just after the most active time block. Rather than put their heads down, the children sit quietly on single rugs or mats which they place somewhere in the room. Here they read a book, work on a puzzle, or play with a toy by themselves. Books and toys for mat time are kept on a special cart and brought out just for this period.

Lunch Time

Does your lunch time arrangement fulfill the daily goal of "helping children work and play together in harmony?" What are its strong points? How can it be improved? Most programs consider eating together family-style in the classroom to be one of the most beneficial ways to enjoy lunch time. Teachers, assistants, volunteers, and visitors sit at the tables with the children, sharing food and conversation. It is a time of enjoyment and relaxation.

Most children love to eat, and even the reluctant eaters find it hard to resist when everyone around them is so completely involved. The wise classroom staff keeps rules to a minimum, discourages nagging and pressure, and promotes a happy atmosphere at the table. Dessert is a nutritious part of the meal, not a reward or bribe for "cleaning your plate."

Children feel good when adults sit next to them at the table and eat the same type of food. They feel even better when adults converse with them as equals. Fascinating information about children's understandings of themselves and their world emerges from lunch-time conversations.

Public schools sometimes require early childhood programs to use the school cafeteria. Alert your staff to the potential difficulties with this arrangement. A noisy cafeteria full of older youngsters presents an intimidating atmosphere for 3- and 4-year-olds, not at all conducive to relaxed eating. If the children must go through the regular cafeteria line, they often receive portions much too large for them to handle and, as a result, end up eating very little. Furthermore, the time pressure to finish up and move out quickly achieves the opposite result. Some programs in these circumstances have been able to arrange with the cafeteria staff to have the food sent to their rooms for family-style eating. School officials will usually cooperate once they understand the situation.

Nap Time

Another of our goals for a particular part of the day was "to improve nap time so that non-sleepers don't disturb sleepers." If yours is an all-day program, you will need to schedule a nap period in the afternoon after lunch. Some children can hardly function without their regular afternoon nap. Others, however, will not need a nap; for them, lying quietly for an hour or so in the same room with sleepers is nearly impossible. Some provision needs to be made for them.

If your center has more than one classroom, you may be able to arrange to use one as the sleeping room and another for non-sleepers. The focus, even for non-sleepers, should be on quiet solitary activities, with the rest of the room sectioned off.

If you have only one room, you can reserve a section for non-sleepers where they can play quietly on mats without disturbing the sleepers. Perhaps the block corner can serve this purpose, if it is well sectioned off. Have a tray, box, or special cart of materials available to the children in this area. If you talk to them in a low voice or whisper, you will soon find the children imitating you. If you have no other means of separating sleepers from non-sleepers, cut apart a large cardboard packing carton and unfold it for a divider.

How do you get children to go to sleep successfully? Some will be ready with no effort on your part, while others will need help relaxing. Dimming the lights or pulling the shades is a signal many will respond to. If you have no shades, use pieces of cardboard to block the windows. A drowsy song on the record player may help. Your reading a story in a low, monotonous voice adds a calming effect. Some children are afraid to let themselves fall asleep in a place other than their bedroom. They may need individual reassurance such as a gentle rub on the back.

Free Choice (P.M.)

How much time is available in your program between children waking up from a nap until their departure? A half hour? An hour? Some activities should be available to children during this late-afternoon time block. Most programs rely on their regular room equipment, but some insist that children not get out all the blocks or dress-up clothes at this time. These restrictions tend to be more for the convenience of adults than for children. You can justify such restrictions as long as you provide interesting substitute activities for the children. Activities different from those in the morning are best.

The answer may be a table with a different kind of art from that available in the morning, or one with different puzzles or manipulative games saved for afternoon play. If you have not used your water or sand table in the morning, this can be an excellent time to open it. You can make this time block both convenient for you and enticing for the children if you and your staff use your imaginations during planning sessions.

Circle Time

Half-day programs often schedule circle time just before lunch or departure. Full-day programs often schedule theirs at the conclusion of the day. The purpose is to pull together the daily happenings and help the children make sense of them. "What did you do this morning, Karen, that you liked best of all?" If teachers listen carefully to children's answers, they can gain valuable insights about the activities that made the greatest or the least impression on the children, and why.

For programs that like to conduct music or story reading in a total group situation, this may be the appropriate time. Invite parents or other special visitors to take part. Guitar players or storytellers might put in an appearance, or the teacher might demonstrate a new game or introduce a puppet who wants to talk with the children.

Circle time should be shorter than most other time blocks because of preschool children's short attention spans and their restlessness in large group situations. Assistants and volunteers can act as listening models for the children to imitate.

Departure

A good ending is as essential as a good beginning. Children need to feel satisfied about the day they have just finished before they can look forward with pleasure to the next. The staff should be on hand to help children prepare to go home. Helping children dress and supporting them in their own efforts, conversing about what they have done during the day, checking out a book or a toy, greeting parents who pick up their children, saying a final farewell and a "See you tomorrow!" — these should be pleasurable activities for all involved. If you have planned well, departure time will signal the end of a happy, satisfying day.

Recording Daily Schedule

You need to write down your daily plans, not as an exercise to please an administrator, but for you and your staff to use. This practice will keep you on target, help you remember what you planned to do, and help staff members keep track of their roles. The plan shown in Table 12.1 involves three staff members: Betty, the teacher, Karen, an assistant, and Pat, a volunteer. The tables referred to are in the art and manipulative areas, the checklist refers to an individual assessment tool to be discussed later. This schedule shows 2 days of the week as planned by the staff on the previous Friday afternoon.

USES TRANSITIONS AND SMALL GROUP ACTIVITIES TO ACCOMPLISH THE GOALS OF THE PROGRAM

Management also involves helping children move from one activity to another with ease. Ordering young children around does not work, nor should it. If we allow the children to choose their own small group activities, we need to involve them in changing from one activity to the next on their own as well. Transition games, songs, and stories allow this to happen. Every preschool teacher needs a repertoire of such activities to use to help children move from free choice to pickup, from snack to playground, or from circle time to departure.

Transitional Activities

Transitional activities might include any of the following, some of which can be made up on the spot, while others are learned from books. Every preschool teacher should collect a card file of them.

Name games
Concept games
Songs
Finger plays
Action chants
Stories
Pick-up games
Follow-the-leader

Name Games

Name games are always popular with children because they love anything that focuses attention on them and their name. While children are waiting for lunch to begin, to go

TABLE 12.1 Daily Schedule

		Monday	Tuesday

Week: October 10
Goal: Better harmony in children's work/play

Theme: Animal pets
Follow up: Apples (last week's theme)

	Monday	Tuesday
Arrival	*Betty:* headbands with animal ears for "check-in" *Pat:* large motor at loft *Karen:* help at cubbies	*Betty:* check in books *Pat:* large motor at loft *Karen:* help at cubbies
Work/Play	(no water table today)	*Pat:* sand table with animal toys
Table 1	*Pat:* cooking—cut apples from field trip; make applesauce	*Betty:* art—coloring with crayons on sandpaper animals
Table 2	*Karen:* collage—from torn paper	*Karen:* sorting squares of materials into boxes
Snack	Cut apples from cooking Milk, crackers	Apple cider and doughnuts
Playground	*Pat:* outside with children *Betty:* checklist observation of Trish	*Karen:* outside with children *Betty:* checklist
Circle	*Karen:* on top of loft with box of kittens from home	*Betty:* under loft with guitar and songs about animals
Lunch	Applesauce from cooking for dessert	Cal's birthday cupcakes
Nap	*Karen:* on loft; read *Pet Show, Curious George* to non-sleepers	*Karen:* on loft; read *Harry, the Dirty Dog,* more *Curious George*
Work/Play	*Betty:* checklist	*Betty:* turtle and books on science table
Table 1	Snack	Snack
Table 2	*Pat:* magazines; cut out animal pictures	*Karen:* sand table
Departure	*Betty:* check out books	*Betty:* check out books
Special Needs	Trish needs support	Trish needs support
Remember	Bring sand, sandpaper, cupcakes	Check on lunches for field trip to animal shelter

outside, or for the bus to come, the teacher can start a name game. One is "Do What the Rhyme Says," in which the teacher says a rhyme about a child's name, telling the child to perform an action. First, the named child does it, then everyone does it. For example:

Billy, Billy,	Sheila, Sheila,
Dressed in blue,	With long hair,
See if you can	Raise your hand
Touch your shoe.	High in the air.
Chris, Chris,	Larry, Larry,
Dressed in brown,	Act like a clown,
See if you can	Jump very quickly
Turn around.	Up and down.

If the named child does not respond, name another child and mention the same action. Make 3-by-5-inch cards with enough rhymes for everyone in your class.

Concept Games

Concept games also involve individual children. Teachers use them to send one child at a time to the next activity, which helps spur the others to get ready for that activity. For instance:

The boy with the red shirt
May go to lunch.

The girl with the blue dress
May get on the bus.

The children who can hold up three fingers
May take a seat.

The children who can make a triangle with their fingers
May sit down for juice.

Finger Plays, Chants

You will also want to invest in a song book and a finger play book to give you more ideas. *Eye Winker Tom Tinker Chin Chopper* (Glazer, 1973) features musical finger plays with guitar chords and finger directions. Old favorites include: "The Wheels on the Bus," "Bingo," "On Top of Spaghetti," "This Old Man," and "Where is Thumbkin?" Finger plays without music are featured in the excellent book *Finger Frolics* (Cromwell, 1976), or you can make up your own:

Caterpillar

Crawl, crawl, caterpillar,	(fingers crawl in air)
Munch, munch, munch;	(fingers chew like mouth)

Chew, chew, caterpillar,	
What's for lunch?	(hold hands in question)
Spin, spin, caterpillar,	(wind hands)
Sway, sway, sway;	(sway hands)
Stretch, stretch, butterfly,	(arms over head)
Fly away!	(arms flap)

Action chants are finger plays done standing in place with the whole body. Again, you can make up your own to suit the occasion:

Lunch Time
Lunch time,	
Munch time,	
Can you wait?	(Jump up and down)
Brunch time,	
Crunch time,	
Don't be late!	(Shake finger)
Here's your table,	
Take a seat,	(Squat down)
Clap your hands,	
IT'S TIME TO EAT!	(Jump up and clap)

Stories

While you wait for children to assemble, you might consider telling a story as a transitional activity to those who have already gathered around you. It is sure to speed up the others as well. You could start with a spooky "tale without an end" done in a deep whisper:

> It was a dark and stormy night. Three robbers sat around the fire. The captain said, "Shorty, tell us a story." So Shorty began: "It was a dark and stormy night. Three robbers. . ."

It is fun for you and the children to make up stories as you go along. Start with a sentence, "On my way to school this morning I was walking along the street when, all of a sudden, I saw something funny. It was a. . . ." You can make up funny, strange, or spooky happenings, or let each child add his or her own idea to the story. If you can't think of something to say, describe the things you really saw that morning, but have them all moving backwards, or upside down, or flying.

Pickup Games

Pickup games are the best way to involve children in picking up blocks, toys on the floor, or clothes in the housekeeping corner. You won't need to scold anyone for not helping with pickup when you do it as a game. In the block corner, you can pretend a large block is a bulldozer that shoves all the other blocks over to the shelves. The block shelves can be a hungry monster that must be fed with blocks. Or you can start an assembly line of children across the room to the shelves and pass the blocks from one to the other until the floor is cleared. Or, you might play a record and see if everyone can clear the floor before it finishes. Or have the children be creatures from outer space who like to eat toys. Use your imagination and the children's to make pickup seem like a game.

Follow-the-Leader Games

Follow-the-leader games can also help with pickup or serve as a transition to move children from one place to another. Have the children follow you around the room in a line, doing what you are doing, for example, picking up items as they weave in and out through the activity areas. This activity is also a fun and effective way to gather up children on the playground when it is time to go inside.

Importance of Small Groups

Because our primary concern in the preschool classroom is for the individual child to grow and develop, we need to structure the organization of the classroom into groups of a size that will not overpower a child. The total group of 15 to 20 children is too large for most preschoolers. These highly self-centered beings, with their demands for exclusive attention, truly feel lost in a group of that size. As a result, they often resort to negative attention-getting devices, or they withdraw.

To help them learn the social skills of taking turns and waiting their turns, as discussed in Chapter 9, the group size needs to be small enough so children do not have to wait inordinate amounts of time. You can also accommodate individual needs much more easily in a small group. In addition, the role of the adult in managing the class becomes easier with small groups, rather than the total group. Because preschool classrooms have at least two, possibly three adult team members, one person can easily be in charge of each group.

Number of Groups

How many groups should you have? That will depend on your particular circumstances. An ideal size is four or five children to a group; thus, you may decide to have three or possibly four groups. If you want an adult in charge of each, the number of classroom staff will have a bearing as well. You also need to take into account the amount of space you have. Three groups may fit well into your classroom size, but four may be too many.

Size of Groups

Each group need not be the same size as the others. Groups can be formed for a variety of reasons, and should not be considered permanent. You may have room for six children to work in a cooking activity one day, while three work with play dough and five play in the block corner. At another time, you may take five children at a time on a field trip to a store, while your staff stays behind with two other groups of five children each.

Forming Groups

How are the groups formed? If you sincerely want children to become self-confident and self-directed in their learning, you should allow them to choose their own groups. This can be done in various ways. You can set up your room with a certain number of chairs at each table where puzzles or play dough are used. You can use a symbol such as a stick figure for the number of children each activity area can accommodate. You might have four stick figures pasted in the block area, as well as in the book corner and at the water table, for example. This means that children can not only choose their own groups but also change when they wish. This self-regulation adds another stepping-stone to the path of independence your children are building for themselves.

Teacher's Role

The classroom team not only sets up the areas ahead of time, but also decides who will be in charge of each activity, if they feel this is necessary. This does not mean, however, that a teacher should hover over children at the water table during the entire free-choice period. Instead, an adult should play an active role where necessary, and act as an observer or supporter at other times.

For instance, one teacher might read a book to a small group in the book area. Another might supervise a cooking activity while a third adult observes or helps a shy child become involved in dramatic play. On another day, all the activity groups might operate on their own while staff members work with individuals who need help or support. Someone could work on a one-to-one basis with a bilingual child who needs help learning English, or help a handicapped child with a small motor game. Another teacher might keep track of overall supervision to make sure the children's self-regulation is working, and assist if things get out of hand.

Total Group

Is there no place for a total group activity within the daily schedule? Many teachers find it valuable to have the whole group together in a circle time, either when they first come in the morning or at the end of the day just before they leave. As mentioned earlier, children have a chance during this time to talk about things that are meaningful to them, to listen to others, and either to hear about the activities planned for the day or to summarize some of the things they have done. Because their attention span is short, children need for total group activities to be brief.

PLANS FOR INDIVIDUAL NEEDS BASED ON CHILD OBSERVATION AND INTERPRETATION

In our discussion of goals, an example of a specific individual goal was "helping Trish to come out of her shell and respond to the other children and activities around her."

Many programs have someone like Trish who may need individual assistance to become involved. To help such children, it is first necessary to find out more about them. Is Trish always withdrawn, or only at certain times? Does she respond to any of the children? Which ones? Any staff? Does she get involved in any activities on her own? Which ones? When?

To find the answers, someone on the staff must step back and unobtrusively observe the child, giving special attention to the identified needs.

Some programs use a checklist to focus on particular behaviors. The Child Involvement Checklist in Table 12.2 is arranged according to the activity areas found in most early childhood programs. The items are stated in positive terms. The observer checks any item the child performs, and places an *N* before any item for which there is no opportunity to observe. The blanks thus may indicate areas of need.

TABLE 12.2   Child Involvement Checklist

Child's Name _____

Time _____   Date _____

Observer _____

(Check items you see the child performing. Use "N" for "no opportunity to observe.")

1. **Child in classroom**
   - _____ Chooses activity area without a fuss
   - _____ Stays with one activity long enough to complete it
   - _____ Changes from one activity to another without a fuss
   - _____ Plays with other children peacefully
   - ___√___ Handles bathroom routine by himself/herself
   - _____ Retreats to private area only infrequently
2. **Child in block building area**
   - _____ Carries blocks, fills and dumps, doesn't build
   - _____ Builds in flat rows on floor or stacks vertically
   - _____ Makes "bridges" (two blocks with space between connected by third block)
   - _____ Makes "enclosures" (at least four blocks enclosing a space)
   - _____ Makes representations, names buildings, role plays
   - _____ Builds in solitary manner
   - _____ Builds parallel to other child(ren)
   - _____ Builds cooperatively with other child(ren)
   - _____ Follows block building rules/limits without a fuss

TABLE 12.2 (continued)

3. Child in book area

____√____ Shows interest in the pictures in a book

_____ Talks about the pictures

_____ Pretends to read

____√____ Recognizes some words at sight

____√____ Handles books carefully

_____ Asks adults to read to him/her

_____ Uses books in dramatic play

4. Child in dramatic play area

_____ Plays a role (pretends to be someone else)

____√____ Makes believe in regard to inanimate objects (pretends about a thing)

_____ Makes believe in regard to situations and actions (pretends to do something or go somewhere)

_____ Stays with role for at least ten minutes

_____ Interacts with others in his/her role

_____ Uses verbal communication during the role play

5. Child in large motor area

____N____ Balances on a board

____√____ Goes up and down steps easily

____√____ Runs without falling

____√____ Climbs easily

____√____ Gets down from high places easily

____√____ Jumps with both feet over an object

____√____ Rides wheeled equipment with ease

____N____ Throws a ball/beanbag

____N____ Catches a ball/beanbag

6. Child in manipulative area

____√____ Stacks objects with ease

____N____ Fastens and unfastens buttons

____N____ Fastens and unfastens zippers

____N____ Threads objects on a string

____N____ Laces shoes or a lacing frame

____√____ Makes puzzles easily

____√____ Traces around an object

____√____ Crayons inside a space fairly well

____√____ Stays with activity until finished

TABLE 12.2 (continued)

7. **Child in art area**

___√___ Handles materials without assistance from teachers or other adults

___√___ Paints with brushes

___N___ Does fingerpainting

___N___ Plays with dough/clay

___N___ Cuts well with scissors

___N___ Uses paste or glue appropriately

___N___ Mixes colors with understanding

___N___ Uses materials creatively

8. **Child in music area**

_____ Plays record player without adult help

_____ Sings songs by himself/herself

_____ Sings songs with others

___N___ Participates in movement activities

___N___ Plays rhythm instrument

_____ Shows enjoyment of musical activities

9. **Child in science/math area**

_____ Explores materials in area

_____ Asks questions about materials

___N___ Brings in new materials for area

_____ Uses senses to examine things

_____ Counts materials accurately up to _____

_____ Sorts materials accurately by size, shape, color

_____ Shows understanding of likeness and difference

___N___ Participates in recording/record keeping

_____ Takes care of classroom plants, animals

10. **Child in sand/water area**

_____ Becomes absorbed in sand/water play

_____ Respects established rules or limits

_____ Helps regulate number of children playing

_____ Can share or take turns with classroom materials without too much fuss

_____ Uses sand/water in imaginative ways

_____ Talks abut what he/she is doing

TABLE 12.2 (continued)

11. **Child in woodworking area**

    _____ Handles tools with confidence

    _____ Pounds in nails

    _____ Saws wood

    _____ Makes things out of wood

    _____ Uses vise without help

    _____ Respects rules or limits

12. **Child in cooking area**

    ____N____ Peels or slices fruit or vegetables with knife

    ____N____ Uses utensils with minimum adult help

    ____N____ Uses names of utensils and foods

    ____N____ Understands recipe chart

    ____N____ Talks with others about what he/she is doing

13. **Child in outdoor playground**

    ____√____ Uses swings without adult help

    ____√____ Uses slides with confidence

    ____√____ Climbs to top of monkey bars

    ____√____ Gets down from high places without help

    ____√____ Runs without falling

    _____ Participates with others in play

14. **Child's health condition**

    ____√____ Has good attendance

    ____√____ Is seldom ill

    ____√____ Looks generally healthy

    ____√____ Seldom complains about feeling sick

    ____√____ Goes to sleep at nap time

    ____√____ Eats most of lunch

    ____√____ Does not get tired easily

15. **Child's visual and auditory skills**

    _____ Makes comments or notices new pictures or materials

    ____√____ Recognizes his/her written name

    _____ Plays lotto or visual matching games easily

    _____ Matches things of similar color

    _____ Matches things of similar shape

    _____ Identifies sounds in sound games

    ____√____ Listens to directions

    ____√____ Listens to stories

TABLE 12.2 (continued)

16. **Child's communication skills**
    - _____ Talks with adults
    - _____ Talks with other children
    - ___√___ Talks with animals, dolls, toys
    - ___√___ Adults can understand him/her
    - ___√___ Children can understand him/her
    - ___√___ Uses whole sentences
    - ___√___ Seldom talks "baby talk"
    - ___√___ Talks spontaneously when playing
    - _____ Talks spontaneously at mealtime
    - ___√___ Uses language props such as toy telephone
    - _____ Starts conversations sometimes
    - _____ Expresses his/her feelings in words

17. **Child's self-image**
    - ___√___ Can identify himself/herself by first and last name
    - _____ Looks at you without covering face when you speak to him/her
    - _____ Seeks other children to play with or will join in play when asked by others
    - _____ Seldom shows fear of new or different things
    - ___√___ Is seldom destructive of materials or disruptive of activities
    - _____ Smiles; seems happy much of the time
    - _____ Shows pride in his/her accomplishments
    - _____ Stands up for his/her rights
    - ___√___ Moves confidently with good motor control

18. **Child with others**
    - _____ Gets along well with other children
    - _____ Gets along well with adults
    - ___√___ Is willing to share
    - ___√___ Is willing to take turns
    - _____ Has special friend or friends
    - _____ Plays table games with another child
    - _____ Joins in group games, activities
    - _____ Is willing to help in cleanup
    - ___√___ Seldom shows hostility toward others
    - ___√___ Generally follows rules

Betty, the teacher in an earlier example, scheduled time in her daily activities to observe Trish. Using the Child Involvement Checklist over a period of several days, she recorded the results.

Using Information from the Observation

As she reviewed the results, Betty was surprised to realize how much better Trish seemed to get along on the playground than inside the classrooms. She decided to concentrate on Trish's strong points to help her overcome what seemed to be a lack of confidence, a shyness, or the fact that she was still not at ease inside the classroom. The staff considered several alternatives for Trish, and finally decided on the activities they listed on the Learning Prescription.

Learning Prescription for **Trish B.**   Date **Oct 14**

Areas of Strength and Confidence

1. Large motor activities (especially outside)
2. Language (talks mostly to inanimate objects)
3. Seems to like books, some art, some manipulative

Areas Needing Strengthening

1. Involvement with other children
2. Self image
3. Involvement in classroom activities

Activities to Help

1. Ask Trish to help Helen on climber
2. Give Trish dolls and telephone to take outside
3. Give Trish puppets. Could one of her puppets tell Helen a story?

Since Trish showed confidence on the climber, the staff felt she might be able to help Helen, a newcomer, learn how to use it. They also decided to let her take some of the dramatic play materials outside, where she seemed to feel more comfortable. They hoped she might let some of the other children get involved in her play with the dolls or the phones, which might then lead her to play with the same children inside the classroom. Because Trish talked well with dolls, Betty thought she might feel comfortable talking to someone else through a puppet. Perhaps Trish could tell Helen a story through one of the puppets.

The staff also recorded these ideas under "special needs" on the Daily Schedule to avoid forgetting them. At the next planning session, the staff could decide how successful they had been and what the next step in helping Trish should be. In this way, individual needs can be incorporated into daily plans for the total group.

If this process seems too complex and time-consuming, remember that you are only looking at one child at a time, and that this is the kind of information you need to be able to help that child. Start by observing children with special needs. Later, as you involve them in activities to improve their skills, you can begin to observe the other children, one at a time, as well.

Don't forget, though, that the raw data, that is, the checklist items, should not be shared with anyone other than the classroom team, that it should be kept confidential. It is your interpretation of that data, such as the Learning Prescription, that you should use for your planning and share with others such as parents.

Almost every person who has taken time to observe and record in this manner has been pleasantly surprised at how many new things they learned about a child that they thought they already knew. You need to step back from the ordinary classroom activities to see with the clear eyes of an observer. It is truly worth your while.

SUMMARY

In developing a professional program based on the needs of individuals, you should assess the needs of individual children by using a focused observing and recording technique such as the Child Involvement Checklist. Then you and your staff will need to interpret the results, and make an individual Learning Prescription from your interpretation. This plan can be incorporated into your weekly plans for your entire class, so that the child will not feel singled out and embarrassed by your attention.

In making plans for your program, you and your staff will also need to keep in mind the goals you have set both for the group and for individuals. Daily goals can be carried out by a program that uses time blocks, since these flexible periods can accommodate activities of varying lengths for individuals as well as small groups. Moving children through a daily schedule works more effectively when you use transitional activities such as games, songs, and finger plays between time blocks.

All members of your classroom team, including volunteers, should be involved in the planning process. Then they will be more committed and willing to carry out the plans. When teams themselves encounter communication problems, a leader can bring them together using verbal and non-verbal communication, as well as writing and listening skills, to resolve the problems.

LEARNING ACTIVITIES

1. Read Chapter 12, "Providing Program Management," and answer Question Sheet 12–A.
2. View Videopak B, "Managing the Daily Program," and answer Question Sheet 12–B.
3. Read one or more of the Suggested Readings, and add 10 cards to your file with specific ideas for managing your program more effectively. Include a reference source on the back of each card.
4. Participate in a team planning session to discuss use of time blocks in planning the daily schedule. Record results and prepare a daily schedule for 3 days.
5. Divide the class into small groups with activities for each, using ideas from the chapter and based on previous planning with the classroom team. (Trainer can observe.)
6. Evaluate three of the time blocks of your program as discussed on page 242.
7. Make file cards for 10 new transitional activities. Use one of them with your children. (Trainer can observe.)
8. Observe a child using the Child Involvement Checklist. Interpret the results and make a Learning Prescription for the child.
9. Complete the Chapter 12 Evaluation Sheet and return it to your trainer or college supervisor.

QUESTION SHEET 12–A

(Based on Chapter 12, "Providing Program Management")

1. What should be the roles of the various staff members during the planning process?
2. If interpersonal communication between team members breaks down, how can it be restored?
3. What do you need to know about your children to plan for their arrival?
4. What are time blocks and for what purpose are they used?
5. Should you have a rest time in the morning? How can you decide?
6. What is the purpose of a total group activity such as "circle time"?
7. What are transitions and how can they be used?
8. Why should small groups be set up for most classroom activities?
9. How should the staff members work with the groups they have set up?
10. How can you plan for an individual child with special needs?

QUESTION SHEET 12–B

(Based on Videopak B, "Managing the Daily Program")

1. Why is balance important in planning the daily program?
2. What kinds of balance are apparent in this particular classroom?

3. How does the room set-up facilitate managing the children?

4. How is the free-choice (work/play) time block in this particular program different from the arrival time block?

5. How is the length of the free-choice time block determined?

6. How is the transition from free-choice time to snack time handled in this classroom?

7. How is the transition from wash-up to lunch handled?

8. What happens to non-sleeping children during nap time?

9. How is the afternoon free-choice (work/play) time different from this same time block in the morning?

10. How can you tell if you have planned your daily program successfully?

SUGGESTED READINGS

Beaty, J. J. (1990). *Observing development of the young child* (2nd ed.). Columbus, OH: Merrill.

Carter, M., & Jones, E. (1990). The teacher as observer: The director as role model. *Child Care Information Exchange, (75)* 27–30.

Cartwright, S. (1987). Group endeavor in nursery school can be valuable learning. *Young Children, 42*(5) 8–11.

Caruso, J. J., & Fawcett, M. T. (1986). *Supervision in early childhood education.* New York: Teachers College Press.

Cromwell, L., & Hibner, D. (1976). *Finger frolics.* Livonia, MI: Partner Press.

Glazer, T. (1973). *Eye winker Tom Tinker chin chopper.* Garden City, NY: Doubleday.

Hildebrand, V. (1990). *Management of child development centers* (2nd ed.). New York: Macmillan.

McAfee, O. D. (1985). Circle time: Getting past 'Two little pumpkins.' *Young Children, 40*(6) 24–29.

Nunnelley, J. C. (1990). Beyond turkeys, Santas, snowmen, and hearts: How to plan innovative curriculum themes. *Young Children, 46*(1) 24–29.

Strom, S. (1985). *The human side of child care administration.* Washington, DC: National Association for the Education of Young Children.

Taylor, B. J. (1989). *Early childhood program management: People and procedures.* Columbus, OH: Merrill.

VIDEOTAPES

Beaty, J. J. (Producer). (1979). Managing the daily program (Videopak B), *Skills for preschool teachers* [videotape]. Elmira, NY: McGraw Bookstore, Elmira College.

Center for Early Education and Development (Producer). (1988). *Looking at young children: Observing in early childhood settings* [videotape]. New York: Teachers College Press.

CHAPTER 12 EVALUATION SHEET
PROVIDING PROGRAM MANAGEMENT

1. Student _____

2. Trainer _____

3. Center where training occurred _____

4. Beginning date _____ Ending date _____

5. Describe what student did to accomplish General Objective

   _____

   _____

6. Describe what student did to accomplish Specific Objectives

   Objective 1 _____

   _____

   Objective 2 _____

   _____

   Objective 3 _____

   _____

7. Evaluation of student's Learning Activities
       (Trainer Check One)   (Student Check One)

   _____ Highly superior performance   _____

   _____ Superior performance   _____

   _____ Good performance   _____

   _____ Less than adequate performance   _____

Signature of Trainer: Signature of Student:

_____   _____

Comments:

13 Promoting Professionalism

General Objective

To continue professional growth as the teacher of young children.

Specific Objectives

- ☐ Makes a commitment to the early childhood field.
- ☐ Behaves ethically toward children and their families.
- ☐ Takes every opportunity to improve professional growth.

What is a *professional* in the early childhood field, and what behaviors are exhibited that make a person a professional? Whether you are a college student, a teaching assistant, a parent volunteer, a Child Development Associate candidate, or a teacher, this is an important question for you to consider carefully. What makes one a professional in this particular field? What will be expected of you that is different from what you are already doing? Although there may be several answers to this question, most early childhood professionals themselves agree that to be a professional in the field of early childhood you must:

1. Make a commitment to the field
2. Behave in an ethical manner
3. Have a knowledge base in the field
4. Have completed some type of training
5. Have completed some type of service

MAKES A COMMITMENT TO THE EARLY CHILDHOOD FIELD

The commitment an early childhood professional makes is an important one. Ours is a helping profession, which means that we must put our clients, the children and families we serve, first in our professional lives. Translated into practical terms, it means that we may have to come in early and stay late to make sure that classes are covered and children are served; that we may have to take children home if the bus breaks down or a parent fails to come; that we may miss coffee breaks or even lunch if there is a classroom problem that needs our attention; that we may have to spend many hours at home preparing activities for the following day.

267

In other words, we must put ourselves and our own needs second when it comes to our professional lives. A professional commitment in any of the helping professions requires us to give of ourselves without expecting to be paid for every hour we contribute. It is also a commitment of time and energy. We may have to work extra hours or even come in when we are not feeling up to par because a particular situation demands it.

This behavior is often quite different from that of the paraprofessional or non-professional. Often people paid on an hourly basis look at their work on the basis of the hours they put in. They are often reluctant to respond to demands made on them outside of their normal working hours. The professional, on the other hand, must take a broader view of program demands and be willing to sacrifice time and energy if the need arises. It is a giving of oneself without expecting a particular reward that marks the true professional in fields such as early childhood.

In addition to putting children and families first, a professional also demonstrates a positive attitude toward them at all times. No matter what the family background, the seriousness of problems faced by the family, or the past behavior of the child and family, a true professional retains an objective view of the situation and treats the child and family in a positive manner. Parents who abuse their children need your help just as much as or more than parents who treat their children positively. Low-income families deserve the same treatment as affluent families. In other words, children are children, to be accepted, respected, and cherished along with their families by the true professional in the early childhood field.

BEHAVES ETHICALLY TOWARD CHILDREN AND THEIR FAMILIES

A second important area of professionalism in early childhood education is that of ethical behavior, including the confidential treatment of information about children and families.

As a preschool teacher, you are probably very much of a "people person." You are probably very interested in every aspect of the children and their families. Your position allows you to find out all kinds of information about them. You'll know good things and bad—health problems, family problems, promotions, firings, new babies, new husbands or wives, and gossip. If you hear other staff members gossiping, you should not join in, but remind them as tactfully as possible that this kind of information is confidential. If parents ply you with gossip about other parents or children, let them know in a diplomatic way that this information should not be shared.

You should not talk with parents about their children when the children are present. These conversations are confidential and can be damaging to a child's self-concept. If parents start talking to you about their child while the child is standing nearby, tell them you prefer to talk at another time or that perhaps the child can play in another room while you chat. Parents who observe your professional treatment of information about them and others are bound to respect both you and your program.

TAKES EVERY OPPORTUNITY TO
IMPROVE PROFESSIONAL GROWTH

The true professional, striving to improve performance, seeks out growth and learning opportunities involving children and families, such as:

1. Reading books and journal articles
2. Viewing films and videos
3. Attending workshops, conferences, in-service training
4. Taking college courses
5. Enrolling as a CDA candidate
6. Joining a professional organization

The principal professional organization in the early childhood field is the National Association for the Education of Young Children (NAEYC), 1834 Connecticut Ave. N.W., Washington, DC 20009. Most large communities have local chapters of this organization that meet on a regular basis. To be considered a true professional in the early childhood field, you should become an active member of such an organization.

The NAEYC sponsors a large national conference each year in a major U.S. city. The conference offers the early childhood professional a wide variety of workshops and speakers, presenting everything from the latest early childhood research to the most effective curriculum materials and strategies. It is an unparalleled opportunity to meet other professionals in the field, as well as authors of early childhood textbooks and outstanding educators from every state and even foreign countries. Membership in NAEYC includes a subscription to *Young Children,* a journal with articles that discuss the latest ideas, findings, and issues in the field and are written for the working professional.

Knowledge Base in the Field of Early Childhood

Professionals in every field must have a familiarity and understanding of the knowledge on which the field is founded. In the field of early childhood, this includes familiarity with the foundations of early childhood education and its principal contributors such as Rousseau, Pestalozzi, and Froebel from the 18th and 19th centuries; Montessori and Carolyn Pratt from the early 20th century; the contributions from the field of psychology by Freud, Gesell, Erikson, Piaget, and Skinner; the kindergarten and nursery school movements in the United States at the turn of the century; the day care movement given impetus during World War II; and Head Start and the compensatory education movement born during the War on Poverty in the 1960s.

In addition, professionals in the field must have a knowledge of child development, health, psychology, sociology, education, and special education, as these fields affect young children and their families. They need an understanding of conflicting development theories such as the maturationist, the behaviorist, and the cognitive/interactionist points of view. They should be familiar with learning theories such as exploratory play as applied to young children, so they can help design a developmentally appropriate curriculum for their own children. They should be aware of various curriculum models and the ongoing research critiquing them.

It is a never-ending task to keep up with developments in this new and dynamic field. True professionals make the effort to acquire this knowledge by taking college courses and workshops, reading textbooks and journal articles, inviting knowledgeable guest speakers to their programs, attending conferences where such knowledge is disseminated, and visiting early childhood programs that feature particular curriculum models.

Training Opportunities

To keep up with the latest information in the early childhood field, you should make training an ongoing part of your life. Like Head Start, many programs have in-service training built into their schedules. The year begins with a pre-service workshop for all teachers and assistants, and continues with on-site or regional workshops in the various component areas such as curriculum, nutrition, health, mental health, career development, and parent-involvement.

Two-year and 4-year colleges also offer courses and workshops in early childhood education. If your local college does not, you might approach someone at the college with the idea of offering workshops in this field. Hospitals are often willing to sponsor early childhood parent training programs, as are agencies such as Cooperative Extension. Libraries will often procure early childhood videotapes for parent groups.

Licensing and Credentialing

Another important mark of the professional in any field is a credential. A professional needs a degree, license, or credential to certify that he or she is qualified in the field. Credentials of various kinds can be awarded to qualified individuals based on college courses or programs completed, workshops taken, training completed, tests taken, or types and amounts of experience. Licensing or credentialing bodies may be colleges and universities, state departments of education, local programs, or national agencies. Types of credentials vary from college degrees to workshop completion certificates.

Early childhood professionals usually complete one or more of the following:

> CDA Credential
> Associate Degree (from a 2-year college)
> Bachelor's Degree (from a 4-year college)
> Master's Degree
> Doctoral Degree
> State teaching certificate/license

Becoming a Child Development Associate (CDA)

In addition to the traditional modes of training for early childhood education, there is another increasingly popular method for developing the necessary competence to teach in the field: Child Development Associate (CDA) training, assessment, and credentialing. CDA training is competency-based and performance-based, which means that a certain percentage of the training must occur in the early childhood classroom and that the trainee must demonstrate competence with children in such a setting.

The Child Development Associate program emerged in the 1970s as a collaborative effort on the part of early childhood professionals and the federal government, represented by the Administration for Children, Youth, and Families (ACYF), to create a new category of early childhood professionals, the Child Development Associate. Initially, the program had two separate parts, training done by local colleges or programs and credentialing done by a national office: the Child Development Associate National Credentialing Program.

Today that program has consolidated training and credentialing under a new CDA Professional Preparation Program offered by:

Council for Early Childhood Professional Recognition
1718 Connecticut Ave, N.W. #500
Washington, DC 20009

Under the new program, a candidate may choose to earn a CDA Credential in one of two ways: the new CDA Professional Preparation Program or by direct assessment. Under the CDA Professional Preparation Program, a candidate for the CDA Credential must complete the following:

CDA PROFESSIONAL PREPARATION PROGRAM

Eligibility
1. Be 18 years of age or older
2. Hold a high school diploma or GED
3. Identify an Advisor to work with during the year of study

Application
1. Submit verification of age and high school diploma or GED
2. Submit name and qualifications of Advisor
3. Submit required fee

On-site Training
1. Complete the readings and exercises in the early childhood studies curriculum in about 8 months
2. Work in a child care setting either as a staff member, a volunteer, or a student during this time

3. Hold a weekly conference with Advisor
4. Complete and submit all assignments to Advisor for verification

Seminar Training

1. Complete 120 clock-hours of classes conducted by Seminar Instructor under the auspices of a local post-secondary institution
2. Complete written sections of the situational assessment

Assessment

1. Be formally observed by Advisor
2. Complete Professional Resource File
3. Distribute and collect Parent Opinion Questionnaires
4. Complete oral section of situational assessment conducted by Council Representative
5. Receive notification of decision by Council about Credential Award

Credential Award

1. Receive CDA Credential

The course of study covered by the seminar includes: an introduction to the early childhood profession; observing and recording child growth and development; establishing and maintaining a safe, healthy, learning environment; advancing physical and intellectual competence; supporting social and emotional development and providing guidance; establishing positive and productive relationships with families; ensuring a well-run, purposeful program responsive to participant needs; and maintaining a commitment to professionalism (Council for Early Childhood Professional Recognition, n.d.).

Direct Assessment Program

A second route to CDA credentialing involves direct assessment by the national program after the candidate has completed the necessary training and data collection. The training can be provided by the early childhood program itself or a local college. This route to CDA credentialing is similar to the program from past years in which training was provided at the local level, and credentialing at the national level. The Local Assessment Team (LAT) meeting is no longer required, nor is there a requirement for a CDA Portfolio. Instead, the candidate must complete the following:

DIRECT ASSESSMENT PROGRAM

Eligibility

1. Be 18 years of age or older
2. Hold a high school diploma or GED
3. Have 480 hours of experience working with children ages birth through 5 years
4. Have completed 120 clock-hours of formal training in early childhood education

Competence
1. Be skilled in the six CDA Competency Areas
2. Have formal observation by an Early Childhood Professional while working with children in a child care setting
3. Distribute and collect Parent Opinion Questionnaires
4. Complete a Professional Resource File

Application
1. Submit application for direct assessment
2. Submit verification of age, high school diploma, and experience working with children
3. Submit a signed ethical conduct statement
4. Submit a verification of formal training
5. Submit a verification of formal observation
6. Submit required fee

Assessment
1. Be present at designated time and place to complete a situational oral and written assessment conducted by a Council Representative
2. Submit the Parent Opinion Questionnaires and the Professional Resource File for review by the Council Representative
3. Receive notification of decision by Council about Credential Award

Credential Award
1. Receive CDA Credential

Professional Resource File

In place of the former CDA Portfolio, candidates must prepare a Professional Resource File, which can be arranged much like the Portfolio in a bound notebook, inside file folders in a box, or in other creative ways. The candidate must be able to carry the Professional Resource File away from a work site, to a home visit, or to a meeting. The File can contain items such as: pamphlets or brochures from early childhood education association meetings; booklets on how children grow and learn that are appropriate for parents; observation tools for recording information about children; agencies in the community that provide help for children with developmental disabilities; emergency telephone numbers; Red Cross certificates; titles of children's books dealing with development of gender identity, separation, or family diversity; goals of your program; favorite poems for children; file cards from the chapters in this text; or list of videotapes on parenting.

Skills for Preschool Teachers is designed to be used in CDA training programs either by individuals who prefer the self-taught module approach (See "Introduction"), or by colleges or training programs who prefer the group or seminar approach. The Teacher Skills Checklist can be used by any CDA trainee or Advisor as an initial assessment tool. Then a Training Prescription can be developed for the trainee to follow throughout training. Each chapter of this book represents one of the 13 CDA Functional Areas derived from the six Competency Goals:

1. Establishing and maintaining a safe, healthy learning environment
   Safe
   Healthy
   Learning Environment
2. Advancing physical and intellectual competence
   Physical
   Cognitive
   Communication
   Creative
3. Supporting social and emotional development and providing positive guidance
   Self
   Social
   Guidance
4. Establishing positive and productive relationships with families
   Families
5. Ensuring a well-run, purposeful program responsive to participant needs
   Program management
6. Maintaining a commitment to professionalism
   Professionalism

Why Become a CDA?

Why should you become a CDA? First, it will help you in your work as a classroom teacher or assistant. It will help you improve your skills in working with young children and their families; setting up an appropriate physical environment; keeping your children safe and healthy; providing opportunities for them to improve their physical, cognitive, language, and creative development; and planning activities and managing individuals and groups.

It will also help you assess your strengths and areas needing strengthening, so you will be able to make the necessary improvements. You will do this not only through your self-evaluation and preparation, but also through the eyes of an early childhood professional, your Advisor, whom you may come to know as a friend.

Receiving the CDA Credential will elevate your status in your program, and the program's status in the community. In some instances, you may receive a promotion or a raise. This credential may be worth college credit at certain institutions. Since the CDA is a national credential, your talents will also be more marketable in other states if you should move.

Finally, the CDA Credential will induct you as a professional into the field of early childhood education. Some professions require a Bachelor's or Master's

Degree for entry; the early childhood field is coming more and more to recognize the CDA as the first professional step in an ever-expanding career.

SUMMARY

To become a professional in the early childhood field, you must first make a commitment to the field by putting children and families first in your professional life. This often means sacrificing time and energy to make sure children and families are served by your program as they should be. It may mean coming in to the program early and leaving late. It means providing services yourself when no one else is available.

A professional also treats information about children and families confidentially. When parents or staff members begin gossiping about children, a professional should not participate and should help others understand why this behavior is not acceptable.

To continue your professional growth as a teacher of young children, you should also take every opportunity to gain knowledge and skills in the field, by joining a professional organization such as the National Association for the Education of Young Children. You should also strive to earn credentials in the profession. One of the important new methods for acquiring competence as well as credentialing in the field is by becoming a Child Development Associate (CDA). This training, assessment, and credentialing program requires trainees to complete a course of study, perform competently in an early childhood setting, assemble a Professional Resource File, and complete a written and oral situational assessment.

LEARNING ACTIVITIES

1. Read Chapter 13, "Promoting Professionalism," and answer Question Sheet 13–A.
2. Read one or more of the Suggested Readings and add 10 cards to your file with specific ideas for improving your professional outlook or that of others. Include a reference source on the back of each card.
3. Make an assessment of another early childhood teacher or assistant using the Teacher Skills Checklist. Summarize the results and discuss them with the teacher or assistant. Make a Training Prescription.
4. Make a self-assessment using the Teacher Skills Checklist, and discuss the results with your trainer after you complete Activity #5.
5. Have your trainer assess you using the Teacher Skills Checklist. Discuss the results and have a Training Prescription prepared.
6. Make a list of organizations or agencies in your community (or county) that are concerned with young children and their families. Attend one of their meetings and write a summary of it.

7. Write to the Council for Early Childhood Professional Recognition for a packet of information on obtaining a CDA Credential. Find out where you can obtain CDA training locally.

8. Obtain a copy of an early childhood professional journal such as *Young Children* and write a summary of interesting ideas from the articles in it.

9. Complete the Chapter 13 Evaluation Sheet and return it to your trainer or college supervisor.

QUESTION SHEET 13–A

(Based on Chapter 13, "Promoting Professionalism")

1. What does it means to be a professional in the early childhood field?
2. What is the difference between a professional and a non-professional in an early childhood program?
3. What kinds of information about children and families must you treat confidentially?
4. What should you do if a parent begins to talk to you about a child while the child is present?
5. What kinds of knowledge should a professional be familiar with in the early childhood field?
6. What kinds of credentials or licenses are available to early childhood professionals?
7. What are two different routes a person could take to obtain the CDA Credential?
8. What is the Professional Resource File and what should it contain?
9. How can this textbook be used to help a person become a CDA?
10. Why should a person become a CDA?

SUGGESTED READINGS

Abbott-Shim, M. S. (1990). In-service training: A means to quality care. *Young Children, 45*(2) 14–18.

Berger, E. H. (1991). *Parents as partners in education: The school and home working together* (3rd ed.). Columbus, OH: Merrill.

Council for Early Childhood Professional Recognition (n.d.). *CDA professional preparation program.* Washington, DC: Council for Early Childhood Professional Recognition.

Cleverly, J., & Phillips, D. C. (1986). *Visions of childhood: Influential models from Locke to Spock.* New York: Teachers College Press.

Feeney, S., Christensen, D., & Moravcik, E. (1991). *Who am I in the lives of young children? An introduction to teaching young children* (4th ed.). Columbus, OH: Merrill.

Gordon, A. M., & Browne, K. W. (1985). *Beginnings and beyond: Foundations in early childhood education.* Albany, NY: Delmar.

Kipnis, K. (1987). How to discuss professional ethics. *Young Children, 42*(4) 26–30.

Morrison, G. S. (1991). *Early childhood education today* (5th ed.). Columbus, OH: Merrill.

Phillips, C. B. (1990). The child development associate program: Entering a new era. *Young Children, 45*(3) 24–27.

Pratt, C. (1990). *I learn from children.* New York: Harper and Row.

Radomski, M. A. (1986). Professionalization of early childhood educators: How far have we progressed?" *Young Children, 41*(5) 20–23.

Spodek, B., Saracho, O. N., & Davis, M. D. (1987). *Foundations of early childhood education.* Englewood Cliffs, NJ: Prentice-Hall.

VIDEOTAPES

South Carolina Educational TV (Producer). Professional behavior. *Caring for pretty special children (abused and neglected)* [videotape]. Columbia, SC: SCETV.

CHAPTER 13 EVALUATION SHEET
PROMOTING PROFESSIONALISM

1. Student _____

2. Trainer _____

3. Center where training occurred _____

4. Beginning date _____ Ending date _____

5. Describe what student did to accomplish General Objective

   _____

   _____

6. Describe what student did to accomplish Specific Objectives

   Objective 1 _____

   _____

   Objective 2 _____

   _____

   Objective 3 _____

   _____

7. Evaluation of student's Learning Activities
   (Trainer Check One)   (Student Check One)

   _____ Highly superior performance   _____

   _____ Superior performance   _____

   _____ Good performance   _____

   _____ Less than adequate performance   _____

Signature of Trainer: Signature of Student:

_____   _____

Comments:

Index